100 YEARS HERITAGE

The work of the
MANX MUSEUM AND NATIONAL TRUST

Devised and edited by
S. HARRISON, B.A., F.M.A.

New colour photography by
DENNIS REED, L.M.P.A.

First Published by the Manx Museum and National Trust, 1986

ISBN 0 948308 04 4
A.H. Jolly (Editorial) Ltd.

Design and artwork by Charles Cannell, B.A.
Printed and bound by Jolly & Barber Ltd, Rugby, Warwickshire

FRONT COVER: Detail from *On the Beach at Douglas* by W. Hardie Hay, 1894

THE CALF OF MAN CRUCIFIXION

The most outstanding of all the Manx Celtic pre-Norse carvings. This fragment of an altar frontal was discovered on the Calf of Man in 1773 and purchased for the Manx Museum by the National Art Collections Fund in 1956.

FOREWORD

by His Excellency The Lieutenant Governor
MAJOR GENERAL L. A. W. NEW, C.B., C.B.E.

I am delighted to accept an invitation to write a brief Foreword to "One Hundred Years of Heritage" particularly in this Manx Heritage Year of 1986 and I do congratulate all those who have been involved in the compilation of this prestigious publication.

It makes fascinating reading and covers the activities of the earliest Trustee Body founded in 1886, its principals and their characters, the search for a permanent Museum premises and a summary of the achievements of past Curators.

Additionally it describes the progression from simple basic studies to major scientific and technical advances within the whole field of Manx Archaeology over the last century and the establishment of a National Gallery, Library and Archives Department of fascinating dimensions.

The Manx Museum and National Trust are to be congratulated on their initiative and foresight in providing, in this book, a true reflection of "Manx Life" past and present.

Their interpretations of "Manx History" in all its forms will serve to enlighten both the present and future generations.

Laurence New

Lieutenant Governor

CONTRIBUTORS

His Excellency the Lieutenant Governor,
MAJOR GENERAL LAWRENCE NEW

J. B. CAINE
Chairman of the Manx Museum and National Trust.

A. M. CUBBON
former Director of the Manx Museum and National Trust.

L. S. GARRAD
Assistant Keeper at the Manx Museum.

A. M. HARRISON
Librarian/Archivist at the Manx Museum.

S. HARRISON
Director of the Manx Museum and National Trust.

CONTENTS

ACKNOWLEDGEMENTS

The Trustees owe their greatest debt of gratitude to the countless donors who, over the last one hundred years have presented a vast array of paintings, archives, objects and memories in order to create the comprehensive and important Museum collections we enjoy today. Without such generous support and foresight, this publication would have been impossible.

This centenary publication has been independently produced by the Trustees of the Manx Museum from private funds. However, the Trustees wish to place on record their sincere appreciation of the generous assistance they have received in this project from a number of other sources.

By happy coincidence, one of our sponsors, the firm of Chartered Accountants Pannell Kerr Forster, are themselves celebrating their centenary on the Island. The firm of Cochran and Walker of Liverpool was appointed auditors of certain Government functions under the Audit Act 1886; the audit file for one of these audits, that of the Trustees of the Common Lands, shows that the earliest accounts were those of the year ended 12th November 1885.

Since 1890 the firm has had premises in Athol Street, and was the first firm of Chartered Accountants to offer services on the Island. It changed its name to W. H. Walker and W. A. Crowe, in 1894; W. H. Walker was succeeded by his son A. D. Walker and W. A. Crowe, and then by the partners still in practice today, since 1971 in conjunction with what is now Pannell Kerr Forster.

In the early days the most notable event was the appointment of W. H. Walker as liquidator after the disastrous collapse of Dumbell's Bank on 3rd February 1900. Apart from this and the Government audit, the firm has been involved widely in the professional and commercial life of the Island in its first century.

Pannell Kerr Forster's generous donation towards this publication provides a splendid example of how the Museum and the private sector can combine to further the aims of Manx Heritage for the benefit of all. In this connection, the Trustees would also wish to express their sincere thanks to the following organisations in the Island:

Friends of the Manx National Trust
Friends of the Manx Museum
Manx Telecom
International Trust Corporation
Manx Helicopters
Manx Technical Publications

PHOTOGRAPHY

The majority of the colour illustrations in this book have been specially commissioned by the Trustees and undertaken by Dennis Reed. However, the Trustees are indebted to a number of other individuals who have provided specific illustrations for inclusion, especially:

John Callister, Walter Clarke, David Freke, Edward Huyton, Jerry Jones, Alexander Maddrell, Basil Megaw, Adrian del Nevo, John Slinn, David Wood, Malcolm Wright.

PREFACE

by S. HARRISON, Director

We all know that Museums are places which are full of fragile and fascinating objects of great age, but when the institution itself reaches its centenary year there is cause for special celebration.

A body of Museum and Ancient Monuments Trustees was established in the Isle of Man by Act of Tywald in 1886 with the aim of preserving the Island's cultural heritage and establishing the first National Museum. In those early days, the search to establish a collection, to find a suitable home and the struggle to obtain the necessary financial support were the formidable obstacles for the dedicated voluntary group of Trustees. A prime mover in the battle to obtain the necessary support to establish the cherished dream of an Island Museum was P. M. C. Kermode, a founder member of the Natural History and Antiquarian Society and a renowned Manx scholar. It was fitting, therefore, that when, in 1922, the old Noble's Hospital building in Douglas was made available for use as a Museum, it was P. M. C. Kermode who was the natural choice as the first Museum Curator.

The headquarters of the Manx Museum today is in the same attractive red-brick Victorian building, but the size, scope, and work of the institution has enlarged considerably, to the extent that it now holds an unrivalled position in the public's esteem and provides a unique educational touchstone to the life and traditions of the Island's cultural heritage. The fact that the Museum's combined operation annually proves to be one of the Island's major visitor attractions is a tribute to those founding fathers and to the succeeding generations who have extended the role of the Museum within the community in a way which belies such humble beginnings.

Despite the major achievements which have been made since the Museum's inception in 1886, the centenary celebrations of the Manx Museum and National Trust are by no means an exercise in self-congratulations. The Museum Trustees have seized the opportunity to commence their second century of existence with an ambitious programme of development and extension of the service offered to the public. Recognising the need to present the Island's history utilising the most modern interpretive methods, the Manx Museum has begun a phased re-design of all its major galleries.

The Trustees have also commenced a major extension scheme in Douglas. This project will provide a lecture and film theatre where visitors may enjoy an exciting introduction to the Island's rich historic landscape before exploring the Museum and countryside. In addition there will be, for the first time, a whole floor devoted to the operation of a Museum Education Service where students of all ages may work in close proximity to the collections of the Island's "treasure house". Coupled with a new exhibition gallery and the extension of the Museum's shop service these new developments will provide the Island with a new focal point for the appreciation of its cultural and natural assets.

By providing new and exciting presentations in addition to the continuance of its established and renowned standards of scholarship and service and through its planned greater emphasis on an outgoing educational programme we can be certain that a foundation is being laid in the young minds of today which will ensure that the Manx Museum and National Trust will be performing a crucial and exciting role in the heart of the Island's community throughout its second century of existence.

IN THE BEGINNING

J. B. CAINE

This book is, amongst other things, a celebration of the first one hundred years since the establishment of The Manx Museum and Ancient Monuments Trustees. However, the idea of an institution designed to preserve and exhibit aspects of the Manx cultural heritage dates back at least another century before 1886 when Bishop Hildesley wrote of his hopes for a museum at Bishop's Court at Ballaugh in the north of the Island. In the first half of the nineteenth century both Trevor Ashe and J. R. Wallace opened private museums in Douglas although their duration was short and we know little of what was on display. Similarly, in 1852 the Reverend J. G. Cumming suggested that a "Manx Museum" be established at King William's College (of which he was Vice-Principal) at Castletown in the south of the Island, and offered his own geological collection as a nucleus of the proposed museum.

THE MANX SUN.

LAXEY CLOVEN STONES.

The Manx Museum.

THE range of this interesting Institution, is now extended to a Library and Literary Lounge.—Mr. Powell, the Keeper of the Museum, has constantly on Sale a select class of Books and Prints of inexhaustible variety and amusement.—Admission is perfectly free from cost; nor is a Visitor under any obligation to make purchases.—Mr. Ashe's "*Manx Sketch Book*" is this day published, price 12s.; also his "*Isle of Man Forget me Not*" price 1s. 6d. The Plates are beautiful and highly finished.

*** The *Museum* is hourly increasing in strength and attractions. It has this week been distinguished by patriotic loans and free gifts of subjects of genuine curiosity from Mrs. Major Glew, Mrs. Deemster Christian, Capt. Moses, Major Tobin, the Lord Bishop, and a Lady of quality,—to whose distinguished taste and patriotism the *Museum* owes its first origin and design.—Mr. ASHE, is proceeding next week to visit an ancient Sarcophagus, and he has great hopes of obtaining a complete Skeleton of an Antediluvian Elk. He invokes the Nobility and Gentry of the Island to visit his MUSEUM, and advance his views.

Museum, Duke Street, August 3rd, 1825.

Above: Illustrated advertisement for the "Manx Museum" established by Trevor Ashe: *Manx Sun*, 6th August 1825.

is now ready for Inspection

J. R. WALLACE'S MUSEUM,

St. George Street, Douglas,

WILL open for Public Inspection on MONDAY 4th May,—containing a Collection of NATURAL HISTORY, viz.:—Beasts, Birds, Reptiles, Fishes, Insects, Crustaceous Animals, and Fossil Remains; 800 Species of Recent Shells. Also, Weapons, Fishing Implements, Tools, Bows and Arrows, Dresses, &c. from New Zealand, the Society and Sandwich Islands, South America, India, &c.; Mummies from the Southern Provinces of Peru, and a New Zealand Chieftain's Head, beautifully Tatooed, in a fine state of preservation; with a variety of other Articles.

The principal part of the above were collected by J. R. WALLACE, whilst abroad.

Admission .... 1s.
Annual Tickets .... 5s.

A Synopsis will be ready for Publication in a few days; in the mean time, J. R. W. will give Visitors all the information in his power.

Open from 10 in the Morning till Dusk.

Douglas, April 30, 1835.

Notice is Hereby Given,

THAT the Right Reverend the LORD BISHOP of Sodor and Man is about to proceed to the CONSECRATION of the Parochial CHURCH of

Left: Advertisement for the opening of J. R. Wallace's Museum in the *Manx Sun*, 1st May 1835.

However, perhaps the most important stimulus towards the concept of a Manx Museum was provided by Governor Loch's invitation in 1865 to the Cambrian Archaeological Association to visit the Island. This visit, together with Governor Loch's appointment of an Archaeological Commission which published its report in 1878, and the foundation of the Isle of Man Natural History and Antiquarian Society in 1879, did a great deal to galvanise public support for the concept of preserving the Island's heritage. This growing level of interest culminated in the Manx Government's official recognition of the desirability of establishing the Island's own statutory body responsible for the protection of ancient monuments and ultimately, the establishment of the first Manx National Museum. The first body of Museum Trustees was established in 1886 and a course was marked out for the preservation of the Island's monuments and the formation of a collection of objects representing the unique Manx cultural and natural heritage.

The development of the Manx Museum and National Trust into the major focus of national culture and identity which it has become has been a long and at times difficult process.

While overall policy has been governed by a body of Trustees which is responsible to Tynwald, the detail and quality of the century's progress inevitably reflects the talents and personalities of its successive Directors. Some of the achievements of these individuals through one hundred years are well worth recording as a backcloth to the story of our National Museum's work today, though the account is necessarily brief.

Philip Moore Callow Kermode

Philip Moore Callow Kermode, the first Director of the Manx Museum was born in Ramsey on the 21st March 1855, the fifth son of the Reverend William Kermode, Chaplain of St. Paul's, Ramsey, and later Vicar of Maughold and Rector of Ballaugh.

Like many Manx clergymen of his day William Kermode engaged in scholarly pursuits and was keenly interested in history and archaeology. He was a founder member of the Manx Society for the Publication of National Documents, usually referred to simply as The Manx Society, in 1858, and a member of the Archaeological Commission appointed by Governor Loch in 1876 to report on the Prehistoric Monuments and the Antiquities of the Isle of Man. Parson Kermode was an early proponent of the formation of a National Museum and Library for the Island.

He had a large family, having fourteen children in all by his three wives though not all of them survived infancy. Several had artistic and literary talents, the best known, apart from Philip, being Josephine, whose poetry and plays in Anglo-Manx dialect have earned her a place in the affection of the Manx people who knew her through her writings as "Cushag". Neither she nor Philip ever married and she devoted her life to his welfare.

No doubt inspired and encouraged by his father, Philip Kermode persued many interests in academic subjects, and during his lifetime amassed a fine, wide ranging, personal library. He was educated in Ramsey and at King William's College, Castletown and later read for the Bar being articled to Mr, later Sir, Alured Dumbell. He was admitted to the Manx Bar in 1878

P. M. C. Kermode, Secretary to the Museum Trustees 1896–1922 and first Curator of the Manx Museum 1922–1932.

and practised as an advocate in Ramsey serving as Clerk to the Justices from 1888 to 1922. He had a great affection for Ramsey and served on the Town Board of Commissioners and was for a period its Chairman. Although it is said that he disliked politics he twice stood, unsuccessfully, as a candidate for the House of Keys, opposing the well-known novelist, Hall Caine in 1901 and 1903.

In 1879 Kermode was a founder member of the Isle of Man Natural History and Antiquarian Society which was later to develop a close and lasting association with the Manx Museum and Ancient Monuments Trust. Kermode himself was the Society's most stalwart member for over fifty years serving as Secretary, Editor, and on three occasions President.

He greatly admired the work of the eminent Manx born naturalist professor Edward Forbes who was a contemporary of his father but had died at the tragically early age of 39, the year before Kermode was born. Kermode described his own work in natural history as walking humbly in Forbes' footsteps. Like Forbes he was a talented draughtsman, a skill he used to great effect in his work on the Manx Crosses.

Although self taught in both natural history and archaeology and at times unduly modest about the value of his own contributions, his work was highly regarded by eminent professional workers in these fields. The lively correspondence he carried on with leading experts and contacts with visiting and local scholars overcame his academic isolation. The eminent glaciologist P. F. Kendal named a hitherto undiscovered species of Nassa (fossil shell), *Nassa kermodei*, an academic honour which must have pleased Kermode greatly.

His travels took him to Italy, where he studied early Christian and Classical antiquities, and to Denmark, Iceland and the Faroe Islands; visits which served to sharpen his appetite for investigating the antiquities of his own native Island.

In 1893, he first excavated the unique megalithic monument on the Meayll Hill, overlooking the south western tip of the Island with Professor Herdman from the marine Biological Station with whom as joint author in 1904 he was to publish a volume summarizing *Manx Antiquities*. Four years later, a remarkable triumph for Kermode was the discovery in 1897 of the almost perfect skeleton of the fossil giant "Irish Elk" *Megaceros giganteus*. A specimen had been found in a marl pit in Ballaugh in 1819 but had been removed from the Island to Edinburgh. It was believed that another specimen might be found at a site at St. John's and Kermode organised an excavation in collaboration with the British Association. The excavation proved successful and the articulated skeleton became one of the most striking exhibits in the temporary museum set up in Castle Rushen in 1905. It has proved to have a particular fascination for younger visitors to the Museum ever since.

In the 1880s Kermode began to press for better preservation of the remarkable Manx Series of monumental crosses advocating that they should be preserved in the parish churches wherever possible or in purpose built shelters in the churchyards. He also started an exhaustive search for other examples and was successful in recovering many which had been lost sight of, often being built into walls and hedges. In his article on Roolwer's Cross published in 1897 he recounted that it had been used for years as a step for a sundial until Dr. Hibbert Ware persuaded the Vicar and Wardens of Maughold to re-erect it on the Green in about 1860. When Kermode's father became Vicar in 1871 he found it thickly covered in bills and posters. Distressed by the condition in which he himself found it when he obtained a cast of it in 1894, Kermode replaced it in a sheltered spot in the churchyard. He asked:

> "When will Manksmen realise that these monuments so few in number, are of priceless value, that their beauty and their interest consists in the intricate details of their sculpturings, and that every year's exposure to the weather alone, apart from the

The Great Deer, excavated by P. M. C. Kermode and somewhat inappropriately displayed at Castle Rushen in 1905.

P. M. C. Kermode making notes on the Norse carvings on a life-size plaster cast of Thorlief Hnaaki's Cross from the parish of Braddan (number 135).

Coloured half title page from P. M. C. Kermode's *Manx Crosses*, published by Bemrose in 1907.

risk of accidental or wanton injury, is depriving future generations of their rights in the only National Art monuments the Isle of Man has produced, and which it should be our greater pride to preserve?"

During his study of the art and iconography of the cross-slabs, Kermode was fascinated to discover that several of them bore pictorial representations of episodes in Norse mythology ante-dating by perhaps two hundred years the earliest surviving written accounts.

For more than twenty years his every available moment was spent in studying the crosses, preparing descriptions, rubbings, life-size drawings, obtaining photographs and directing the preparation of cast replicas made by Mr. T. H. Royston. The fruits of this study appeared in papers in learned journals and were finally brought together in his inaugural opus "Manx Crosses" published by Bemrose in 1907. This finely produced work was undoubtedly the single most important work on Manx archaeology to be published although now inevitably out of date in some respects.

Investigation of an early keeill site at West Nappin, Jurby circa 1891.

Following this major achievement, Kermode was typically reluctant to relax the pace of his endeavours and in the following year he instigated a full field survey of Manx archaeology commencing with the excavation and documentation of the Island's early chapel (Keeill) sites and associated burial grounds. Four reports were published between 1909 and 1915 and the published survey of this class of monument was finally completed in 1968.

In 1896 Kermode became a member of the Manx Museum and Ancient Monuments Trustees and was appointed its Secretary in 1905. He was a tireless worker for the conservation of the Island's monuments and in the struggle which lasted over thirty years to secure permanent premises for the establishment of the Manx Museum. When in 1922 the long hoped-for institution became a reality he was appointed its first Curator, a post for which he had in effect spent his life in preparation, he was then 67. He embarked enthusiastically on the task of bringing together the collections from the temporary museum in Castle Rushen, those stored at Peel, Government Office and several other locations together with the Manx items from the Antiquarian Society's collections in Ramsey. In addition, Kermode brought together an initial collection of local prints and pictures including the Baume bequest of works by the distinguished Manx artist J. M. Nicholson.

The building which provided the first permanent house for the Trustees' scattered collection was the former Noble's Hospital in Douglas which had been made available by the Henry Bloom Noble Trustees following the move of the hospital to new premises. By an appropriate coincidence, the foundation stone of this original hospital building was laid in 1886, precisely the same year in which the Museum and Ancient Monuments Trustees were established by Act of Tynwald. It had taken thirty-six years for the momentous union to take place. (Although a number of additions to the original building occurred in the 1930s, it is equally fitting that the second foundation stone marking a major extension to the Manx Museum was laid in 1986, the Trustees' Centenary Year.)

The new Museum was opened by His Excellency the Lieutenant Governor Sir William Fry and his opening remarks, as reported in the *Isle of Man Times* for 4th November 1922, remain a true appreciation of the Museum's role in the community today:

> "I think, on behalf of all here present, we shall desire to congratulate the Trustees of this Museum on the fulfilment of what has been a long hoped and long worked-for event – that is the establishment of a Manx Museum. Everyone who calls himself a true Manxman or Manxwoman is, I am sure, delighted that this Museum has been established at last, because it is more essential now than ever it was for all people who desire to preserve their nationality and their own character that they should have a storehouse for the antiquities and history of the past. (Hear, hear.) That has at least been accomplished. Some may think this Museum rather small; but when you go round, you will find a very large number of exhibits which we owe to the kindness of many donors. . . . All museums must have small beginnings; but there is no reason why this Museum should not grow. We have the ground for extension, and already plans are in view whereby it may be enlarged. . . . It has always been in the minds of the Trustees that this should be an educational centre for the Island. Everybody who has studied modern education will know the enormous use made of museums in the training of young children. One hour spent in a museum will be worth many hours spent over books. . . ."

Top: The original Noble's Hospital building converted to house the Manx Museum in 1922.

Right: The scene at the opening of the building as a hospital in 1886.

The public was first admitted to the new premises on 2nd November 1922 when the Lieutenant Governor Sir William Fry and Lady Fry were the first to enter. For Kermode this was the realisation of the project he had dreamed of and striven for all his adult life.

William Cubbon was appointed Secretary and Librarian and was the perfect complement to Kermode, his bubbling enthusiasm and extrovert character balancing the more severe aspect of Kermode's serious but kindly nature.

Over the next ten years Kermode laid the foundations of the academic standards on which his successors have built, an achievement the more remarkable since he started his curatorial career at an age when most men today would have already retired.

He actively continued his archaeological work excavating the neolithic burial site at Ballafayle, Maughold in 1926 and the Viking Ship Burial at Knock-e-Doonee in 1927 at the age of 72. In the following year he published his fifth paper describing the cross-slabs discovered since the publication of "Manx Crosses".

The University of Liverpool conferred the degree of M.A. (*Honoris causa*) on him in 1929, and on the very day of his sudden death, the 5th September 1932, news came that the Government of Iceland had made him a Knight of the Order of the Falcon.

His long life spanned the "Heroic Period" of Manx Studies. He had been a member of the Council of the Manx Society, he was the founder of the Isle of Man Natural History and Antiquarian Society and its only surviving original member on its fiftieth anniversary. He was the driving force behind the establishment of the Manx Museum, and its first Director.

He was buried in the churchyard at Maughold near the largest single parish group of the ancient cross-slabs he had laboured so long to preserve. Kermode built his own lively monument in the shape of the first permanent Manx Museum. In addition, his great book on the memorials of our Celtic and Scandinavian forebears will help to bring this period of history to life in the imagination of archaeologists and historians for generations to come.

P. M. C. Kermode addressing a visiting party of archaeologists from the cross-shelter at Maughold parish church, shortly before his death in 1932.

William Cubbon

William Cubbon, Secretary and Librarian of the Manx Museum 1922–1932 and the second Curator, from 1932–1940.

William Cubbon was promoted to the position of Director of the Manx Museum in succession to Philip Kermode in 1932 having previously served in the dual function of Secretary and Librarian since the Museum opened in 1922.

Born on 30th May 1865 the son of James Cubbon, a master mariner engaged in the local fishing industry, he spent many of his childhood days in the company of farmers and fishermen from whom he first absorbed the language, customs and lore which led to his deep patriotic love for his native Island.

He related that his first job was leading a pony and sled taking "jumpers" (the long heavy chisels used for drilling shot holes in the mines at Ballavarkish) to the Level Smithy to be resharpened.

At the age of fifteen, Cubbon was apprenticed to a printer in Douglas but he soon developed an ambition to become a journalist. About three years later he joined the editorial staff of the *Isle of Man Examiner*. By 1889 he had risen to the position of manager and acting editor.

In July 1900 he became joint owner of the *Manx Sun*. When the partnership of Cubbon and Lightfoot took over, the paper announced that:

> "The aim of the paper would be to promote Manx National interests, to create a higher ideal among the people as to their duty to the country, and to influence a higher degree of patriotism."

These were the ideals Cubbon was to follow all his life. It was once said of him "Never has the Isle of Man been loved more deeply by any of its children".

Cubbon continued to work as a journalist until 1912 when he became Borough Librarian of Douglas. He continued to write for the local press and periodicals as a freelance journalist. He was associated with all the leading figures in the resurgence of Manx studies which was taking place at that time. While working for the *Examiner* in the 1880's he had arranged for the publication in its columns of J. J. Kneen's early writings on Manx Gaelic. These attracted the attention of Speaker A. W. Moore and after several private discussions they called a public meeting at which it was agreed to form a Society to promote the use and the preservation of the language: *Yn Cheshaght Ghailckagh* – The Manx Language Society. A. W. Moore was elected President and Cubbon Treasurer. Letters of encouragement were read from supporters who were unable to attend, including P. M. C. Kermode who was elected a Council member at the next meeting. Cubbon became President in 1916.

Cubbon enthusiastically co-operated with other workers in the field of Manx studies and local creative writers, impressing upon them the importance of getting their work into print. His support greatly assisted Kneen in the compilation and publication of his *Place Names of the Isle of Man* (for which Cubbon prepared the Treen maps) published by *Yn Cheshaght Ghailckagh* (The Manx Gaelic Society) in 1926–28, the *Grammar of the Manx Language* in 1931 and *Manx Personal Names* in 1937. This last work was published by the Museum and Ancient Monuments Trustees with financial assistance from Tynwald. He was also associated with the Society's fine periodical "Mannin" edited by Sophia Morrison which ran to nine issues from 1913 to 1917.

A. W. Moore's *Manx Worthies* and C. Roeder's *Manx Notes and Queries* also benefitted greatly from his co-operation with the authors. He was interested in poetry, and published an anthology, *A Book of Manx Poetry*, in 1913.

Cubbon joined the Antiquarian Society in 1898 acting as Secretary from 1920–1924 and President in 1925. He contributed many valuable papers and conducted several important excavations, notably that at Cronk-yn-Howe, Lezayre with J. R. Bruce.

As a keen collector Cubbon delighted in the contacts he had with book-sellers and other collectors especially G. W. Wood of London. He was instrumental in the acquisition of many important books and manuscripts against the day when a major Manx Museum reference library should, as he fervently hoped, be formed.

In 1916 he left the Douglas Library to become the manager of the Manx Government Labour Exchange.

When in 1922 the great ambition he and Kermode had cherished so long was fulfilled through the establishment of the Manx Museum he was appointed Secretary and Librarian under Kermode's Directorship. Cubbon then began what could truly be called a labour of love, the formation of the Museum's National Reference Library containing almost every printed work ever published concerning the Isle of Man.

Cubbon's work on cataloguing the growing collections led to the production of his comprehensive two volume *Bibliography of the Literature of the Isle of Man* published in 1933 and 1939, which has become an indispensable tool for all workers in Manx Studies.

In 1924 he was concerned with the important publications dealing with historical records – the facsimile edition of the *Manx Chronicle* and Talbot's translation of the *Manorial Roll of the Isle of Man 1511–15*. Both of these amply illustrate the bibliophile's delight in the physical form of finely produced books though it is a matter of regret that the "Chronicle" was issued only in a limited edition of fifty copies.

From 1930–40 Cubbon edited the *Journal of the Manx Museum* which brought the work of the Museum to the attention of a wide and appreciative audience. The Journal's long series of *Unpublished Documents in the Manx Museum* stimulated great interest in the Museum's archive collections.

With his friend J. J. Kneen he contributed much linguistic and historical information to the studies of Carl J. G. Marstrander, Professor of Celtic in the University of Oslo. It was during a visit to Norway to see Marstrander that Cubbon was seized by the work undertaken by the Scandinavian Museums, and cherished the hope that similar development might be undertaken in the Isle of Man.

It was only six years after he succeeded Kermode as Director of the Manx Museum that Cubbon was able to plant the first seeds of this vision through the formal opening in 1938 of Harry Kelly's cottage at Cregneash as the nucleus of a Manx National Folk Museum. Indeed, this formed the basis of the first publicly owned and administered "open-air" folk museum in Britain and although considerably enlarged by his successors, Cubbon's original foresight has provided the Island with one of its most prized conservation projects.

In 1952 his book *Island Heritage* was published containing a series of historical essays written for the enjoyment and indeed delight of the non-specialist audience. The proceeds of the sale of this volume formed the nucleus of a fund used to assist the publication of original work in Manx Studies.

Cubbon's patriotism was not the narrow nationalism which seeks to vaunt the achievements of one nation over another's. It sought rather to advance the intrinsic merits and self esteem of all. Like Kermode he strove all his life to convince those of his countrymen, who needed to be convinced, that not only was their cultural

William Cubbon (right) with Professor Carl Marstrander in his studio in Oslo.

and linguistic heritage well worthy of preservation but that its value extended far beyond the shores of their own little Island, and above all "That it is no mean thing to be a Manxman".

The University of Liverpool conferred on him the degree of M.A. (*Honoris Causa*) in 1940 and in 1947, the Norwegian Government made him a Knight of the Order of St. Olaf (first class).

Having succeeded Kermode as Director in 1932, William Cubbon retired from the post in 1940 at the age of 75, but was retained as Honorary Consultant until he died, on New Year's Day, 1953.

Basil R. S. Megaw

Basil R. S. Megaw, Museum Secretary 1936–1940 and Director from 1940–1957.

Basil R. S. Megaw became Assistant Director of the Manx Museum under William Cubbon in 1936, having recently graduated in Archaeology and Anthropology at Cambridge University. Although originally from Belfast, Megaw had an affinity with the history, traditions, and the people of the Isle of Man which was to become clearly apparent through the work he initiated during his twenty-one year period at the Manx Museum.

Following his academic training at Cambridge, Megaw continued his researches into aspects of current archaeology, including the new-found wealth of Manx material. In 1938, a monograph on British decorated bronze axes was published under the joint names of Basil Megaw and Eleanor Hardy (younger daughter of the biophysicist Sir William Bate Hardy). This collaboration had begun when both authors were students at Cambridge and the association was made permanent on 6th September 1939 when they were married and established their home in the Island. The advent of War however meant that the honeymoon they had planned to take in France was spent in an equally delightful, but somewhat more convenient location – Peel!

The relationship between the venerable Museum Director, William Cubbon and the new graduate from Cambridge proved to be stimulating and the two men developed a relationship and a far-sighted approach to the Museum's work that was to characterise its achievements for many years to come.

On arrival at the Manx Museum, Basil Megaw was immediately involved in the provision of a series of extensions to the display space available. This was a result of William Cubbon's success in winning the financial support of Tynwald for a phased building programme which was to add four new display galleries to the old hospital building between 1933 and 1939. This programme was a typical example of William Cubbon's desire to present the Manx people with a rich tableau of the country's cultural heritage which formed so firm a stand in his own national pride and which was enthusiastically adopted and developed by Basil Megaw. Cubbon took pains to share with Megaw his extensive knowledge of the Manx countryside and, perhaps more importantly, to introduce him to the people of the countryside with whom he had developed such a warm and beneficial relationship. Thus, when William Cubbon retired as Director in 1940 his successor was in a position to continue and enlarge the work of the Museum in preserving and collecting the "folk-life" of the Island as well as maintaining the standard of work in more traditional areas. It is interesting to read Basil Megaw's own account of how this section of the Museum's work was enlarged, as described in a paper delivered to the Isle of Man Natural History and Antiquarian Society on 3rd November 1939, which begins:

"It is strange how seldom the things of daily life attract the attention of scholars. . . . Yet, while recognizing that our predecessors deserve the highest credit for initiating the study of the traditional life and institutions of the people, we must also recognize that their chief energies have been directed towards the preservation and interpretation of such outstanding relics as the cross slabs and the keeills, as well as towards the study of purely constitutional history. Indeed, until very recently, the Folk Collection has been the Cinderella of the Manx Museum. . . . Interest in the traditional culture of the Manx folk is as old as, and indeed older than, this Society, yet no survey of the subject has been attempted, and I remember that when I first came to the Museum, three and a half years ago, very little interest was taken in the Folk Section either by the public or by the Trustees. The whole collection was crammed into the single room which now contains the Manx Farmhouse, and the collection itself was not much larger than it had been before the Great War. It is due to Mr. Cubbon that room has been

The Manx Farmhouse interior modelled on and using the original hearth of a farmhouse from Jurby, recreated in the Museum galleries by William Cubbon and Basil Megaw.

provided for the proper display of these exhibits in the New Gallery, completed in 1937, and from the first he insisted on the creation of a farmhouse interior. When the necessary space was available to make an attractive display to illustrate the life and industries of the people, we saw the very obvious gaps in the series of exhibits. How could we make the exhibits tell a story? . . . We resolved on a campaign of field work in the country, on the principle that we would not obtain what we required unless we went to look for it. Such work had to be carried out after Museum hours, as it was considered rather frivolous. It was our intention to create a small group of voluntary helpers who should actively support us in the collection of exhibits and of information to serve as a basis for a survey of Manx Folk Culture and (most important) to try to interest more and more of the Manx people in the aims of their National Museum."

This brief extract gives some indication of the various difficulties which Cubbon and Megaw experienced in trying to establish Folk-Life studies as a respectable and worthwhile discipline within the Island. The fact that the embryonic work the Folk-Life Survey (described more fully in a later chapter of this book) proved so valuable is a tribute to the pioneering work of Cubbon and Megaw and a full justification of their efforts to promote what was initially seen in more traditional quarters as a "rather frivolous" activity.

Basil Megaw's concluding paragraph in his 1939 address is a firm and eloquent statement of the guiding principle which must have sustained him in the face of such official apathy:

"A people which deliberately breaks all links with the traditions and inherited knowledge of their forebears is like a tree without roots. By the addition of a Folk Section to the Museum we are able, for the first time, to appreciate the continuity of development in Manx domestic life from remote times to present day; to understand the essential needs of Manx folk, from age to age, and to see the means whereby those needs have been supplied. Indeed it is only the realisation of the common fund of experience, traditions and history revealed in the Folk Section which entitles us to call ourselves a nation. By renewing contacts with the past and by helping people to appreciate their indebtedness to their predecessors, the Museum endeavours to fulfil a truly national service."

This philosophy was given wider expression in connection with the development of the Cregneash Village Museum project which, following the opening of Harry Kelly's Cottage in 1938, became one of Basil Megaw's prime interests and achievements. In addition, his published articles on traditional Manx farms, cornmills, agricultural hand-tools, Manx fishing craft, and other aspects of Manx traditional life, did much to establish a firm academic base for this most important branch of Manx studies.

In January 1942, Megaw left the Museum to take up duties with the Ministry of Aircraft Production, completing his war-service in 1946. During this time his wife, Eleanor Megaw, was Honorary Acting Director apart from a short period of absence when this role was fulfilled by Mr. B. E. Sargeaunt the Museum's librarian/archivist.

The onset of war brought many difficulties in staffing and the need for stringent economies, but still much valuable progress was made, especially in the field of archaeology. The distinguished German archaeologist Gerhard Bersu and his wife Maria were among the many foreign nationals held in camps on the Island under the British Government's policy of internment of aliens. Arrangements were therefore made with the authorities allowing Dr. Bersu and a selected group of assistants to perform excavations under armed guard which resulted in the excavation of several highly significant sites. In fact Bersu remained on the Island until 1947 to complete this important work. However, internment proved to be a mixed blessing as camps which were established at Port St. Mary and Port Erin led to the restriction of public access to Cregneash and the Folk Museum was, perforce, closed until the summer of 1942.

On his return from war service, Basil Megaw continued the advancement of Manx archaeological studies. He undertook a number of small but important excavations including, in 1953, the famous neolithic burial monument in the parish of Lonan known as King Orry's Grave. He also instigated a thorough recording format for archaeological artefacts and played a leading role in the Field Section of the Natural History and Antiquarian Society. He was also careful to continue and to build on the pioneering work of P. M. C. Kermode with regard to the corpus of Manx cross-carvings, publishing the new finds since Kermode's death, including the prized fragment of an altar slab known as the Calf of Man Crucifixion. Megaw's further articles on the early Christian and Mediaeval periods of Manx history remain standard references for students and scholars today.

Basil Megaw was ever vigilant to seize opportunities of expanding the role of the Museum and the scope of its collections with a view to presenting the people of the Isle of Man with a fuller view of their own cultural achievements. One such opportunity presented itself in 1950. During a visit to Blair Castle in Perthshire to consult the Atholl family papers, Megaw discovered a marvellous and previously unknown sequence of twenty-six water-colour paintings of the Isle of Man executed by the noted eighteenth century artist John "Warwick" Smith. Basil Megaw did not fail to capitalize on such a discovery and persuaded the Duke of Atholl to allow the series of paintings to be loaned to the Manx Museum for exhibition in the Art Gallery. Megaw was subsequently able to encourage a private benefactor to purchase the entire collection for the Museum thereby providing a major addition to the collection of Manx-associated works of art.

In 1951, under Megaw's Directorship, two further major additions were made to the scope and nature of the Museum's work. The opening of a new Nautical Museum in Castletown provided the second branch of the Manx Museum centred on the oldest surviving Manx-built ship, the "Peggy", rediscovered just before the outbreak of war in an eighteenth-century building adjacent to Castletown harbour. The building, together with this unique survival was presented to the Museum Trustees in 1941 and on his return from war-service, Basil Megaw completed the programme of necessary repairs and conservation to provide the public with this new dimension for the interpretation of Manx history.

Megaw's wide vision of the potential role of the Museum within the Manx community had led to his deep concern for the preservation of the Manx countryside. He shared this concern with a small number of other individuals, notably Deemster Percy Cowley, who were actively acquiring areas of land for preservation pending the establishment of an officially responsible body. As a result of such activities, Megaw was able to assist in drawing up a Manx National Trust Bill to provide a measure of statutory protection for the scenic Manx landscape. The Bill was duly steered through Tynwald and finally became law in 1951, in consequence creating the single combined body of Trustees known as the Manx Museum and National Trust.

Thus, when in 1957, Basil Megaw resigned from the Directorship of the Manx Museum to become Director of the School of Scottish Studies at the University of Edinburgh, he left behind an institution which had been enlarged in both size and scope from the original concept and which contained the hard-won elements of a modern museum service for the nation.

A. Marshall Cubbon

A. Marshall Cubbon became Director of the Manx Museum on the 1st September 1957 on the departure of Basil Megaw. He had joined the staff seven years previously as Secretary and Assistant Director in succession to Eric Cregeen.

It had been Marshall Cubbon's intention to pursue a career in teaching and he had qualified at Sheffield Teacher-Training College before being called for service in the Army. After demobilisation he taught for a period and then entered the University of Manchester where he read for a B.A. Hons. Degree in Geography.

On taking up work at the Manx Museum his first major task was the development of the geological collections and initial displays of the rocks and minerals of the Isle of Man. In this project he had the valuable collaboration of Dr. David E. Owen on secondment from the University of Liverpool.

This was followed by work on the early printed maps of the Isle of Man. Gaps in the collection were identified and these were filled with the generous financial assistance of the Friends of the Manx Museum, all the more valuable in the financial stringency of the post-war years.

Marshall Cubbon wrote a guide to the map collection, the first in a valuable series of booklets produced over a period of years which included, *inter alia*, Guides to the Manx Museum and the Branch

A. Marshall Cubbon, Secretary and Deputy Director 1950–1957, Director 1957–1984.

Museums, the Ancient Monuments of the Island and The Art of the Manx Crosses.

On becoming Director, Marshall Cubbon took over responsibility for the archaeological work of the Manx Museum. He himself carried out many important excavations, notably the prehistoric burial site at Kitleaba, Ramsey, which was reported in the Proceedings of the Prehistoric Society.

A policy of inviting expert archaeologists from other institutions to the Island was established. In this connection the invaluable contribution to Manx archaeology of the late Peter Gelling of the University of Birmingham, himself a Manxman, which extended from 1950 until his death in 1983 is gratefully acknowledged. This, and the work of other visiting specialists is mentioned in more detail in a later chapter of this book.

In 1971 negotiations with the British Government led to the Treasury's agreeing to the presumptive right to Treasure Trove found in the Isle of Man passing from the British Museum to the Manx Museum. This bore fruit in 1976 when the silver coins and armlets found in the churchyard at Kirk Michael were ruled to be Treasure Trove at the first inquest of its kind held since that on the Douglas Hoard in 1894, and were later acquired by the Manx Museum.

Subsequent discoveries, one accidental, and others made with the use of metal detectors, led to the accumulation of an important corpus of coins of the Viking period and to the identification of a Hiberno-Manx coinage by the late Professor Michael Dolly.

In the years 1962–64 Marshall Cubbon supervised an extensive programme of gallery reconstruction made possible by the relocation of the library collection in the

Marshall Cubbon lecturing to the Anglesey Antiquarian Society at King Orry's Grave, Lonan, 1970.

newly erected book stack. A "reshuffle" took place resulting in the creation of a larger map room, a larger, improved Art Gallery and the creation of the Upper Folk Life Gallery. However several years were to elapse before funds became available to construct the new reading room originally planned to complement the book stack.

Marshall Cubbon exploited the greater potential of the new Art Gallery in 1964 with the exhibition of the avant-garde abstract sculpture of the Manx-born artist Bryan Kneale; a fine example of whose work "The Watcher" stands on a site near the base of the book stack, appropriately commanding a wide view of Douglas Bay. Exhibitions of the work of two other outstanding Manx artists, Archibald Knox and John Miller Nicholson followed.

In 1973 a major fund-raising effort was mounted, involving many organisations both on and off the Island, to purchase four outstanding eighteenth century portraits of members of the influential Manx family, the Taubmans. Three are by Romney and the fourth is attributed to F. Cotes. The acquisition of these fine portraits considerably enriched the quality of the Museum's art collection.

Marshall Cubbon was deeply involved in the work of the Manx National Trust from its inception in 1951 and was instrumental in the acquisition of many of its properties.

In 1952 the Calf of Man was leased at a peppercorn rent from the National Trust for England and Wales who had acquired it in 1937. At first the property was farmed but in 1959 it became a Nature Reserve and Bird Observatory under the Wardenship of Einar Brun. Through the efforts of succeeding Wardens and the continuing help of the British Trust for Ornithology it has gained a place in the front rank of Bird Observatories.

During Marshall Cubbon's time at the Manx Museum he implemented a programme of considerable expansion of branch museum activity. A major expansion of the Nautical Museum in Castletown was undertaken in 1967 and in 1970 the mediaeval Chapel of St. Mary, later the Old Grammar School, at Castletown which was under threat of demolition was purchased and a programme of excavation and reconstruction carried out thus preserving the oldest surviving roofed building on the Island.

In 1978 the first branch museum in the north of the Island was established with the opening of the Grove Rural Life Museum at Ramsey. Under Marshall Cubbon's vigilant control and with the assistance of a number of specialists in the field, this comfortably proportioned Victorian house was restored to provide an authentic and vivid picture of domestic and agricultural life at the turn of the century.

In his capacity as Inspector of Ancient Monuments Marshall Cubbon continued the Trust's policy of providing better protection for the ancient cross-slabs by repositioning them wherever possible outside the parish churches and commenced a scheme for the erection of a shelter for the cross-slabs at Lonan Old Church.

His published work includes papers on cross fragments found at Maughold and Braddan and descriptions of the Early Christian and Viking heritage in the Island.

Marshall Cubbon was involved in professional Museum activities outside the Island and was elected a Fellow of the Museums Association and of the Society of Antiquaries of London, and he takes an active part in the affairs of the Isle of Man Natural History and Antiquarian Society, presiding as President during the Society's Centenary Year.

In 1967 he was awarded a Winston Churchill Travelling Fellowship which enabled him to travel for three months studying museums and their service to the communities in the United States of America, Mexico and Iceland. This outstanding opportunity to widen his professional experience produced a valuable feed-back to his work in the Manx Museum.

He was invited to read several papers at annual conferences of the Museums Association and was elected a Member of the Council of the Association from 1970 to 1973 serving as Chairman of one of its standing committees from 1972–76.

He was invited to prepare specialist reports on nine museum development projects in both England and Ireland on behalf of the Carnegie U.K. Trust, and was commissioned to report on the development of the museum services of the county by Cumbria County Council.

In 1975 he was awarded an O.B.E. for his services to the Manx Museum and National Trust, which he viewed as an honour to the work and standing of the Trust. He served as President of the North West Federation of Museum and Art Galleries from 1978 to 1979.

Throughout his Directorship he strove to strike the essential balance between popular presentation of the Island's heritage and academic scholarship, which he viewed as vital to the integrity and professional standing of any good museum.

SOME MANX CROSSES

Irneit's Cross-Slab, Maughold (No. 47).
The inscription within the circle, in debased Roman characters, records a Celtic bishop, Irneit.

The fourteenth century Maughold Pillar-Cross standing in Maughold churchyard. There are various heraldic and other carvings on the head including a representation of the crucifixion and an early example of the Manx armorial bearings of the "three legs", the spurs on the armoured legs being clearly visible.

Dragon Cross-Slab, Michael (No. 117).
A late Scandinavian style cross with skilled interlace on both faces and stylised dragons in the side panels.

Thorwald's Cross-Slab, Andreas (No. 128).
A most significant cross in the corpus of Manx carved stones. One face is decorated with a graphic scene from the last great battle of Norse pagan mythology, Ragnarok, when Odin is devoured by the Fenris Wolf.
On the other face, a belted figure carries a book and a cross and tramples on a serpent next to the early Christian symbol of a fish.
An incomplete runic inscription down the edge of the stone reads: "Thorwald raised this cross . . ."
This tenth-century cross may well be reflecting the contemporary decline of pagan beliefs and the coming of Christianity.

Below left: St. Patrick's Chair, Marown (Nos. 6 and 7).
These two slabs of local slate, each marked with a simple cross and set into a small rectangular dry-stone base in the middle of a field, may mark the site of an early Christian preaching station.

Below right: Wheel-Headed Cross-Slab, Lonan (No. 73).
Impressive cross-slab some five feet high, standing in its original socket-stone outside Lonan old church. Possibly dating from the tenth century, its decoration consists of typical Celtic interlace.

DIGGING UP THE PAST

A. M. CUBBON

The Isle of Man, in common with the antiquarian movement in Britain generally, was influenced by a small but active and often remarkably well-informed group of nineteenth century amateur scholars, who in general avoided the excesses of unbridled romanticism and recognized the value of objective, scientific scholarship. Much of the important pioneer studies of antiquities in the Island was incorporated into the publications of the Manx Society for the Publication of National Documents, which issued thirty-three volumes between 1859 and 1894. An awareness of history in the countryside, and a growing recognition of the new dimension that the developing science of archaeology could give to the earlier periods of Manx history, was much in the minds of these pioneers who saw the need for a national museum service for the Isle of Man. In this, as in so much of the formative thinking behind the embryonic Manx Museum, the leading figure was to become that of P. M. C. Kermode. When the first Manx Museum Act was promulgated from Tynwald Hill in 1886 it was the preservation of the Island's ancient monuments that formed the first major role of the new Trustee body. In the first year of its existence a report was produced on the ancient monuments in need of protection, with an understandable and proper emphasis on the preservation of the Island's great heritage of carved stone cross-slabs.

It would appear that in its early decades the Trust saw its role in the countryside primarily as protecting the surviving monuments. Excavation was being undertaken to a limited extent, but privately and through the Isle of Man Natural History and Antiquarian Society (established in 1879). Excavation in those early days did not require the now necessary licence of the Museum Trust. Local antiquarian literature records early finds of weapons, urns and runic inscriptions, and later refers to deliberate excavation such as the opening of tumuli and the discovery of urns on Peel Hill in 1878. Frederick Swynnerton excavated, recorded and published what might be regarded as perhaps the first scientific archaeological excavation in the Island when at Port St. Mary in 1887 he recognized the importance of the stratigraphical relationship of an early Mesolithic occupation deposit into which and onto which later cist burials had been dug. In one of his

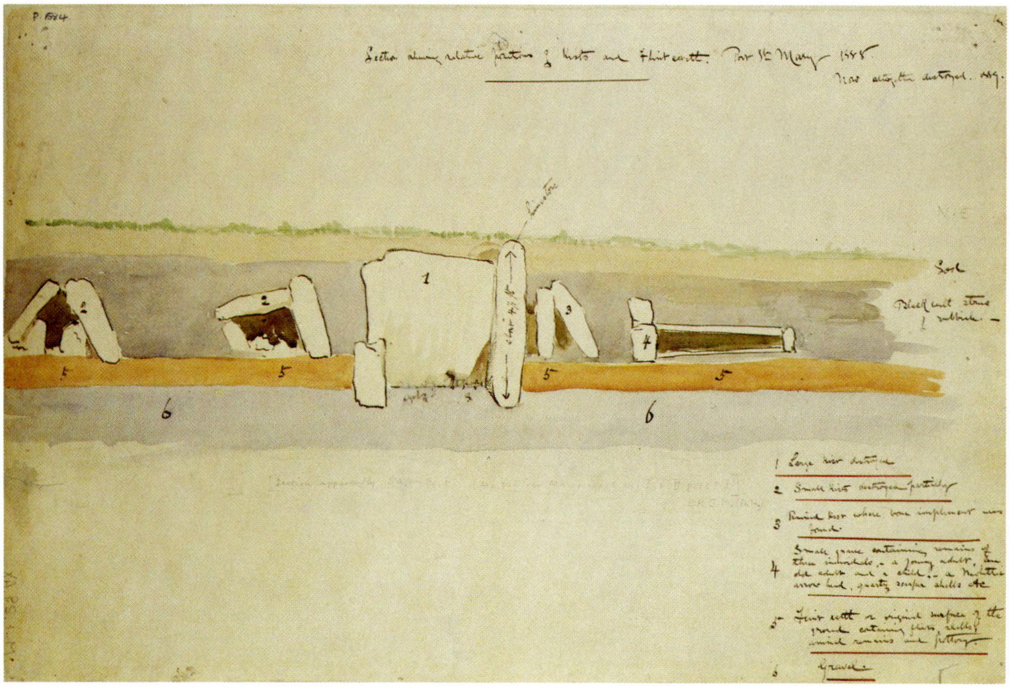

Frederick Swynnerton's watercolour tinted sketch of his 1888 section across the megalithic burial cists found when the Alfred Pier was built at Port St. Mary. It illustrates his superiority as an archaeologist over most of his contemporaries and many of his successors.

published accounts he deprecates his own work as "'rooting' (mostly done with a large nail!)"; but this shows his awareness of the care that excavation demanded, contrasting with the pick and shovel approach of antiquarian treasure hunters. The *Proceedings* of the Isle of Man Natural History and Antiquarian Society records much of the early archaeological activity in the Island, and continues as a major organ for the publication of important excavation reports to the present day. P. M. C. Kermode, the virtual founder of the Society, had become the dominant figure of Manx archaeology by the end of the nineteenth century. In particular his detailed study of the Island's great corpus of Celtic and Norse carved cross-slabs culminated in the publication of his monumental *Manx Crosses* in 1907.

Philip Moore Callow Kermode, pioneering Manx archaeologist and first Director of the Manx Museum. He is pointing out the features of a cross-slab found at Andreas and carved with "bind-runes".

By the early years of the twentieth century the Museum Trustees' particular concern over the preservation of the Island's cross carvings led to the bringing together of these outstanding monuments at their respective parish churches, and the erection of shelters to protect them from the elements. This process was taken further over the last thirty years by moving more of these priceless memorials of the Island's early Christian heritage inside the churches, or under effective shelter, with much more meaningful interpretation of the carvings, particularly at Andreas, Bride and Lonan.

Above: The cross display at Andreas parish church where the standards of preservation and display established by Kermode in relation to the crosses has been continued and enlarged by his successors. The majority of these ancient gravestones and memorials are preserved in the church of the parish in which they were found, as a fitting reminder that they are Christian monuments of the Island's past.

In 1908 a major – indeed staggeringly ambitious – step forward was taken when, under the tireless drive of Kermode, the Manx Archaeological Survey was launched, which aimed "to make inquiry as to the number and position of all the Historic and Pre-historic Remains in the Isle of Man, to conduct a careful and systematic examination of such Remains, and to draw up a full and particular Report thereon". The Manx Museum and Ancient Monuments Trustees were co-opted *ex-officio* to the organising body, which was chaired by H.E. the Lieutenant Governor, Lord Raglan, and the decision was taken to concentrate first on the early Christian keeills (chapels) with their associated burial grounds. Throughout the rest of his life Kermode, the secretary and prime mover in the scheme, pressed ahead with this survey – and in most cases excavation – of the keeill sites, though understandably the project slowed down markedly when, in 1922, his dream of the establishment of a national museum was realised and he was appointed as the first director of that institution. Four reports covering four of the six sheadings of the Island were published between 1909 and 1915, but the fifth report, largely compiled by Kermode in 1918, only got into print (as a posthumous tribute to its author by the

J. R. Bruce (1895–1986) who, while not himself a Manxman, made a major contribution to the study of the Island's archaeology, not least as Vice-Chairman of the Manx Museum Trustees (1962–1976) and as compiler of the sixth volume of the Manx Archaeological Survey.

Museum Trustees) in 1935. It is gratifying that the project so far as the keeills were concerned was completed many years later by a long-serving and highly respected member of the Trust, J. R. Bruce, who as a young man had assisted Kermode in sorting the initial collections of the Manx Museum. Bruce's report covering the keeill sites in the sheading of Rushen was published by the Museum in 1968.

Kermode's archaeological work however was certainly not confined to the Early Christian period, although his name will always be associated with the Manx crosses and the keeill sites of the Island. In 1893 (and again in 1911) with Professor Herdman he excavated at the Meayll Circle, on the moorland between Cregneash and Port Erin. This unique monument, with six pairs of burial chambers, arranged in a circle, each pair approached by a stone-sided passage from the outside of the circle, yielded evidence of cremated burials with flint implements and a range of decorated pottery bowls, some of a type unparalleled until similar pottery was recovered at Ballaharra, Isle

Above: This unique megalithic ritual and burial site on the Meayll Hill was placed in the care of the Manx Museum and Ancient Monuments Trustees in 1907.

Right: The Ballafayle long cairn at Maughold.

of Man in 1971, a site which yielded radio carbon dates of *circa* 2300 B.C. A small jet bead was also recovered from the Meayll Circle excavation, from beneath the flooring slabs of one of the burial chambers. In 1926 Kermode excavated another Neolithic burial site in the megalithic tradition of chambered tombs, at Ballafayle, Maughold. Here again cremation was the burial rite, and evidence of funeral pyres was recovered from the trapezoid cairn behind a concave forecourt flanked by large upright stones. The funeral fires must have been burning as the cairn was built up, as in places there was clear evidence of the vitrification and fusing of the cairn stones by heat.

Perhaps the most dramatic excavation by Kermode was that of a pagan Viking boat burial in 1927, from a conspicuous mound on the summit of a morainic hill at Knock y Doonee, Andreas. The site commands sweeping views southwards over the northern lowland plain of the Isle of Man to the Manx hills beyond, and northward across the ayres, the gravel beach which forms the northern coastline of the Island, and on a clear day across the sea to the long vista of the coast of southwestern Scotland. This typical setting for a Viking ship burial yielded evidence of a well-furnished burial of a typical farmer-warrior, with sword, spear, axe and shield, together with smith's tools, iron cauldron, knives, stone sharpening hone and lead fishing line weight. His horse had been slain, and buried with the dead warrior, together with its harness, while the handsome silver-inlaid bronze penannular brooch was recovered which would have secured the Viking's cloak at his shoulder. The surviving – if rusty – iron clench nails marked the outline of the ship in which the dead warrior was buried in the cairn, very probably on the highest point of the farmstead he had seized when he settled in the Isle of Man in the mid to late ninth century.

Above: Some of the finds from Kermode's excavation of the Norse burial mound on Knock y Doonee, Andreas, the first ship burial to be excavated in the British Isles.

Below: Detail of the silver-inlaid bronze pennanular brooch from this pagan grave.

Another notable excavation of the late 1920s was J. R. Bruce's and William Cubbon's investigation at Cronk yn Howe, Lezayre, which revealed early Christian graves, cross-slabs, objects attributed to the Norse Viking period (a glass bead, iron hinges from a wooden casket and iron tools) and the foundations of a rectangular keeill. Bruce's meticulous excavation records mark a significant advance on the over-hasty digging of earlier periods.

After the death of Kermode in 1932 a number of excavations were carried out in the Island during the 1930s, at the invitation of the Manx Museum, by Professor Fleure and a number of his students from Manchester University. Fleure was a brilliant and inspiring teacher in the field of human geography, and a number of his outstanding students have for a generation made a major impact on geographical, ethnographical and archaeological studies in Britain.

Fleure excavated the striking neolithic chambered tomb at Cashtal yn Ard in Maughold, and the then enigmatic site at the Braaid. His excavation techniques would now be regarded as not of the highest, but his broad interests and experience in European historical geography brought a valuable dimension to Manx studies at that period. Cashtal yn Ard was recovered from a heavily overgrown state, cleared and restored to a meaningful condition. It is of course only the skeleton of its original form; the cairn material has been

stripped away throughout past centuries, and only the largest and firmly-set stones survive. In places Fleure re-erected fallen stones, or even re-set stones in positions where sockets made it clear that major upright stones had formerly stood. All such repositioned stones were clearly dated by the excavator, and the result was a meaningful representation of the monument. Its overall dimensions were shown, and also an internal kerb of stones which probably retained the cairn of an earlier phase of the site. In particular the enormous stones incorporated into the semi-circular forecourt at the western end of the cairn were cleared, flanking the portal entrance way, leading from the forecourt into the long burial chamber of five compartments running down the long axis of the site. Western neolithic pottery was found in the course of the excavation, showing that the site was typical of the chambered tombs of western Britain, and the recovery of unburned bone indicated that interment rather than cremation was the burial practice.

Left: A general view looking east through the curved entrance to the ritual and burial site now known as Cashtal yn Ard, Maughold. Although it was investigated successively by the Rev. S. N. Harrison and Professor H. J. Fleure it remains something of an enigma.

Right: A view of the five burial chambers.

An aerial view of the Norse homestead at the Braaid, Marown, including a boat-shaped hall, and what is assumed to be an earlier round house, excavated by Professor Fleure and, later, by the Manx archaeologist, P. S. Gelling.

When Fleure switched his attention to the site at the Braaid he was still thinking in prehistoric terms, and the large, undressed slabs of local slate (so similar to those at Cashtal yn Ard) were interpreted as a Bronze Age circular henge or "temple", with associated processional alignments of standing stones (reminiscent of Stonehenge and Avebury). The clearing of the site produced no dateable finds. The now accepted interpretation of the cleared structures as a circular Celtic house and Viking boat-shaped and rectangular buildings was first made by Gerhard Bersu in 1941, and Fleure and Dunlop incorporated the suggestion, with acknowledgement, in the latter part of their report on the site, which appeared in print in 1942. In 1962 Peter Gelling re-excavated a limited area of the site, and found traces of a turf gable wall at each end of the Viking boat-shaped house. The work on this site is a nice illustration of how the developing and improving science of archaeology can revise and refine the interpretation of a monument.

In the later 1930s the excavation of a group of dry-stone circular huts and associated features near the Balthane Road, between Ballasalla and Derbyhaven, was necessitated by the development of Ronaldsway Airport. This so-called "Ronaldsway village site" produced an imortant range of finds including both metalwork and pottery, covering early Christian and probably Viking times, together with prehistoric features; but inadequate recording unfortunately reduced the importance of this potentially significant site.

In 1936 Basil Megaw, recently graduated in Archaeology and Anthropology at Cambridge, was appointed as Assistant Director of the Manx Museum, where he became Director from 1940 to (after war service) 1957. His work on the growing collections built on the foundations laid by Kermode, and his reorganisation ensured the development of the institution beyond its formative stage. With William Cubbon (his Director) he played an important part in drafting the 1938 Act of Tynwald, which extended and strengthened the Manx Museum's position in relation to the protection of ancient monuments, and made necessary the reporting of archaeological finds, the licensing of all archaeological excavation, and of the removal of archaeological objects from the Island. In legislative terms the Isle of Man can show the way ahead to the United Kingdom.

The 1939–45 war and the immediate post war years might have been expected to be a period of restricted archaeological activity. In the Isle of Man however the fortunes of war resulted in this being a period of outstanding and exciting archaeological advance. The brilliant German archaeologist Gerhard Bersu, with his wife Maria, out of favour with the Nazi establishment in Germany, had been excavating in Britain during the summer of 1939. After the fall of France in 1940 all enemy aliens were interned, and both the Bersus were imprisoned in the Isle of Man (at first unaware of each other's whereabouts, but later in the war together in a mixed internment camp in Port Erin).

The Museum's third Director, B. R. S. Megaw, being helped to measure the promontory fort at Cronk ny Merriu, Santan, by H. M. Rogers, a member of the Isle of Man Natural History and Antiquarian Society.

Dr. Gerhard Bersu, the great German archaeologist, who was interned in the Isle of Man during the Second World War and consequently did so much to further Manx archaeology. *(Photograph by courtesy of B. R. S. Megaw and Dr. I. Scollar.)*

After a small geological prospecting excavation in which Bersu located limited deposits of manganese (a valuable mineral under wartime conditions) had shown the practicability of such operations, and with the encouragement and sponsorship of the Society of Antiquaries of London, the camp authorities were persuaded to permit Bersu to undertake archaeological excavation, using parties of volunteers from the camp, working under armed guard. The excavations which followed must have been a somewhat bizarre experience for those concerned, but they represented a sustained programme of archaeological research at the highest level, co-ordinated by the Manx Museum.

Bersu of course was working under all the difficulties of his wartime circumstances, with in particular no access to academic library facilities, no trained support, other than that of his wife, and no possibility of direct professional consultation other than with the Director of the Manx Museum (however the Museum functioned as a line of communication, and occasional visits by leading British archaeologists took place). On the other hand Bersu had no other professional pressures to divert his interest, and from 1941 to 1946 he could devote all the time when he was not actually digging to study and interpretation of his results.

Of the three Celtic round house sites which he dug between 1941 and 1944 he told the writer "Never again will a site of this type ever be excavated in such detail". These circumstances were perhaps just as well as the sites, two adjoining houses at Ballacagen, half a mile north-west of Castletown, and one at Ballanorris, half a mile further north-west, were multi-period and exceedingly complex, producing timbers and postholes from in all nine different house plans.

This model of the round house at Ballacagen was made by a fellow internee, under the supervision of Dr. Bersu, to embody the results of his excavations of this important site prior to final publication of the excavation's findings.

These successive, large timber-framed houses, up to 25 metres in diameter, were completely roofed (apart from a smoke hole above the central hearth) by a covering of sods, supported on a timber framework carried on concentric rings of substantial timber uprights. The boundary rings, which are now all that show on the sites, mark the position of the surrounding ditch and the earth ramp raised against the outer wall of the house to help take the strain of the outward thrust of the huge timber roof structure. In the course of the excavation evidence was produced that the nine houses built on these three sites had incorporated the trunks of over 4000 mature oak trees. It was clearly these Celtic Iron Age farmers who played the major part in clearing the thick tree cover which in prehistoric times had covered much of the lowlands of the Isle of Man. Much of this timber had of course decayed away long before Bersu's excavations, but in the water-logged soil conditions of these sites, in marshy lowland near to a stream, the footings of some of the timbers survived in embarrassing quantities. It is ironic to realise that these excavations occurred just before the days of radio carbon dating of organic material, and such was the problem of the quantity of unworked timber being produced by the site that it was used to cook the wartime sausages of the diggers' lunch! Fortunately however specimens were preserved at the Manx Museum which in due course yielded radio carbon dates of the third century B.C. for the early levels of occupation, which probably extended over 200 to 300 years. The sites yielded finds of crude pottery, ornaments of bronze, glass, amber and stone, bone objects, worked stones, querns and crucibles, which represented the occupation debris of these large Celtic Iron Age farmsteads. Post war pressures and Bersu's appointment to the directorship of the Deutsches Archaologisches Institut at Frankfurt-am-Main, long delayed the full publication of these outstandingly important excavations, but a full and definitive report was eventually published by the Manx Museum in 1977. Behind the analytical scientific evidence of this report one should recall a picture of small groups of internees, travelling with their armed guards by the local narrow-gauge steam railway from the barbed wire enclosure of the camp at Port Erin to the sites in the meadows north of Castletown; and of representatives of the Manx Museum visiting the site to inspect progress, and surreptitiously dropping little tins of his beloved snuff into the wellington boots of Gerhard Bersu!

Aerial photography showing the remains on site of the two round houses at Ballacagen excavated by Dr. Bersu.

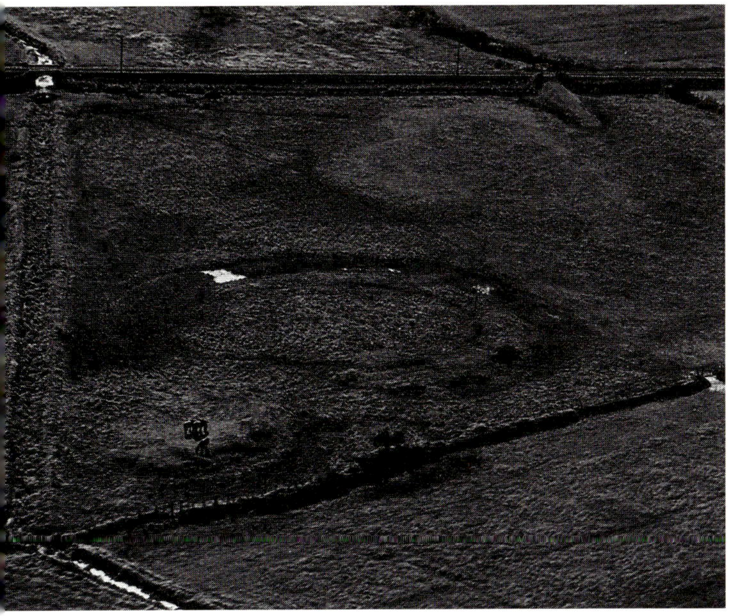

Above: Polished axe-heads and other wood and leather-working tools typical of the Ronaldsway culture.

Left: Finely-worked slate plaques, recovered from the emergency excavation by J. R. Bruce and Mrs. E. M. Megaw in 1943 of a house site revealed by the construction of Ronaldsway Airport. Two have incised decoration which is only wholly paralleled by a further plaque excavated at Ballavarry in Andreas and some sherds from Glencrutchery, Onchan. Like the stone axes above, they are typical of the Isle of Man's unique first farmers' culture now known, after the house site, as the Ronaldsway neolithic.

While Bersu was digging at Ballacagen, just north-west of Castletown, another major site was uncovered at Ronaldsway Airport, just to the north-east of the town. The enlargement of the airport, at that time also a Fleet Air Arm station, uncovered the remains of a neolithic house, which had to be hurriedly but expertly excavated by Eleanor Megaw (Basil's wife, he being away on war service) and J. R. Bruce. The Ronaldsway rectangular neolithic house yielded much characteristic pottery, asymmetrical stone axeheads, finely-worked flint implements, and five enigmatic incised small stone plaques. It forms the type site giving its name to the distinctive Manx "Ronaldsway" secondary neolithic culture.

At the end of the war in 1945 Bersu was excavating at Chapel Hill, Balladoole, a fortified Celtic iron age site west of Castletown, which proved also to be the site of a pagan Viking ship burial. The wood of the vessel had, of course, long decayed, but the iron clench nails securing the timbers of the ship gave its position and dimensions. A well-equipped man was found in the vessel, as well as the body of a woman. The man's personal ornaments, his horse's harness, his spurs, stirrups, shield boss and iron cauldrons show how his personal equipment had derived from Ireland and Scotland, Scandinavia, Anglo-Saxon England and the continental Carolingian empire. The pagan burial had been sited directly over a Celtic Christian cemetery. The human dimension of Bersu's work at Balladoole is shown by an entry in the midst of the technical records of his field notebook, recording that the policeman had arrived with the news that the war in Europe was over. The impact of such news for an internee can be imagined.

Above: Chapel Hill, Balladoole, one of the Island's most important sites occupied from earliest times. Kermode excavated the rather late keeill (early Christian chapel) and Dr. Bersu investigated the perimeter iron age defences and a pagan Viking burial (marked by an oval of stones in the photograph).

Below: Some of the iron harness of the pagan Viking, including a spur and a stirrup.

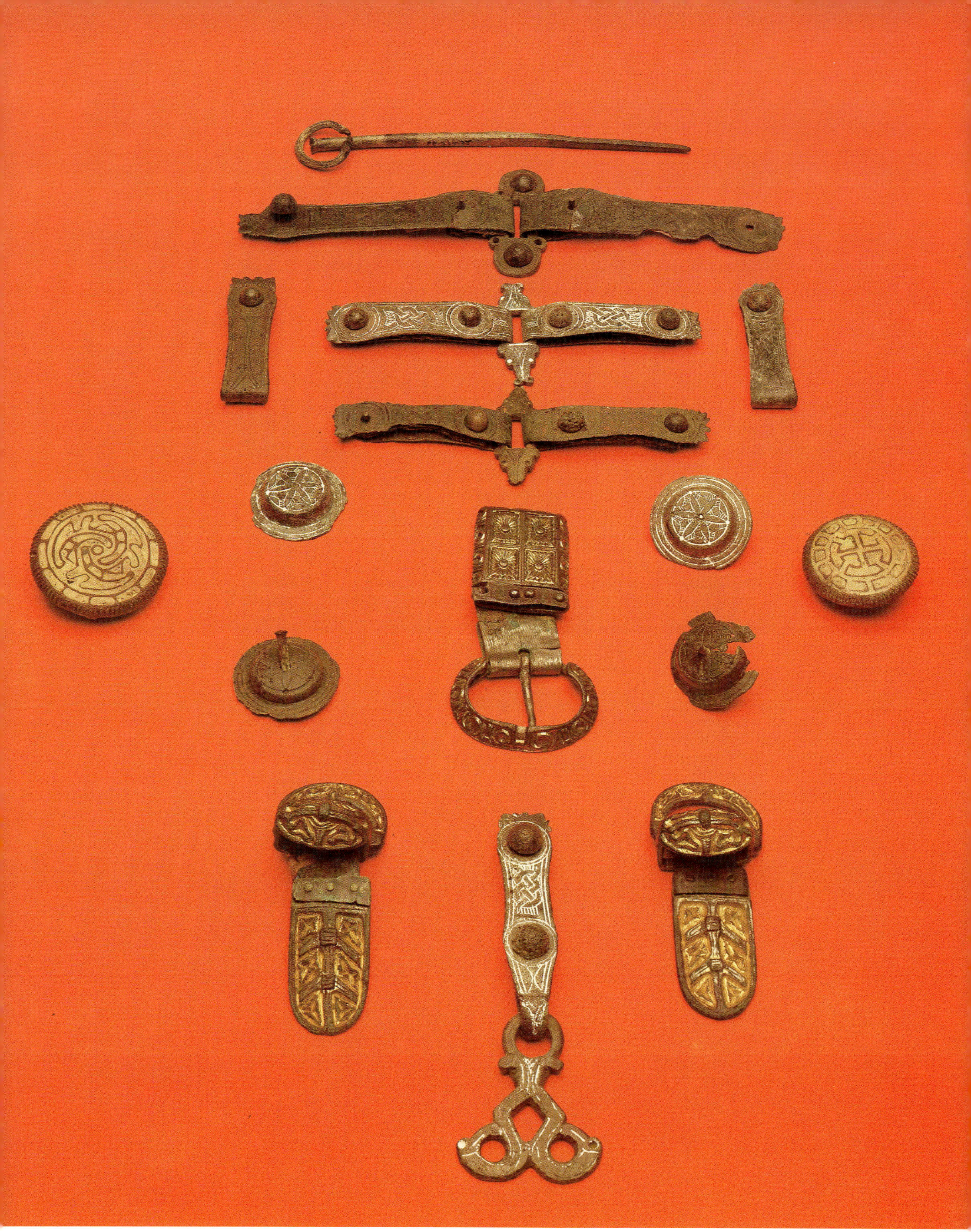

Left: The finer ornaments of the Balladoole Viking, stemming from disparate sources within the trading world of the Norsemen. The bronze mounts with incised decoration belong to the horse's bridle. The more elaborate bronze buckles, slides and strap-ends decorated with silvering and gilding were part of the warrior's spur fittings.

Below: The weapons from the pagan Viking grave excavated by Dr. Bersu at Cronk Mooar, Jurby. Such weapons seem customarily to have been damaged before burial – swords are found broken and shield bosses dented – either to release their "spirit" for the use of the dead man, or to minimise the attraction of grave-robbing. (Broken sword, spear, shield-boss and knife.)

Bersu remained in the Island until 1947, and following his meticulous excavation of the ship burial at Balladoole, he excavated two further pagan Viking burials in Jurby parish, at Cronk Mooar in 1945 and Ballateare in 1946. These were both coffin burials, yielding fine Viking swords (recovered in their scabbards thanks to Bersu's outstanding excavation techniques), as well as spearheads, shield bosses, and dress ornament. Textile fragments of the Viking's shaggy, woollen cloak were recovered at Cronk Mooar, while traces of plough marks in clay sub-soil beneath the burial mound, suggested extended farming activity or technological advance in ploughing associated with the Viking settlement of the Isle of Man. At Ballateare, where the burial mound had survived, this yielded evidence that it had been formed of top sods, possibly representing a sacrifice of the fields of the farmstead of the Viking settler. Near the top of the mound a layer of

A macabre find from Dr. Bersu's excavation of a pagan Viking burial at Ballateare, Jurby. The back of the skull of this young girl was sliced away with a sword as a sacrifice to accompany her dead master into the burial mound.

cremated animal bone – ox, horse, sheep and dog – represented a sacrifice of the dead farmer's livestock, while the top of the mound also yielded the most dramatic evidence of sacrifice – the skeleton of a young woman, the back of whose skull had been cut away by the blow of a sharp implement. As the young woman had been killed prior to being placed on the mound, this implement may perhaps have been the fine sword with its handsome guard inlaid with silver, which had later (in its scabbard) been broken into three pieces before being placed within the wooden coffin in the grave pit under the mound.

During the summer of 1947 Gerhard Bersu returned briefly to the Isle of Man to direct his last excavation on the Island – a series of long exploratory trenches within Peel Castle. A young Manx student assisted on this dig, which encouraged him to make a career in archaeology. Peter Gelling graduated at Cambridge and later became a lecturer in archaeology at Birmingham University. In 1950 he commenced the first excavation he directed in the Isle of Man – the promontory fort of Cronk ny Merriu, Port Grenaugh – on the day that the writer started work as assistant director of the Manx Museum. This was the first of many excavations by Gelling in the Island; indeed apart from the disrupted year of the seamen's strike he excavated in the Isle of Man every year up to his death in 1983. This sustained programme (with financial assistance from the Manx Museum and the Isle of Man Natural History and Antiquarian Society) has contributed significantly to the advance of Manx archaeology over the past 35 years, particularly in relation to the Celtic iron age and Viking periods. Apart from the two sites on which he was engaged at the time of his untimely death every one of his Manx excavations has been published.

Left: P. S. Gelling explaining the results of his work on the site of an iron age and Norse promontory fort at Cronk ny Merriu, Santan.

Below: The carefully chosen defensive site of Cronk ny Merriu guarding the entrance to Port Grenaugh.

From 1950 to 1957 Gelling excavated three coastal promontory forts, Cronk ny Merriu, Close ny Chollagh and Cass ny Hawin, each of which yielded a Norse style house, with indications of an earlier period of occupation. This earlier period was fortunately preserved at Close ny Chollagh, which revealed the foundations of four well-built stone circular huts, with a range of finds giving a date of the first century B.C. to first century A.D. The study was extended to an inland promontory fort on Ballanicholas, Marown (excavated 1957–9), which produced evidence of a Celtic timber-framed house, smaller but clearly in the tradition of Bersu's sites at Ballacagen and Ballanorris, with a penannular brooch indicating a similar date in the Celtic Iron Age.

Below: The successive iron age stone-built round houses that preceded a later Norse house in the promontory fort at Close ny Chollagh, Malew, excavated by P. S. Gelling.

Bottom: An ancient safety pin with a tale to tell – the "Colchester fibula" that provided a date for the iron age occupation of the Close ny Chollagh promontory fort.

Gelling's study of habitation sites continued with the excavation of a number of mounds at Block Eary (1958–60) and Injebreck (1961), which proved to be built up from the collapse of successive wattle and daub huts. These had been occupied as shieling habitations in the summer months, when the high pastures were grazed by flocks and herds driven into the hills from the lowlands. This practice, and the huts, clearly extended over a very long period, but an English penny of King Stephen from one of the Block Eary huts demonstrated that the practice was in use in mediaeval times.

In the early 1950s Basil Megaw excavated and cleared the north-eastern end of the megalithic chambered tomb known as "King Orry's Grave" at Laxey. The excavation revealed lengths of well-preserved original dry stone walling, and the sockets of former standing stones, as well as finds of pottery and flints, and resulted in this portion of this sadly mutilated monument being accessible to the public in a meaningful state for the first time. Megaw also excavated a Bronze Age burial mound at Bishopscourt Farm, which covered two cists, one containing a crouched burial and the other a cremation. Each cist also contained a pottery food vessel.

A cairn excavated by Marshall Cubbon at Clay Head (1961–2), enclosed within the grounds of a new bungalow was thought to be a similar Bronze Age tumulus, but it (and an adjoining mound) proved to be multi-period cooking place sites with boiling troughs, which produced radio carbon dating which, when calibrated, indicated extended use from late Neolithic through to mid Bronze Age times, from approximately 2200 to 1050 B.C.

Peter Gelling excavated at the Island's major hill top fort on the summit of South Barrule, 1,585 feet above sea level, in the summers of 1960, 1961 and 1968. It was a blissful spot, with superb panoramic views when the weather was kind, but its altitude and total lack of shelter could be all too real in bad weather, even in summer. He sectioned both of the concentric ramparts that encircle the site, and excavated four of the complex of over seventy huts which are discernible within the inner rampart, and which produced pottery. Charcoal from a hearth in one of the huts yielded a radio carbon date of circa 523 B.C.

Gelling contributed further to his research on Viking houses in the Isle of Man by his re-excavation of the large "boat-shaped" house at the Braaid in 1962, and by his excavation of a Norse type farmstead at Dooarlish Cashin, Patrick, in 1970 at an altitude of about 700 feet. The discovery of such a house – together with a corn-drying kiln, implying arable farming – on such marginal land appears to be striking evidence of the density of occupation at the time of the Viking settlement in the ninth century; the latecomers had to make do with marginal hill land.

King Orry's Grave – the remains of what was once perhaps Man's greatest ritual and burial site. This ruinous but still impressive megalithic monument is under the protection of the Manx Museum Trustees and was excavated by B. R. S. Megaw with the assistance of P. S. Gelling prior to the building of the adjacent houses.

The major hillfort on the summit of South Barrule. Trial excavations by P. S. Gelling suggest that it was occupied at the end of the bronze age, at a time when the climate was generally much worse than it is now. The people must have been under great threat to take refuge on such an exposed site.

The late 50s and 60s also saw the excavation of important mediaeval sites in the Isle of Man. A. M. Cubbon excavated the mediaeval chapel (later the Old Grammar School) at Castletown, producing stratigraphy and pottery which, with the architectural features of the building – notably its fine Romanesque arcade – made possible the working out of the history of this uniquely interesting structure. It was built originally by the monks of Rushen Abbey *circa* 1200, continuing in use as the town chapel until 1702; it was already being used also as a school as early as 1570, which role it continued until 1930. The building had only been saved from demolition by the Museum Trustees nailing a preservation order onto its door in 1950, the Museum later purchasing the building and restoring it. The main wing is the oldest roofed structure in the Isle of Man – older than all but the lowest courses of masonry of Castle Rushen.

Proposals to re-roof the ancient mediaeval cathedral of St.German's on St. Patrick's Isle at Peel led to Dr. Ralegh Radford undertaking further important excavations there in 1962, both at St. German's and also at the still older St. Patrick's church near to the round tower, giving evidence that the earliest St. Patrick's church was a tenth or eleventh century structure in the tradition of important early churches of this period in Ireland.

In 1966 the proposed erection of a new vicarage at Braddan, in a corner of the "camp field" with its impressive if enigmatic series of substantial earthworks, led to A. M. Cubbon excavating the threatened area. This produced structural features and

Above: "The oldest roofed building in the Isle of Man", the Old Grammar School, Castletown. The building incorporates the medieval chapel of St. Mary which is older than all save the lowest courses of Castle Rushen. It was only saved for posterity when the Trustees of the Manx Museum took the unprecedented step of nailing a preservation order to its door. It was subsequently excavated internally by A. M. Cubbon, re-roofed and protected against various threats from development.
Inset: the interior of the old chapel showing the impressive original arcade.

Left: Dr. C. A. Ralegh Radford's excavations of St. German's Cathedral on St. Patrick's Isle, Peel, 1962.

finds indicating mediaeval iron working, and an extensive range of mediaeval pottery, with a silver penny of Edward III, of 1351 to 1361, providing a central dating to the three centuries of occupation represented by the excavated portion of this large site, which appears to represent the remains of an important mediaeval farmstead.

In the late 1960s R. A. Curphey excavated the remains of the late seventeenth century battery at Ronaldsway, complementing his detailed documentary research into the coastal batteries of the Isle of Man, while Dr. Larch Garrad undertook a number of small-scale excavations in Castletown, which produced a range of mediaeval and post mediaeval pottery. F. J. Radcliffe commenced the excavation of interesting occupation midden deposits in the floor of a cave at

Some of the varied finds from H. M. Sloop of War "Racehorse", Captain Suckling commanding, wrecked off Langness 14th December 1822. The wreck was purchased by the Isle of Man Sub-Aqua Club, with the assistance of the Manx Museum which houses thc finds from their several seasons of scientific investigation of the site.

Perwick, which included the bones of the extinct Great Auk, revealing a glimpse of the hunting, fishing and fowling activities of the inhabitants, dated by radio carbon to the first few centuries of the Christian era. In the field of nineteenth century industrial archaeology the Manx Mines Research Group cleared an area of the extensive washing floors at Beckwith's Mines at Glen Rushen, revealing buddles, ducts and the water supply for the wheel that powered the plant. About the same period the Isle of Man Sub Aqua Club commenced their excavation of the wreck of the "Racehorse", a British Navy sloop lost off Langness in 1822, which yielded an interesting range of finds, and represents the first submarine excavation to be carried out in Manx waters.

At Killeaba, south of Ramsey, prior to the erection of a housing estate, Cubbon excavated an important Neolithic and early Bronze Age burial site, with "Ronaldsway" Manx secondary Neolithic cremation burials in timber-lined pits and miniature stone cists associated with urns, in close association with typical early Bronze Age cists with crouched or flexed inhumations with pottery food vessels.

Miss Audrey Henshall, of the National Museum of Antiquities of Scotland, following her masterly published survey of the chambered tombs of Scotland, accepted an invitation to undertake a reappraisal of the Manx sites of this type, and as part of this research project undertook a limited excavation of the unique Meayll Circle of chambered tombs near Cregneash. A further new Neolithic chambered tomb was revealed by gravel extraction at Ballaharra, German, and excavated (1971) by Miss Sheila Cregeen. This important emergency excavation produced an extensive cremation deposit, near to the large though disturbed chamber, a fine range of flint implements and pottery, including some with distinctive decoration only previously known from Kermode and Herdman's pioneer excavations at the Meayll Circle. Radio carbon dating places the Ballaharra site at circa 2300 B.C.

The traditional "Dark Ages" of the Celtic Iron Age have become less misty as a result of the last two major excavations undertaken by Peter Gelling. From 1962 to 1967 a site at the edge of the Lhen Valley at Kiondroghad, Andreas revealed the existence of a seventh to ninth century metal worker's hut, yielding bronze objects, stone moulds, pattern stones and whetstones, as well as the structural evidence of the hut itself. From 1973 to 1981 he had worked at a somewhat similar, but larger and more complex Celtic Iron Age habitation site, in its later phases of the seventh or eighth century at Purt e Candas, German. This excavation though well advanced was unfortunately not finished at Peter Gelling's untimely death, but it is hoped to produce a report from his records and the mass of finds from his work.

Above: Three bronze age food vessels from the excavations at Killeaba, south of Ramsey.

Below: A reconstructed bowl from the Meayll Hill megalithic site, excavated by Kermode and Herdman and a large sherd from the ruined megalithic site at Ballaharra, German, where Miss Sheila Cregeen conducted a rescue excavation necessitated by sand and gravel extraction.

P. S. Gelling excavated an important metal-working site at Kiondroghad, Andreas, that has now been levelled by agricultural improvement. The finds included iron ore, almost certainly from Maughold, and debris from its processing, together with evidence of finer work, such as this sandstone pattern stone with a trial design and the enamel-inlaid bronze latchet disc.

In its earliest days, in a unanimous resolution of 1894, the Museum Trustees strongly deprecated "the removal of the recent treasure trove in Douglas from the Island", and although most of this hoard was subsequently returned to the Isle of Man for display in the Manx Museum its removal had strengthened the case for a national museum in the Island, and led to the establishment of the first temporary displays in Castle Rushen. The special case of treasure trove however had been highlighted, though it was to be the 1970s before significant finds of this category were again to come to light. In 1967 however the Trustees had again raised at Governmental level the question of the Manx Museum having the pre-emptive right to the possible acquisition of treasure trove found in the Isle of Man, which right was eventually conceded.

The first fruits of this decision became apparent in 1975, when a hoard of English, Irish, Norman and Manx silver coins of the tenth and eleventh centuries, with silver armlets, was taken in to the British Museum on behalf of a workman who stated they had been found by him on a building site in the Isle of Man. They were immediately taken to the Manx Museum where they were held pending a treasure trove inquest. The police enquiries preceding the inquest suggested their discovery was in the course of the digging of a grave in Kirk Michael churchyard rather than on a building site, and eventually, with the permission of the family and the church authorities, the re-excavation of the grave in question led to the recovery of 17 more English, Irish, Norman and Manx coins, with fragments of two more silver armlets. The inquest jury eventually declared the finds treasure trove and this important Viking hoard was acquired by the Manx Museum – with a greatly reduced reward being paid to the finder. Under normal circumstances, where a finder has acted promptly and properly he will receive the full value of treasure trove acquired by a museum. Since 1976 eight treasure trove inquests have been held in the Isle of Man relating to Viking or mediaeval hoards, several of which have come to light from the use of metal detectors. This approach to digging up the past can be very dangerous if approached irresponsibly, as the vital stratigraphical evidence on which the archaeologist depends for his interpretation of the history of a site is likely to be totally unrecognised by a metal detector enthusiast only interested in treasure hunting. However the Manx Museum has established a valuable liaison with the Manx Metal Detector Club, which has worked well to the benefit of both parties.

The Manx Museum of course has always had to contend with the archaeological challenges and opportunities represented by rescue excavations, and the museum staff – and its appropriately experienced voluntary supporters – have undertaken numerous investigations of this sort, often with significant results. Examples of such from the last decade include Dr. Larch Garrad's excavation of an early Christian lintel grave cemetery near Santan Church, A. M. Cubbon's excavation of a Bronze Age cist at Cronk Coir, Ballaugh, and Garrad's investigation of a number of sites in the north of the Island which have been revealed by the sustained and skilled observations of Mr. A. Skillan, a redoubtable voluntary archaeological field walker.

Above: A very small portion of the second hoard to be found within the parish churchyard at Kirk Michael, subsequently declared to be Treasure Trove. This was partly recovered by a temporary gravedigger, the balance coming to light only when A. M. Cubbon re-excavated the grave on behalf of the Manx Museum and with the permission of the family. The coins:- *Top left:* Hiberno-Norse; *Right:* Anglo Saxon; *Middle left:* Hiberno-Manx; *Right:* Normandy denier. *Top centre:* Part of the original eleventh century cloth bag which held the hoard of over 79 coins. *Below:* Two of the three silver armlets discovered in the hoard.

Left: A handsome gold ring of intricately plaited heavy gold wire dating from the tenth or early eleventh century, discovered at a farm at Greeba and declared Treasure Trove at an inquest in 1983. It is the first ancient gold artifact found in the Island this century.

In 1979 the blade of a sword, bent to a right angle was exposed literally in the grab of a mechanical digger on a building site at Claghbane, Ramsey, but thanks to prompt reporting and the careful marking of the spot by the bulldozer driver, Marshall Cubbon and the Museum's maintenance men were able to excavate the undisturbed hilt of the Viking sword and nearby the iron boss of the accompanying shield, recovering also the soil-stains from rusted shield fastenings which indicated the diameter and thickness of the long-decayed wooden shield. The excavation evidence also made it clear that surprisingly the sword and shield were not associated with a pagan Viking burial but instead represented a ritual burial of these weapons.

From the late 1970s the Manx Museum has extended the practice of inviting appropriate archaeologists to undertake specific excavations in the Isle of Man. Dr. Lawrence Butler of Leeds University excavated the chancel, eastern portion of the nave and the adjoining areas of the cloistral buildings at Rushen Abbey in 1978 and 1979. This investigation of the Island's principal late mediaeval monastic site (following early digging in the 1920s and 1930s) was extended in 1984 when Dr. Garrad directed the excavation of walling and a charnel deposit associated with the abbey church which was exposed in the course of building work in the yard of the adjoining Abbey Hotel.

Right: The square tower at Rushen Abbey, Ballasalla. The site was investigated in the 1930s by its then owner, W. C. Cubbon, and more recently by Dr. L. A. S. Butler of Leeds University at the invitation of the Manx Museum.

Below: Druidale, Michael. The site of a keeill not investigated by the Manx Archaeological Survey, was to be destroyed during construction of the Sulby Reservoir. Mr. Chris Morris of Durham University was invited by the Manx Museum to excavate this important site.

In 1979 and 1980 Mr. Chris Morris of Durham University directed the excavation of the early Christian keeill at Druidale, high up the Sulby valley. This excavation was occasioned by the site being doomed to flooding by the construction of the new Sulby reservoir, but the time schedule for the excavation was drastically shortened when it was learned that the spur on which the keeill was sited was to be blasted away to provide hard core for the dam-head. The excavation showed that the keeill itself had undergone two periods of construction, and that a yet earlier structure (possibly secular) had occupied the site. Although a series of early cross-slabs had been built into the walls of the keeill no graves were found in the area, probably reflecting the fact that this keeill high in the uplands was primarily serving the temporary population that occupied the upland sheilings during the summer months only.

Right page: Druidale, Michael.
Top: The keeil cleared of vegetation.
Bottom: The keeil after meticulous excavation.

St. Patrick's Isle, Peel, a site of major archaeological importance. Small-scale investigations had taken place in the past but a major five-year programme of excavation began in 1982, licensed by the Museum Trustees and undertaken by David Freke of Liverpool University. Major new discoveries have subsequently been made which emphasise that this is one of the Island's most important historic sites.

Peel Castle – recent excavation in progress. *(Photograph: David Freke.)*

In 1980 Miss Sheila Cregeen excavated a richly furnished Bronze Age cist at the Cronk, Upper Lhergydhoo, German, and later that year was assisted by Professor Rynne from University College, Galway, in excavating a nearby Bronze Age urn with a cremation burial. In 1983 Professor Peter Woodman of University College, Cork, following up a prolonged study he had undertaken of the earliest Mesolithic hunter-fishermen of whom we have evidence in the Isle of Man, excavated an exposure of a settlement of this period near Cass ny Hawin, east of Ronaldsway Airport. The full report is still awaited, but for the first time we have a radio carbon dating for a Manx mesolithic site of approximately 5500 B.C.

Arising from a report on Peel Castle and necessary maintenance of the standing masonry there, it was recognised that archaeological excavation would be a necessary preliminary to any disturbance to this major Manx monument, and that such excavation should be undertaken under the auspices of the Manx Museum. In consequence in 1982 the Museum invited Mr. Peter Gelling to excavate the Half-Moon Battery, west of St. German's Cathedral, and Mr. David Freke, then Director of Liverpool University Rescue Archaeology Unit, to excavate the "Earl of Derby's apartments", the run of roofless buildings to the north of the chancel of the cathedral. Such was the success of that initial season that the St. Patrick's Isle Archaeological Trust was founded to expand and advance this major excavation programme. Unfortunately the untimely death of Peter Gelling prevented him from completing his work on the Half-Moon Battery, and this also passed to David Freke, who was appointed director of the excavations of the Archaeological Trust. The work at St. Patrick's Isle, developed in close association with the Manx Museum, has aimed at an initial five year excavation programme, digging each Easter and Summer, with the necessary post-excavation work on the finds being virtually continuous, and has yielded spectacularly successful results. The major discoveries of the work to date, in chronological order – very different from the order of discovery, as the excavated area has been extended over successive seasons – may be summarised as follows: a mesolithic deposit of worked flint microliths; a circular timber structure, possibly of the Celtic Iron Age; an early Christian lintel grave cemetery of a Celtic monastery of the pre-Norse period; richly-furnished "pagan" Norse Viking graves of women and children in the Christian cemetery, which cemetery continues in use into late mediaeval times; a hoard of eleventh century silver coins of the Norse Viking Kingdom of Dublin; a large timber hall of quite sophisticated construction of the mid-twelfth century, possibly a royal or ecclesiastical palace, of the hey-day of the Norse Viking Kingdom of Man and the Isles; foundations of successive phases of the mediaeval masonry defenceworks of Peel Castle; evidence of the structural development of successive buildings culminating in the post mediaeval Earl of Derby's apartments. From all these different phases an important corpus of finds has been recovered and subjected to detailed specialist study, the results of which enormously expand knowledge of the site and the people who have lived and worked and died there over the centuries. The exhibition of a selection of finds at the Manx Museum has been of outstanding interest. All the finds will be housed in the Manx Museum when their scientific examination is completed. The St. Patrick's Isle project represents a high water mark of archaeological activity in the Isle of Man.

a. Naturally shaped slate stone with incised cross dating from c.700 A.D. – found re-used in a pre-Norse lintel grave, 1983 Peel Castle excavations. *(Photo: D. Freke)*

b. Tenth century gilt bronze strap-end, possibly part of a gilt plaque looted from an Irish reliquary or book-cover – from a male Viking grave, 1984 Peel Castle excavations. *(Photo: D. Freke)*

c. Tenth century bronze buckle with bronze bosses and animal head motif – from a male Viking grave, 1984 Peel Castle excavations. *(Photo: D. Freke)*

d. Viking gold pin-head with filigree decoration – 1983 Peel Castle excavations. *(Photo: D. Freke)*

e. Tenth century silver wire tassels, possibly from a cloak – from a male Viking grave, 1984 Peel Castle excavations. *(Photo: D. Freke)*

A spectacular necklace, originally consisting of over 60 glass and amber beads, found in a richly furnished female grave at Peel Castle. This is the first female Viking grave to be found in the Island and also contained a cooking-spit (wrapped in textile), two knives, a decorated bone comb, a bag with two needles and a pair of small shears.

This outline account of Manx archaeological work has perforce omitted many excavations, though all have contributed to the growing body of evidence of the Manx past held at the Manx Museum. Some early explorations were simply not recorded in sufficient detail; rescue operations on varying scales have always been mounted by the Museum in response to chance finds occasioned by farming activity or building work. An emergency excavation haversack, ready packed with the necessities for examining and recording chance discoveries always sat in the corner of the writer's office when he worked at the Museum, and bringing it into use could always be relied on to get the archaeological adrenalin running! The now routine checking of all planning applications has resulted in some areas of potential archaeological interest being examined prior to disturbance, or being subject to inspection while building work is proceeding, on occasion with very worthwhile results. The Manx Museum has however always gained handsomely by the support and interest of the Manx people in all parts of the Island, who have time and again let the Museum know when archaeological finds or features have unexpectedly come to light. May it long continue.

BRANCHING OUT

S. HARRISON

The main Manx Museum in Douglas provides unrivalled potential for displaying the full historical story of the Isle of Man, from prehistoric to modern times. However, it was recognised at an early stage that there were limitations to what could be achieved within the confining walls of a single building and that there were aspects of the cultural and natural heritage which should ideally be preserved *in situ* to provide the fullest educational potential for the people of the Island and to maintain the historic and scenic integrity of the Manx landscape. Similarly, an important aspect of policy was established at this time with the realisation that the work of the Museum should permeate the community it serves, and should not confine its activities to the Island's capital.

Thus, for many years after the search for an initial home had proved successful, the Trustees cherished hopes of establishing a branch museum which could provide a fuller and more effective picture of traditional Manx life. Accelerating developments of modern society, the continuing demands of a thriving tourist industry and the changing structure of the Manx economy all presented a considerable threat to the customary lifestyle of the Manx countryside which had played such a vital role in developing the national character.

As the years passed, the Trustees' concern at the loss of traditional buildings from the countryside and of the customs, crafts and skills associated with the old rural communities, was seen to be well-founded as the fragile evidence of a long and precious heritage rapidly disappeared. It was fortunate, however, that other people were also conscious of this alarming trend and were prepared to take practical steps to preserve these aspects of their heritage for future generations. It was a direct result of such efforts, guided by the ever vigilant William Cubbon, that Cregneash village became the setting for the first publicly owned "open-air" folk museum in Britain.

CREGNEASH VILLAGE FOLK MUSEUM

Until the beginning of this century, Cregneash was a typical upland crofting village, or *clachan*, isolated from modern developments in the rest of the Island, and preserving the old customs and traditions handed down from father to son through generations of Manxmen. Perhaps strongest of all these traditions was the Manx language itself, for "y Ghailck" was spoken by all the inhabitants of Cregneash within living memory. Indeed, it was partly due to the encouragement of Professor Carl Marstrander, a Celtic scholar from Oslo who had been making wax cylinder recordings of Harry Kelly's Manx speech, that Harry Kelly's cottage was donated to the Trustees by a member of the Kelly family and in 1938 became the first building in the village to be opened as a museum.

At the opening ceremony, William Cubbon, the then Director of the Manx Museum, reflected on the spirit of the old crofting communities living on in the cottage, and dedicated the house as a memorial to them and as a reminder of the environment in which they lived and worked.

Right page.

Top left: Harry Kelly outside his cottage at Cregneash c. 1930.

Top right: Professor Carl Marstrander who made the first wax-cylinder sound recordings of Harry Kelly's Manx speech.

Right: Harry Kelly's cottage, interior.

Inset: At the opening ceremony of Harry Kelly's cottage, 1938.

Top: Cregneash village in 1896.

Bottom: Cregneash village 1986.

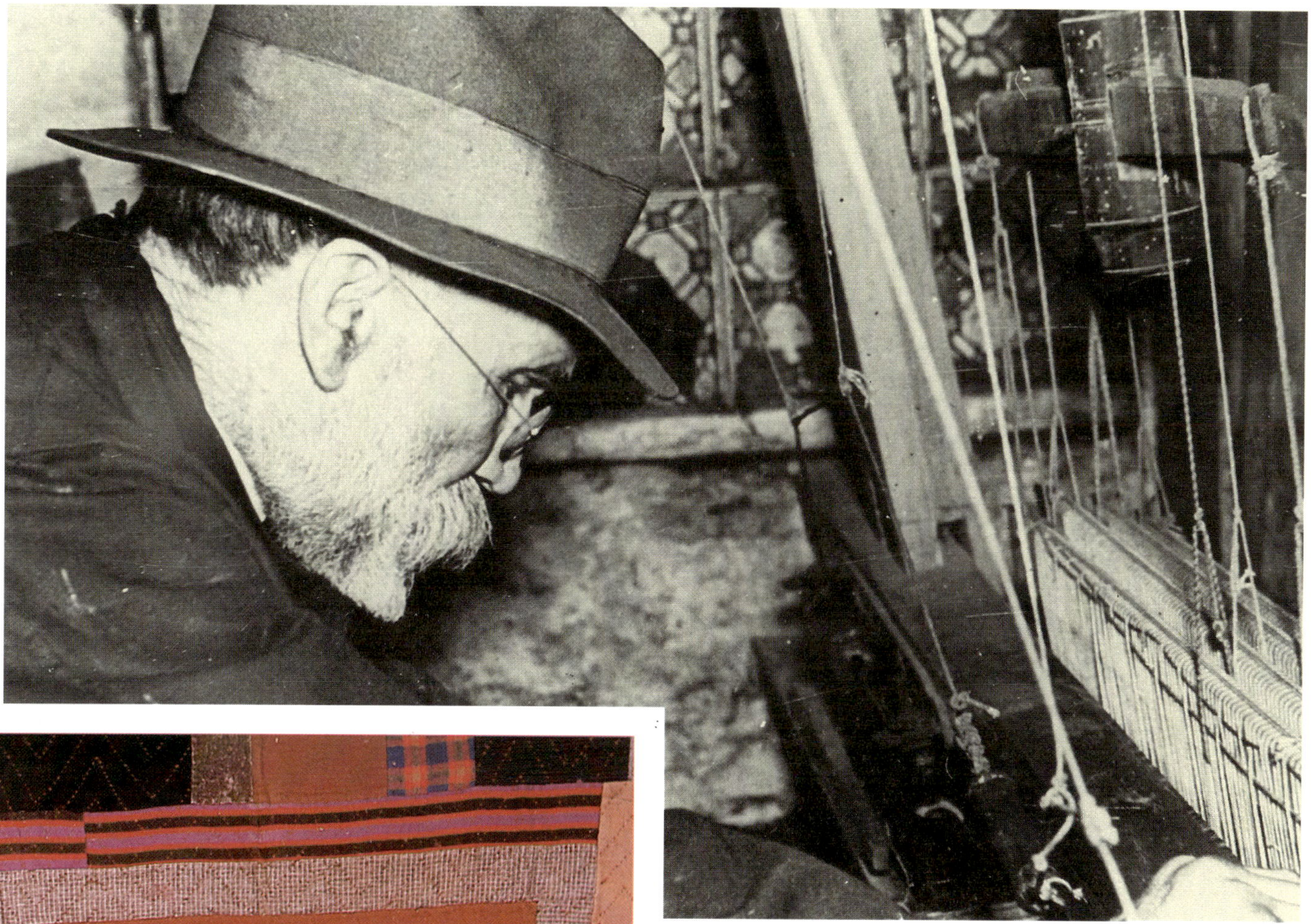

Above: Alfred Hudson, weaver and owner of the last handloom in the parish of Rushen which is now preserved in the weaver's shed at Cregneash.

Left: A Manx bed-cover of woollen patchwork in a traditional "framed" pattern.

Since 1938, other buildings in the village have been acquired to enlarge the picture of crofting life and to show the diverse crafts, upon which the crofter depended for his livelihood.

In 1939 the story extended to the Weaver's House where the last handloom in the parish of Rushen was re-erected in the thatched loom-shed or *Thie Cogee*. The manufacture of cloth from both flax and wool was a vital part of the crofter's domestic economy, and in 1850, there were at least five weavers (or *fidderyn*) in Cregneash. The weavers made most of the cloth needed by the village for clothing, blankets and quilts, although much of their work would be done in the winter after the demands of the fields and the fishing season had been met, or at night by the light of home-made candles. The loom on display in the shed belonged to Alfred Hudson of Ballafesson known as *Hudgeon y fidder* (Hudson the weaver), whose family had produced generations of weavers.

Above: Shearing a healthy loghtan can often be a two-man job!

Right: A blanket in tartan-style overchecks, hand woven by Mr. Kermeen of St. Jude's, Andreas, 1949.

Alfred Hudson used the loom until 1922. It is still in perfect working order and demonstrations of hand-loom weaving are frequently given throughout the summer.

Although it was the men of the village who were mainly responsible for the weaving, the women were kept busy preparing and spinning wool and flax for the loom. Much of the woollen cloth was dyed, often using wild fruits and plants, but a distinctive and popular cloth was produced from the undyed brown wool of the native Manx sheep, the loghtan. This attractive and rare breed of sheep, which is possibly descended from Viking times, was in danger of extinction by 1950 until the Manx National Trust secured a small flock for preservation. Happily, this has been achieved and there is now once more a healthy number of loghtan sheep in the Island. Part of the Trust's flock is kept on the Calf of Man, but loghtans may also be seen at the thatched farmstead in the village.

Above: Spinning demonstrations are regularly given at Cregneash during the summer.

Above left: The type of spinning wheel made by the Callisters of West Craig which would have been in operation in most houses in Cregneash supplementing the crofter's income.

Left: Demonstrating the treadle-lathe once used to turn out spinning wheels by the Callister family of West Craig, Andreas.

In the nineteenth century almost every house in the village would have had a spinning wheel and the women would spend many long hours rocking the treadle as the clipped fleece was spun into yarn. This process too can still be seen at Cregneash as regular spinning demonstrations are given during the summer.

The Callister family of West Craig, Andreas, were renowned in the Isle of Man as manufacturers of spinning wheels and the lathe upon which many of these wheels were turned is preserved in the wood-turner's shed across the road from Harry Kelly's cottage. It is driven by a large treadle wheel, and formed part of the Callisters' country joiner's shop, one of those which provided an essential service to small isolated communities when so many of the daily domestic utensils, tools and furnishings were made of wood.

The country joiner would often work in conjunction with the local blacksmith, and between them, they provided the manufacturing skills for most village needs. The original Cregneash smithy building has long since disappeared and seems to have ceased operation at the beginning of this century. But the ringing of the anvil may still be heard, for in 1959, a suitable ruined building was restored, and converted to house a typical small upland smithy with an adjacent shoeing shed. For this careful measurements and photographs were taken of a number of smithies throughout the Island, and valuable practical advice, as well as tools and equipment, was obtained from the remaining blacksmiths, to ensure that the smithy forge could once again take its rightful place in the heart of Cregneash.

Much of the blacksmith's work would be repairing agricultural equipment, for farming was an essential part of the crofting economy. At the Karran farmstead, the Museum preserves one of the last traditional Manx farm crofts. The two thatched buildings flank the stackyard or *haggard* where the results of the harvest's labour would be stored in small circular stacks or *thurrans* with conical thatched tops, which are so much a feature in old photographs of Cregneash. In such an isolated community, farming small areas of rough land, the success of the year's work in the field depended upon co-operation between crofters to till the land and claim the crop. Livestock and equipment were pooled at vital times, such as for ploughing, and the women of the village were often left to tend the fields until the men returned from "the fishing" to gather in the harvest. Long winter nights would follow when groups of men gathered to thresh the grain with flails, leaving the unbroken straw for thatching the roofs.

Left: Some of the blacksmiths who gave generous help with the reconstruction of the Cregneash smithy.

Below: Mr. L. Maddrell working at the forge of the reconstructed Cregneash smithy.

Corn was stored in the *thurrans* until the winter months when the men gathered in small groups to undertake the laborious task of threshing with flails.

Below: Cregneash village from the south c. 1900, showing a number of conical, thatched corn-stacks or *thurrans*.

Harvesting wheatstraw in the traditional way at Balladoole farm, utilising the binder and threshing machine rather than a combine harvester. Such methods are essential for preserving the water-proof unbroken straw required for thatching at Cregneash.

The Manx Museum and National Trust has attempted to preserve at Cregneash, examples of the traditional thatched roofs of the Isle of Man as they rapidly disappear from the rest of the countryside. Modern harvesting methods break the straw, making it useless for thatching, so a wheatcrop is specially harvested in the traditional way each year to provide thatching straw for Cregneash. For this, the Museum is indebted to the Moore family of Balladoole farm, who help to preserve the traditional farming methods by growing the wheat on their own farm and by using the old style binder and threshing machine instead of a modern combine harvester. A tractor has taken the place of the horse today, but the crofter's spirit of co-operation is still evident on threshing days when all available hands help to fork the straw, feed the machine, stack the bundles of threshed straw, and carry away the sacks of grain.

Of course, the story does not end there, for when the threshing drum stops turning, the work of the thatcher begins and as traditional Manx straw thatch only lasts about five years, the Museum thatchers are kept busy with a continual round of repair and replacement. In the nineteenth century community, every crofter would have been able to repair his own thatch, but nowadays this skill is a rarity, and the Museum is proud to be helping to preserve the traditional skills as well as the artefacts of the Manx cultural heritage.

The thatching of roofs at Cregneash is a great commitment for the Trust's staff but the importance of preserving this skill is increasingly emphasised as the numbers of thatched roofs in the rest of the Island decreases.

Times change, however, and requirements of modern life do not always fit happily in the traditional scene. The Museum is well aware of the needs and necessities of today's community, but seeks, whenever possible, to prevent these improvements from marring the appearance of one of the Island's most traditional settings. For example, from 1973–77 an ambitious project was carried out to replace the unsightly poles and overhead wires that lined the narrow roads of the village, by underground cables. The difference to the appearance of Cregneash and its surroundings has been remarkable, and resulted in a special award for the scheme from the Civic Trust. Similarly, the Museum strives to preserve other characteristic features around the village like the narrow strip fields and dry stone walls, the tholtans and the village wells.

Some properties owned by the Museum are not open to the public, but are privately tenanted. The interiors are designed for modern living, but the Museum maintains the exteriors to retain their traditional appearance in the landscape. In having some of its houses for people to live in, the Museum is helping to maintain Cregneash as a *living* village throughout the year.

However, buildings and objects alone cannot tell the whole story of a crofting community like Cregneash. The character of the Manx people who lived here and continue to live here is what ultimately determines the character of the place.

Individuals like Harry Kelly will always be remembered. So too will the old families of Cregneash with names like Maddrell, Crebbin and Karran, some of whom still live in or near the village – and in the stories and poems of Ned Beg Hom Ruy we have a lasting picture of their hopes and fears, their hardships and achievements. The Museum and the Manx nation, owe a great debt to these people, and also to the more recent generations of Cregneash folk who have by their generosity, encouraged and furthered the aims of the Museum.

Over the years, the historical integrity of Cregneash Museum has sustained its position as one of the most important long-term preservation projects in Britain. Since the advent of the Manx National Trust in 1951, it has been possible to preserve not only the buildings but also large areas of the surrounding countryside which are so vital to the natural and historic setting of the village. Cregneash now reveals how the joint responsibilities of the Manx Museum and National Trust run perfectly together, providing a unique and positive contribution to the Island's past, present and future.

Background: Aerial view of Cregneash today.

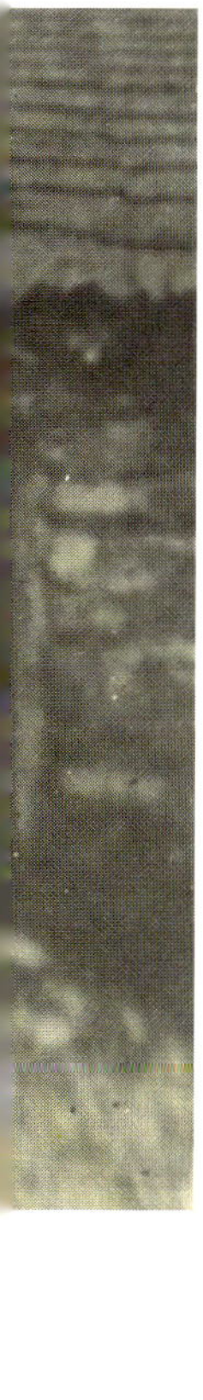

Inset.

Top left: Ned Beg Hom Ruy, crofter and village poet.

Bottom left: One of the "big Karrans" of Cregneash outside the Karran farmstead.

Bottom right: Messrs. Griffin and Karran outside Ned Beg's cottage.

Top right: Harry Kelly outside his cottage.

THE NAUTICAL MUSEUM: CASTLETOWN

The second branch of the Manx Museum came in a more unexpected fashion than the long cherished and well-planned development at Cregneash.

In 1935, a dramatic discovery was made in the cellar of an eighteenth century building backing on to Castletown harbour. Cocooned in a subterranean vault adjacent to the Quayle family home of Bridge House, a remarkable survival of nautical history precipitated great excitement amongst enthusiasts and scholars throughout Britain.

An eighteenth century schooner-rigged armed yacht, the *Peggy*, built for George Quayle in 1791, had remained undisturbed and almost forgotten in her walled-up boat cellar since the death of her owner one hundred years before. This unique survival from the period of the French Revolution prompted the Society of Nautical Research to despatch one of their researchers to make detailed plans of the vessel and these drawings were subsequently put on display at the Science Museum in London. Interest in this discovery was such that a family descendant of George Quayle generously offered the *Peggy* in her original boathouse to the Manx Museum Trustees, and this exciting development was announced in the Trust's annual report for 1942:

"The oldest surviving Manx-built ship, together with her original boathouse at Bridge House, Castletown has been offered to the Trustees by Mrs Pharo-Tomlin and gratefully accepted . . . It is hoped to restore it after the war as a small nautical museum."

As the Director of the Museum, Basil Megaw, was absent from the Island on war service, the realization of the potential of this new property was delayed. However, this time was utilised to effect the necessary repairs to the building and some limited restoration of the *Peggy* herself, prior to the official opening of this new branch museum in 1951.

Figurehead of the schooner *Spray*, carved by James Hudson of Port St. Mary. The *Spray* was built by Thomas Gale of Port St. Mary in 1877 and lost off the east coast of Scotland c. 1900.

Above: The *Peggy* in the boat-cellar below George Quayle's cabin room where she was rediscovered in 1935.

Left: View across Castletown harbour showing the walled-up entrance to the boat-yard.

Although the star attraction was undoubtedly the preserved vessel in her original boatcellar, the new Museum provided its visitors with much more of historical interest as a result of the activities of the remarkable George Quayle.

The Quayles of Bridge House were a leading Manx family throughout the eighteenth century, being actively involved in the Government, trade and financial sectors of the Island. George was the eldest son of John Quayle who, like three other members of his family, was Clerk of the Rolls. George, however, was to involve himself more directly in the Island's Government, maintaining his seat in the House of Keys for 51 years and playing a leading military role in connection with the Manx forces raised at various times after 1793 to counter the threat posed to Island security by the war with France.

However, it is George Quayle's more eccentric activities which are revealed in the boathouse adjoining Bridge House. Built between 1789 and 1791, the building which now comprises the Nautical Museum fully reflects its original owner's personality and interests. His abilities as a scientist and inventor are evidenced by his original lathe and wood-framed telescope which remain in the workshop loft which now houses an atmospheric recreation of a sail-maker's workshop. His slightly idiosyncratic enthusiasm for the military concerns of the day are revealed behind a secret wall-panel in one room, where his design plans for a gigantic invasion barge capable of transporting 30,000 troops across the English Channel to Napoleonic France are still preserved.

Below: Recreation of a typical Manx sail-maker's loft. This area was where George Quayle *(inset)* had his workshop and his original lathe can be seen in the background.

George Quayle must have taken great delight in the design of his boathouse for the rooms are provided with a full complement of trap-doors, hidden doorways and architectural jokes like the fireplace positioned under a window. His *piece de resistance* was the cabin room above the boatcellar which he constructed as a replica of a stern cabin from a naval warship of the "Nelson" period. Its wood panelling, slanting stern windows and domed ceiling, combined to provide a unique meeting place for Quayle's friends and associates. A letter of 1791 reveals the excitement that was felt as this construction neared completion:

> *". . . The boathouse is growing apace . . . the apartment over it will be quite an oddity, the interior alterations, ornaments and decorations are not to be described to the Vulgar until finished and even then to be seen only by the elect."*

George Quayle's original recreation of the stern-cabin of a ship from the Nelson period.

Above right: Quayle's original boat-house design is full of ingenious and amusing architectural features, including this fireplace below a window.

Right: The remains of the original paintwork on the transom stern of the *Peggy*.

A rigged sailing model of the *Peggy*.

The cabin room is directly above the boatcellar which has been the home of the *Peggy* for 150 years, since the original archway allowing direct access into Castletown harbour was built up. Fortunately the damp conditions in which the vessel was entombed proved to be almost ideal for preservation of the clinker-built hull, with its transom stern still displaying the original paintwork of 1791.

Quayle used the *Peggy* for communication with British ports and small trading excursions but it has not been proved that she was actively engaged in "the running trade", or smuggling, from the Island which caused the British Government so much concern at this time. In these turbulent times it is no surprise that George Quayle equipped his small craft with eight small cannons as well as six "fowling pieces", as protection against the unsolicited attentions of other vessels patrolling or marauding in the Irish Sea.

Top: Boats of the southern Manx fishing fleet with their Castletown (C.T.) registration numbers.

Left: Hauling in the herring nets c. 1920.

Above: A ship's biscuit making machine from Dale's grocery store, Crown Street, Peel.

However, the *Peggy* was no mere general purpose vessel, for George Quayle applied his ingenuity for design and invention to create a swift and elegant racing craft which could also satisfy his sporting instincts. Quayle was particularly proud of his modification to incorporate drop or "sliding" keels which were put fully to the test in 1796. In that year, the *Peggy* was sailed across to the Lake District and transported overland to Lake Windermere to take part in the prestigious Windermere regattas where she attracted considerable interest and achieved some success. The return journey however, was somewhat traumatic and put both the captain and his vessel to a severe test:

". . . we put down the sliding keels and that enabled us to stand on, now and then letting fly the foresail and continuing our tack we fetched about three leagues to the leeward of the Calf. The wind now changed to the westward and by one tack we fetched this (Castletown) Bay . . . the quarter cloths were of very great protection, without them I believe we had gone to Davy Jones' locker, and without the sliding keels we could not have carried sail enough."

By 1967, the purchase of the coach-house and stable complex adjoining the boathouse, had provided the opportunity to extend the museum to include a wider picture of Manx nautical history in the days of sail.

The fishing gallery reflects the importance of this industry for the Isle of Man in the nineteenth century. In 1883, it was estimated that the Island had over 450 boats worth £240,000, producing an annual yield of £140,000. Some 3,500 people were directly or indirectly employed and about a quarter of the population was dependent on the fishing for its livelihood. On display in the gallery is a fine series of models of local fishing vessels and associated equipment together with an evocative series of photographs depicting the people and supporting crafts of a vibrant industry which was soon to suffer a rapid decline.

Further expansion is planned at the Nautical Museum to enlarge the picture of this intrinsic theme of Manx history. Although the story now portrayed extends far beyond George Quayle's boathouse and cabinroom, the museum still preserves the spirit of his original concept and the spirit of adventure, skill and determination which characterises the tradition of Manx seafaring.

Figurehead of the schooner *Progress*, built at Port St. Mary in 1868.

THE GROVE MUSEUM

In the summer of 1838, Duncan Gibb, a prosperous Liverpool shipping merchant, visited the Isle of Man with a friend. The professional interests of these two men caused them to travel to the Point of Ayre to inspect the most modern lighthouse in the Irish Sea area at that time. Driving back to Douglas in their carriage, they passed a cottage for sale on the outskirts of Ramsey and it was decided to break the journey for a tour of inspection. Duncan Gibb emerged as the new owner of the cottage and thereby commenced a sequence of events which was to lead to the establishment of a third branch of the Manx Museum some one hundred and forty years later.

Duncan Gibb aged sixty, the Liverpool shipping merchant who enlarged the Grove to its present size.

The Misses Gibb whose generous bequest formed the basis of the Grove Museum.
Left: Miss Alice Gibb, shortly before her death in 1971 aged over ninety.
Right: Miss Janet Gibb who died a few weeks after her ninety-sixth birthday in 1974.

Below: The formal opening of the new Grove Museum in June 1978 was performed by Dr. (later Sir) David Wilson, Director of the British Museum. *Left to right:* J. Crellin, W. Radcliffe, Dr. D. Wilson, A. M. Cubbon, Major T. E. Brownsdon.

"Poplar Grove", the original cottage, was enlarged by Gibb to provide a modest sized Victorian mansion as a summer home for himself and his family. His ownership of a large area of adjoining farmland encouraged him to erect a number of agricultural buildings at the rear, including a barn to house a threshing mill driven by a horse-walk outside.

When Duncan Gibb died in 1867, the legacy of this summer retreat in the Isle of Man passed down through the family and until 1971 was the home of his two granddaughters, the Misses Janet and Alice Gibb. For many years, the Misses Gibb had lovingly preserved their grandfather's legacy including the vast majority of its original furnishings and fittings, and their concern for the house's preservation after their deaths increased as they observed modern developments in the vicinity.

Through the good offices of Mr J. C. Crellin, a friend of the two ladies and a Museum trustee, the Director of the Museum was invited to take tea at The Grove to discuss the future preservation of the property. The result of these discussions was that the Museum was given an option to purchase the property and its entire contents on very favourable terms, with the request that it be preserved as a period museum on the demise of the owners.

The Manx Museum Trustees had been hopeful for some time previously of combining a new branch museum in the north of the Island with a fuller interpretation of the Victorian period of Manx domestic and agricultural history. The Grove property, with thirteen acres of adjoining land, offered an ideal opportunity to fulfil this ambition and to fulfil the terms of agreement with the Misses Gibb to the benefit of the Manx public.

Following the death of the longer surviving sister, Miss Janet Gibb, in 1974, the Museum exercised its

Below: The front entrance and gardens of the Grove, an elegantly proportioned, small, early Victorian mansion house.

Bottom: The yard and outbuildings to the rear of the main house with displays of agricultural equipment and transport, including the original phaeton used at the grove.

The Kitchen: dominated by the cast-iron coal-burning range which provided the means of cooking and obtaining hot water for the house. A rocking chair is provided for the cook's rare leisure moments.

The Scullery: where vegetables and other foodstuffs would be delivered and prepared and where the dirty pots would have been washed.

option to purchase the property and its contents and began the prodigious task of recording three generations of the family's accumulated possessions and restoring the main building to its original Victorian appearance. By the summer of 1978, the new branch museum was ready for opening to the public who entered through a new interpretative centre before enjoying the short walk through the grounds and garden to the house. Subsequently, the original out-buildings were developed to show a range of nineteenth and early twentieth century agricultural equipment and transport and the garden is in process of being restored to illustrate typical Victorian trends in horticulture.

Most of the furniture in the restored period rooms are original pieces handed down through successive generations of the Gibb family and the house now provides today's visitors with a vivid and intimate insight into the domestic arrangements of a prosperous Victorian family's country home.

Outside, displays of agricultural transport and equipment in the original outbuildings provide a picture of farming life in the rich lowland areas of the Isle of Man which contrasts markedly with the more basic requirements of the upland crofting community depicted at Cregneash.

The Grove Museum now represents an important and popular addition to the service offered by the Manx Museum, providing another unique touchstone to the Island's social history and development.

The Dining Room: with mahogany furniture dating from the 1840s and the original late Victorian colour scheme of olive and gold wallpaper, lined in the traditional manner with family portraits.

The Drawing Room: redecorated in late Victorian style but with many of the original contents from 1870.

Main Bedroom: set to represent the return from a well-documented holiday in France in 1908. A half-unpacked trunk occupies the middle of the floor, and French hats are souvenirs of the trip.

Left: Child's Bedroom: perhaps originally furnished with items discarded from other rooms in the house, this room has a distinct charm for today's visitor.

Right page.

Top: A small selection from the many beautiful Victorian greeting cards preserved by the previous owners of the Grove and which now form a fascinating part of the Museum's displays.

Bottom left: Sewing Room: originally the dressing room for the main bedroom and now displayed as a sewing room, most of the items being from the original Grove house contents.

Bottom right: One of the bedrooms has been converted to house a display of costume. This leno dress with green satin stripes, was worn by a member of the Corrin family of Castletown c. 1880.

A Happy
Christmas
Wishing
you a happy
Christmas

May every Birthday add but Joy to Joy.
With the
Compliments of the Season
Jollification
A Very
Happy
New Year.
Wishing you a
Happy New Year
With the compliments
of the season

THE NATIONAL ART GALLERY

S. HARRISON

When permanent premises, in the shape of the former Noble's Hospital in Douglas, were finally acquired to establish the Island's National Museum, the Museum Trustees prepared for the first time to achieve the potential for presenting a comprehensive display of the Manx cultural heritage.

It is significant that from the outset, it was recognised that one of the great strengths of the new institution was its ability to draw together object, documentary and art collections, thereby providing the Manx people with an homogeneous educational and cultural resource which had few parallels in Britain.

Therefore, when the new Museum opened to the public on 1st November 1922, an important feature in the Eastern gallery was a series of oil paintings and drawings by the renowned Manx artist, John Miller Nicholson, with a smaller adjacent room being devoted to local views,charts, maps and prints.

In subsequent years, the importance and range of the art collections has increased greatly while always retaining its precise Manx relevance and associations. The space devoted to this aspect of Manx culture within the institution as a whole has been enlarged accordingly over the years in line with the Museum's expanding role and responsibilities, major re-allocations of display space taking place in 1935 and 1960.

In addition to its primary role as the home of the National art collection, the Museum Art Gallery has, from an early stage in its evolution, provided a forum for a wide ranging series of temporary exhibitions of non-Manx art and an annual series of illustrated public lectures and films on a variety of cultural topics. These two additional facilities have enjoyed the enthusiastic support of the Manx public who have consistently filled the gallery to capacity to hear a distinguished sequence of visiting speakers and to enjoy exhibitions drawn from the international field of artistic achievement.

The Manx Museum Art Gallery now represents the primary exhibition area for Manx art and its changing exhibitions reveal the great depth of artistic talent which has been and continues to be associated with the Isle of Man.

HISTORY IN PICTURES

All pictures in the permanent collections of the Art Gallery of the Manx Museum have qualified for acceptance by virtue of being works of quality by Manx artists or by artists depicting Manx subjects. This strict collecting policy provides the unifying strength of the art collection brought together over the last hundred years.

However, a number of these paintings exhibit an additional quality of extreme importance providing fascinating and often unique glimpses of the Island's social, political and physical history. The Museum visitor who looks beyond an initial artistic appraisal of many works is rewarded with a wealth of topographical and architectural detail of places and buildings which have been transformed beyond recognition over the years or which have vanished from the modern scene completely. Similarly, many topographical paintings will reveal, often as a casual addition to the main theme, a host of important references to traditional social practices of the time. Thus, details of contemporary dress, transport, agriculture and manufacture may all be represented, providing vital additional information concerning Manx life in previous centuries.

Similarly, the Museum's small but important collection of portraits provides a vivid realization of some of the major personalities of Manx history, bringing into sharp human focus our rich collection of documentary and object sources.

The Seventeenth Century

One of the Daniel King's drawings of Castle Rushen. Note the two horsedrawn sledges or *caayr sleod* loaded with straw in the centre, and the sloping "counter scarpe" or glacis of the castle.

The earliest known views of the Island are in the form of a series of monochrome wash drawings executed by Daniel King of Chester. They are of prime importance in providing us with a view of the Island in the middle of the seventeenth century when civil unrest and political intrigue were building to a climax which was to have a lasting effect on Manx society.

Daniel King of Chester was a pupil of W.Hollar (one of the most important illustrators and topographers working in England in the seventeenth century) and drew many views of buildings for Dugdale's *Monasticon* and also for his own folio of *Cathedrals*. Between 1643 and 1651 at the height of the Civil War activity in the Isle of Man, King produced sixteen monochrome wash drawings of important buildings and natural features. These drawings were subsequently used to illustrate *A Short Treatise of the Isle of Man* by James Chaloner (a Commissioner in Man on behalf of Lord Fairfax and Governor from 1657–1660) which appeared as an appendix to King's *Vale-Royall of England, or The County Palatine of Chester Illustrated* published in 1656.

The original drawings are housed in the British Museum but the Manx Museum exhibits a full series of facsimiles undertaken in the nineteenth century.

The scope of King's work clearly reflects the nature of his commission, concentrating on the portrayal of the important centres of Governmental, military and religious authority. The collection comprises no less than eight views of Castle Rushen, one of Peel Castle, and four of Bishop's Court, all of which are important in recording the precise appearance of these buildings in the mid-seventeenth century.

However, despite this architectural emphasis in his drawings, King's eye for social detail provides us with valuable information on some infrequently documented aspects of social life including early forms of transport and contemporary dress.

Against this early physical background portrayed for us by King, we are able to set a number of important

Yn Stanlagh Mooar, "The Great Stanley", James, the seventh Earl of Derby, Lord of Man. The painting is attributed to the Van Dyck studio.

Charlotte de la Tremouille, Countess of Derby, wife of the seventh Earl.
Charcoal drawing attributed to the Van Dyck studio.

seventeenth century portraits of key figures in the political and social events of these turbulent times.

Foremost among these was the Seventh Earl of Derby (*Yn Stanlagh Mooar*, "The Great Stanley") who, with his Countess, Charlotte de la Tremouille, held the Isle of Man as one of the last strongholds of the Royalist cause during the struggle for power in the English Civil War. As Lord of Man, the Earl and his Countess established a secondary Royalist court at Castle Rushen after the loss of Charles I's cause in England, the Countess finally surrendering this offshore stronghold to the forces of the Commonwealth in 1651.

The portrait of the Seventh Earl is attributed to the Van Dyck studio and is one of the finest quality paintings in the Museum's collection. The subject is presented in a typically military setting. The Earl appears attired in plate armour of the period holding a musket in his right hand, his sword hanging from his waist. In the background, his cavalry assembles by the campaign tents which proudly flourish the Royalist flag and the Derby family's emblem of the Eagle and Child.

The charcoal study of Charlotte de la Tremouille, purchased by the Friends of the Manx Museum in 1954, provides us with a reminder of the Countess's courageous role in supporting her husband's ill-fated cause. When the Earl of Derby left the Island to join battle for the Royalist cause in England for the last time, he knew he was leaving at Castle Rushen, a Countess who had already proved her courage and fortitude during the long seige of a family seat at Lathom House in Lancashire. Indeed, the Countess may well have held the Island against the Parliamentary forces had it not been for the devastating effect of the sudden news of her husband's execution at Bolton, combined with the famous deeds of the Manx patriot William Christian, or as he is more popularly known, *Illiam Dhone* ("Brown-Haired William").

Illiam Dhone and the Seventh Earl of Derby are the two dominating protagonists of Manx politics in the mid-seventeenth century. When the Earl left the Island for the last time in 1651, William Christian remained as one of the Countess's principal officers, holding the positions of receiver of revenues and major-general, and also having control of the local militia.

Following news of the Earl of Derby's defeat and capture, Illiam Dhone and an influential group of Manxmen saw an opportunity to redress the community's long-standing grievances regarding the traditional system of land lease and the burden of supplying the Governmental troops. Fearing that the Countess Charlotte would not consider the Island's traditional constitution and customs in any agreement of surrender, Illiam Dhone and the militia obtained control of all the forts except Peel and Castle Rushen in an effort to guarantee a surrender of the Island to the Parliamentary forces on favourable terms to the Manx people.

Castle Rushen fell without a siege, apparently through deception from within but Illiam Dhone and his supporters did not enjoy the change in circumstances they had hoped for from their new rulers. With the restoration of King Charles I in England, Charles Stanley, the eighth Earl of Derby resumed his family's rule as Lord of Man. Despite a pardon from the King, the eighth Earl was determined to exact revenge on Illiam Dhone and his fellow conspirators, and the Manx leader was executed at Hango Hill near Castletown for his betrayal of the Countess Charlotte and the Derby lordship.

Although Illiam Dhone had conspired against the prevailing Government, he was mourned by the Manx as a martyr to his country and the cause of the common people, his name being commemorated in an heroic Manx ballad.

(The Manx Museum also houses a cap, reputed to have belonged to Illiam Dhone, which is very similar to the one he wears in the portrait.)

William Christian, *Illiam Dhone*. Executed at Hango Hill in 1663 for his part in the Manx Rebellion of 1651 which led the Countess of Derby to surrender Castle Rushen to the English Parliametary forces.

Inset: Silk embroidered linen cap, dating from the early seventeenth century and said to have belonged to Illiam Dhone.

The Eighteenth Century

Above: Moses Griffith's accurate depiction of Peel Castle in 1774.

Right: Castle Rushen by Moses Griffith, showing the original dormer windows with diamond-leaded panes of the seveteenth century mansion built within the castle walls by the seventh Earl of Derby.

Chronologically, the next important collection of Manx topographical paintings are those undertaken by *Moses Griffith* in 1774.

Griffith was one of a number of artists who came to the Isle of Man with Thomas Pennant, the noted Welsh writer, naturalist and antiquary, to provide accurate illustrations of hitherto little known natural and historic features within the Island.

The party which visited the Isle of Man in 1774 included Pennant, Griffith and Captain F. Grose, an antiquary and draughtsman. Grose, the author of *Antiquities of England and Wales* (1773–1787) enjoyed a considerable reputation for his work on topographical surveys and his work undoubtedly influenced the younger Griffith.

Many of the illustrations undertaken during Pennant's several tours of the British Isles between 1769 and 1783 were later copied by contemporary engravers and published as book illustrations, but Griffith's work remained unpublished and relatively unknown until the Pennant library was sold at Christie's in 1938. The Manx Museum acquired a small number of these original eighteenth century "tinted" paintings at this time, including views of "Balasala Abbey", Tynwald Hill, Ballaugh Church and Peel Castle.

After the Second World War, the Friends of the Manx Museum generously donated a further selection of Griffith's paintings which add considerably to our record of the Island in the eighteenth century.

The third important collection of pre-nineteenth century topographical works takes the form of twenty-six exquisite water-colours painted by *John "Warwick" Smith circa* 1795. The existence of these paintings, comprising the largest selection of eighteenth century views of the Island by a single artist, was unknown to the Manx Museum until 1950 when they were discovered by the then Director, Basil Megaw, gracing the walls of Blair Castle in Perthshire, the residence of the Duke of Atholl. The Atholl family had preserved this remarkable collection as part of the family history, reflecting the influence of their name in the history of the Isle of Man since the Lordship passed to the Atholls from the Derbys in 1736. Indeed, the paintings were probably commissioned by the fourth Duke of Atholl, Governor-in-Chief of the Island from 1791.

John Smith was of Cumbrian extraction and enjoyed the patronage of several members of the English landed gentry, including the Earl of Warwick and John Christian Curwen who came from a notable Cumberland/Manx family. The artist's nick-name of "Warwick" or "Italian" Smith was derived from his protracted visits to Italy between 1776 and 1781 undertaken with financial support from the second Earl of Warwick. However, it was his work as a British water-colourist which earned Smith his high reputation amongst his contemporaries, and he was responsible for several other topographical series including views of Perthshire and the English Lakes. Following his death in 1831, Smith's work suffered a decline in popularity, but his artistic legacy has in recent years gained a greater appreciation. In terms of the Isle of Man's artistic legacy, his contribution is outstanding and his series of twenty-six paintings provide a major category in the art collections as well as an important source of reference for the Island's appearance and development at the close of the eighteenth century.

Laxey in 1795: showing the village focussed at the river-mouth with the bridge carrying the old highway from Douglas to Ramsey. Note the "bleaching fields" on the river bank where the long lengths of linen cloth were laid out to dry.

Above: Laws on the Tynwald, 1795: the earliest known picture of the Manx national assembly. The riotous collection of figures may have been painted by J. C. Ibbetson who is known to have worked with Smith.

Below: North view of Peel Castle, 1795: the Castle and Cathedral ruins viewed from the sands of the bay. The chancel is still roofed, and the west gable of the old St. Patrick's Church is still standing. Meanwhile, fishermen and women collecting driftwood go about their work.

Thomas and Ann Durie: an eighteenth century Douglas merchant and his wife.

As in the seventeenth century period, we are also fortunate in having a number of portraits of notable eighteenth century personalities which provide flesh for the bones of Manx social history before the age of photography. A particularly fine pair of portraits depicting Thomas Durie, an influential eighteenth century Douglas merchant, and his wife Ann, allow us the facility to enter the world of eighteenth century trade and social status revealing numerous insights into the Island life at this time.

(The following description is extracted from an article by A. M. Cubbon in Volume VI of the Journal of the Manx Museum.)

"In his elegant light blue coat and waistcoat, with gold braid and buttons, and lace at neck and cuff, with his well-powdered wig and his kindly but shrewd eye, Thomas Durie makes a striking figure. He typifies the merchant class whose activities led to the rapid and significant growth of Douglas as the major port of the Island during the eighteenth century.

"Ann Durie, Thomas' wife, is depicted as a shepherdess, an interesting illustration of the romantic treatment practised in feminine portraiture of the time. Her dress, however, provides an insight into the attire of the wife of a prosperous Manx merchant of the period. A charming little vignette worked into the background of the painting shows a large merchantship with furled sails riding at anchor beside a fortress, presumably a slightly stylised representation of the old fort of Douglas, which at that period still stood guard at the Douglas harbour mouth. It was from the maritime trade of this harbour that both the Duries and the Fines (Ann's family) derived their substance.

"Douglas had become during the eighteenth Century not only the principal Manx port, but an important entrepôt centre of Britain, with merchantmen flying the flags of many countries frequently in its harbour. Trade flourished, and the merchant class of Douglas was an important element in the social structure of the Island. The seventh Earl of Derby a century previously had declared 'This Isle will never flourish until some trading be', and from an economic point of view at least the growth of eighteenth century Douglas was to prove the wisdom of his remark.

"The Durie family was of Scottish extraction, and was in fact related to the Forbes, ancestors of the famous Manx naturalist, Professor Edward Forbes. In 1771, indeed, Thomas came into the estate of David Forbes, the naturalist's great-grandfather, who had settled in Ramsey early in the century. Thomas Durie was a successful merchant of Douglas, while his brother John traded in Ramsey. Thomas had no children, and only two daughters of the Ramsey branch of the family lived to reach maturity, so that the name died out in the Island. Thomas Durie, however, was an influential figure of his day, and resided for many years at the Nunnery, which he apparently rented from P. J. Heywood, prior to its purchase in 1776 by John Taubman. It in fact appears likely that Thomas Durie continued to reside at the Nunnery even after the sale of the property, and may have remained there up to the time of his death in 1779. Durie also owned a large house in the 'town of Douglas', which not only became known as Durie House but gave the name Durie (later corrupted to Drury) to the lane in which it stood, in that part of old Douglas which was swept away in the town improvement programme of the nineteen thirties. The Museum collections in fact contain the fine brass door knocker and a marble eighteenth century mantlepiece obtained from Durie House at the time of its demolition.

"Ann, the daughter of William Fine, another Douglas merchant, married Thomas Durie at Malew parish church on 12th May 1760. She died at Douglas in 1815 at the age of 80, the contemporary newspaper account of her death stating, 'Her suavity of manners endeared her to all ranks in society .. Her habitation was that of delight and cheerfulness'.

"Thomas and Ann Durie are intriguing figures of their time in their own right, but in addition typify the mid-eighteenth century merchant class which played such an important role in the economic development of the Island."

In the latter half of the eighteenth century, Manx merchants like Thomas Durie displayed great enterprise in developing trade routes around the world. The more affluent merchants were heavily involved with the many ships which operated out of the Isle of Man under a variety of flags of convenience, trading with ports in France, Spain, Italy, Sicily, the Baltic and even the United States.

One such ship involved in this far-flung and highly lucrative trade was the Brig "Caesar" of Douglas. In 1935, a dusty and neglected water colour painting of this proud vessel was brought into the Manx Museum thereby providing a rare illustration of the Island's eighteenth century maritime history.

The vessel is depicted at anchor in the bay of Naples in 1788, flying a flag bearing the Union Jack and the Manx Three Legs emblem. The interest of the painting was greatly increased with the subsequent discovery of

An eighteenth century trading vessel, the Brig *Caesar* of Douglas.

the ledger of John Joseph Bacon, one of the foremost Douglas merchants of the eighteenth century. The ledger, dealing with the "adventures" of Bacon's many vessels trading in foreign ports, reveals a wealth of detail concerning the "Caesar's" voyages, her main cargoes being barrels of red and white herrings. In the same year as her depicted visit to Naples, the "Caesar" sailed to the West Indies, no doubt with a cargo of herrings, perhaps intended as food for the black slaves during their long sea-journeys to a life of servitude on foreign shores. She returned with a rich cargo of West Indian sugar and rum.

The last recorded transaction in the ledger is for the year 1792 when 614 barrels of herrings delivered to Naples made a handsome final profit of £921 15s. 5d.

An equally stimulating insight in eighteenth century maritime affairs is provided by Richard Wright's painting *The Squadrons of Thurot and Elliot in Ramsey Bay, 1760*. However, this splendid picture of English and French naval ships lying perfectly calm at anchor, belies the history of the violent naval engagement which immediately preceded the artist's tranquil scene.

The following description of the battle and the painting is extracted from an article by A. M. Cubbon in Volume VI of the Journal of the Manx Museum.

"On 28th February, 1760, during the Seven Years War between England and France, residents in the North of the Isle of Man witnessed a stirring naval engagement fought off the Ballaugh coast. Three French ships, under the command of the redoubtable Monsieur Thurot, had been plundering at Carrickfergus, in Northern Ireland, and the young Captain Elliot had been despatched with a squadron of three English ships to redress the dishonour suffered by the British Navy from these presumptuous activities of enemy vessels in British waters. The engagement off the Manx coast was fierce and decisive, and ended in a complete English victory. Thurot was killed in the battle, and all three Frenchmen were captured. After the battle the English commander sailed his ships and his three French prizes round to the sheltered anchorage of Ramsey Bay to repair the ravages of the engagement.

"The centre of the picture is occupied by Thurot's captured flagship, the Maréchal Belleisle, with its mizzenmast shot clean away, and its French colours (the fleur-de-lis on a white background in those pre-

The squadrons of Thurot and Elliot in Ramsey Bay, 1760 by Richard Wright.

tricolour days) flying beneath the Union Jack at the stern. The artist's viewpoint must have been in the neighbourhood of Gob ny Rona, near Port y Vullin, and the coast south from Ramsey is indicated towards the left of the picture, with Ballure chapel just discernible. The painting also shows local Manx shipping, and is particularly valuable in illustrating examples of the old 'square sail' fishing boats of the Isle of Man, the earliest illustration known of this now obsolete type of craft, descended from the Viking ships. In the right foreground such a vessel carries a party of gentry on a pleasure cruise, complete with fiddler, doubtless taking the opportunity to view the warships at anchor in the bay. A flag, bearing the three legs of Man, flutters in the stern sheets. This is one of the earliest representations of the Island's flag, and another point of particular Manx interest in the painting.

"The canvas is not signed, but fortunately contemporary record, coupled to expert assessment of the artist's treatment of his medium, leaves virtually no doubt concerning his identity. A letter from Douglas, Isle of Man, dated 4th March, 1760, appeared in Whitworth's Manchester Advertiser, which in describing the scene of the squadrons in Ramsey Bay, and in particular the carnage on Thurot's ship, states: 'Mr Richard Wright, painter, formerly of Liverpool, was on board, and is now drawing a sketch of the whole'. Further confirmation is given given by an entry in the Belfast Newsletter of 15th April, 1760, inviting subscriptions to support the publication of 'two elegant copper-plate Prints, representing the engagement on the North side of the Isle of Man, wherein monsieur Thurot's squadron was taken; and a Representation of the Ships in Ramsey Bay, taken on the spot after the Battle . . .'. 'Mr Wright, the Undertaker, engages to have the Plans engraved from a Painting of his own'. Still more conclusive evidence is afforded by the engraving itself, published on 30th May, 1762, of the ships in Ramsey Bay, which shows the identical scene. This is captioned 'J. Goldar, Sculp.', 'Richd Wright Pinx', and is dedicated:

> " 'To the Worshipful Corporation and Merchants of LIVERPOOL this Print being a View of both Squadrons Lying in Ramsey Bay in the Isle of Man, after the defeat of the Daring Monsr. THUROT who was killed in the Action the 28th of Feby 1760, is most humbly Inscribed by Gentleman Your most Obedt. Servant Richard Wright. Engraved from the Original Painting Drawn from the Real Ships by Permission of Capt. Elliot, in the Collection of a NOBLE-MAN.'

"Expert opinion by no less an authority than Messrs. Thomas Agnew & Sons, the well-known London Art Dealers, confirms that the treatment is by Wright, the one aspect of the painting which does not appear to be characteristic of the artist – the representation of the flat calm – again being borne out by contemporary record; Mark Hildesley, Bishop of Sodor and Man, writing in May, 1760, recorded that 'during the eight days the victors, with their captives, lay in the bay . . . there was the most perfect calm ever remembered, at that or any period of the year".

Richard Wright was born in Liverpool circa 1720 and later became sometimes known as "Wright of the Isle of Man". Self taught, he began life as a house and ship painter in the literal sense, but won his reputation as an artist, and was at one time engaged by Sir Joshua Reynolds to paint in the background scenes to his naval portraits. At Hampton Court there is a picture by Wright of "The Royal Yacht bringing Queen Charlotte to England in a Storm", while his best known work, "The Fishery" formed the basis for Woollet's engraving. Wright died about 1775.

As one of the first artists of note to paint in the Isle of Man it is most gratifying to have this worthy example of his work in the collections of the Manx Museum. Competent marine paintings, especially of the eighteenth century, are always much sought after, and this picture possesses several points of particular and outstanding interest for Manx people.

The Nineteenth Century

The nineteenth century saw the rise in popularity of the Isle of Man as a place to visit and the flow of visitors to the Island was radically accelerated by the introduction of regular steamship sailings from England in the 1830's.

The splendour of this age of paddle-steamers is given vibrant expression in several marine paintings by Samuel Walters in the Museum collection. His portrayal of the Isle of Man Steam Packet Company's first ship the *Mona's Isle I Leaving Douglas Harbour* is an horrendous reminder of the latent malevolence of the Irish Sea but it is also a fitting illustration of the pride attached to the operation of this Island lifeline of communication and trade.

A much gentler, and hopefully more typical, view of nineteenth century activity is depicted in W. Hardie Hay's painting *On the Beach at Douglas 1886*. Here a variety of detail is presented for our modern-day scrutiny as a profusion of Victorian holiday-makers partake of traditional sea-side delights.

There is a rich source of contemporary social detail to be found in the paintings of a range of nineteenth century artists whose artistic eyes were drawn to the bustling activity of the Manx ports set against dramatic coastal scenery. These views have great importance as social records before the popular introduction of photography.

A number of them also exhibit high artistic quality, reflecting the attraction the Isle of Man presented to some of the leading artists of the day.

However, the nineteenth and twentieth centuries were also notable for marking the appearance of talented insular artists whose artistic achievements and importance grew to belie their isolated working environment. A summary of notable contributions made by several Manx artists is given in the following section.

The paddle-steamer *Mona's Isle* leaving Douglas harbour, by Samuel Walters.

Right: On the Beach at Douglas, 1894 by W. Hardie Hay, provides a marvellous record of contemporary activities at the Victorian seaside.

Below: View of the North Quay, Douglas from the Nunnery Howe, painted in oils by Jacob Strutt R.A. in 1833.

SIX SELECTED ARTISTS

George Romney: 1734–1802

The Isle of Man's isolated geographical position belies the extent to which its people have impressed themselves on the attention of other nations through their deeds, achievements or acquired status.

In the field of art therefore, it is no surprise that over the centuries, leading social figures of the day who were directly or indirectly associated with the Island have employed their patronage to encourage the leading contemporary artists to contribute to the corpus of Manx-associated works.

As a result of this tendency in the seventeenth and eighteenth centuries the Museum Art Gallery can proudly exhibit the works of Daniel King, the "Van Dyck Studio", Moses Griffith and Warwick Smith. These riches were further enhanced in 1973, when the Museum was fortunate enough to acquire three paintings with strong Manx associations executed by the leading London portrait painter George Romney.

The paintings are portraits of the Taubman family of Douglas, an influential family in the eighteenth century who had lived at the Nunnery mansion on the outskirts of the city for over one hundred and fifty years. When the modern-day owners of this historic property decided that the contents should be sold, the Museum acquired the three Romney portraits and one other family portrait (originally attributed to Romney but now thought to be by F. Cotes, a London contemporary) which together formed a group of four.

Miss Christian Taubman, aged twenty-eight painted by Romney in 1781.

(The following details are extracted from an article by A. M. Cubbon in Volume VII of the Journal of the Manx Museum.)

"Romney was born at Beckside, Dalton-in-Furness, Lancashire, in 1734, and first practised portrait painting at Kendal. It may have been that the Taubman's connections by marriage with some of the leading families of the Lake District led to their decision to have their portraits painted by Romney, though these portraits were executed long after his move to London, which took place in 1762. He visited France in 1764, and studied art in Italy from 1773–75. Although he had established a reputation as a good portrait artist earlier, his 'high period' commenced in 1776, after his return from Italy, when he set up his studio in Cavendish Square, London. An indication of the growth of his reputation and popularity is given by the prices he charged. The cost of a normal portrait on a three-quarter canvas which fetched 15 guineas in 1775 had risen to 30 guineas by 1790. His well-known association with Mrs Emma Hart (later Lady Hamilton) whom he painted many times, commenced in 1782, and his health and (it is generally considered) his artistic abilities declined after his contact with her ended in 1791.

"The three Taubman Romneys all date from his best period. They are all of three-quarter size (30 ins × 25 ins). Fortunately, from the detailed diaries of the artist which survive, the actual dates of the sittings for the Taubman portraits are known.

"The earliest is that of Miss Christian Taubman (who later became Mrs. Cunninghame). She had sittings on June 4th–10th, 13th and 15th, 1781. She was then aged twenty-eight.

"Next to be painted was Christian's mother, Mrs Esther Taubman, whose London address is also recorded, 'No. 19, Cecil Street, Strand'. She sat for the painter on 29th April and 3rd and 4th of May 1786, when she was seventy-three years old. The diaries also record '1786, July, received of Mr Taubman, for Mrs Taubman's portrait . . . £21.'

Mrs. Esther Taubman, aged seventy-three, painted by Romney in 1786.

Captain John Taubman, painted by Romney in 1788.

"Finally Captain John Taubman had sittings on 4th, 9th, 10th, 22nd and 29th April and 2nd and 6th May 1788. His address then was 31 Leicester Square. The record ends 'Paid for, by Capt. Taubman, in full, 25 gs., June 24, 1788; sent off, June 27, same year'.

"The painting of these portraits by a leading London portrait painter, and their transport by stage coach probably to Whitehaven for shipment to the Isle of Man gives a graphic glimpse of the social life of a well-to-do Manx family during the second half of the eighteenth century. It is indeed gratifying that these outstanding treasures – both as fine portraits and significant social records – have now been safely returned to the Isle of Man to hang in the Manx Museum."

John Martin: 1789–1854

One of the Island's most accomplished artistic visitors in the nineteenth century was John Martin who was eminent as a painter, engraver, London town-planner and socialite during the first half of the century. Born at Haydon near Hexham in Northumberland in 1789, Martin enjoyed a great artistic reputation, exhibiting eighty-seven works at the Royal Academy, thirty-seven at the British Institute and sixty-two at the Royal Society of British Artists. He was also well known to a more general audience through his highly acclaimed illustrations for Milton's *Paradise Lost* and for certain editions of the *Bible*.

A historical and landscape painter in both oils and water-colours, Martin also became an accomplished engraver of his own pictures. However, his enduring reputation derives from his large canvases depicting religious or "sublime" scenes characterised by sweeping swirls of turbulent colour, full of atmosphere and emotion, depicting such biblical scenes as *The Last Judgement*, *The Great Day of His Wrath* and *The Deluge*.

Towards the middle of the nineteenth century, Martin spent a number of his summers and autumns in the Isle of Man, staying at the home of a distant relative, Thomas Wilson, a leading draper and social figure in Douglas. Martin's son, Charles, himself a noted portrait painter, actually came to live in the Isle of Man and later married Mary Anne Wilson of Harold Tower, Douglas. In October 1853, Martin left his home in London to visit his son in Douglas, and it was at this time that he embarked on his representation of *The*

Plains of Heaven having completed a water-colour depicting *Joshua Spying Out the Land of Canaan* in 1851.

One month after his arrival in Douglas, Martin suffered a paralytic seizure which left him without the use of his right hand and which quickly affected the use of his other limbs and eyesight. His English doctor and longstanding friend declined to come to the Isle of Man, describing in a letter, the inevitability of Martin's decline:

> *"I have known John Martin for years, and have made him my particular study. The attack was one to be calculated upon at any time, it being the result of an over-wrought brain. With him, ten years were equal to a life-time of those with the average mould."*

Martin died at 4, Finch Road, Douglas in 1854 and was buried in Kirk Braddan cemetery in the vault of the Spittal family. Through the generosity of the Friends of the Manx Museum, in 1934 the Museum was able to acquire from Martin's nephew the remarkable portrayal of *Joshua Spying Out the Land of Canaan*, thereby reflecting the close association between the Isle of Man, and this major British artist. The significance of this association was reflected in an article in the *Mona's Herald* following the artist's death, which stated:

> *"Henceforth, the deathless name of Martin, associated with that of our lovely Isle, like the great Napoleon's linked with St Helena, will invest it with an interest and celebrity which will endure to the end of time; and we may truly predict that strangers from all parts of Europe, landing on these shores, will, like pilgrims journeying to some far-famed distant shrine, visit the grave of Martin."*

Joshua Spying Out the Land of Canaan, watercolour painting by John Martin, 1851.

John Miller Nicholson: 1840–1913

J.M.N., as he often signed his work, is perhaps the most accomplished of all Manx artists. Comparisons with Turner are frequently cited with regard to the quality and style of his work and the fact that his ability is not more widely regarded is a result of the artist's own self-effacing non-commercial attitude and the Island setting chosen for his life's work.

Born in Douglas on the 29th January 1840, the son of a housepainter, the young Nicholson was from the beginning surrounded by the sights, sounds, colours and activities of an expanding Victorian town and port which by the time he had reached adulthood had become the official capital of the Island.

On leaving school, where his artistic ability had already become apparent, he became an apprentice painter in his father's expanding business in Well Road Hill, Douglas, and was also able to develop and refine his natural skills in draughtsmanship.

The exploration of his talent with a pencil and his experimentation with the artistic use of colour was given ample scope around the bustling streets and quays of Douglas. The minute details of the Victorian town, its buildings, people and shipping, together with the ever-changing reflected colours across the bay, were

Left: John Miller Nicholson, self portrait aged thirty-nine.

Below left: Nicholson's box camera made by W. W. Rouch and Co., London, with a number of prints from the artist's original glass negatives.

meticulously and swiftly transferred into sketch books for future reference. These early sketches in pencil, together with copious margin notes in his distinctive minuscule handwriting noting details of weather conditions, light and shade, provided a source for many of his later oil and water-colour paintings. At this most formative stage of his artistic career, the sights, sounds and textures of Douglas were systematically absorbed and became part of him.

His ability to capture in pencil the tonal effects of changing light coupled with his remarkable visual memory for detail, inspired his experimentations in photography. Using a wooden-cased quarter-plate camera manufactured by Rouch & Co. (now in the Museum collections) he amplified his collection of sketched sources with realistic visual records which, none the less, betrayed the critical artist's approach. Typically, he excelled in this allied field of new technology and in 1891 was awarded medals in photographic exhibitions at Liverpool, Leeds and Gloucester.

Through the good offices of Lady Loch (wife of the Island's Lieutenant Governor), John Ruskin, a driving force of the Victorian Arts and Crafts movement, became an admirer of Nicholson's work and purchased

Right: One of Nicholson's early paintings of Douglas harbour in a realistic style which was later to become more "impressionistic".

Below: A detailed pencil sketch of Nicholson's observations at Douglas harbour on 27th September 1880. Note the artist's meticulous attention to detail and his precise margin notes on colours, "veiled sunlight" etc., which would enable him to reproduce the scene as a full-size painting at some future date.

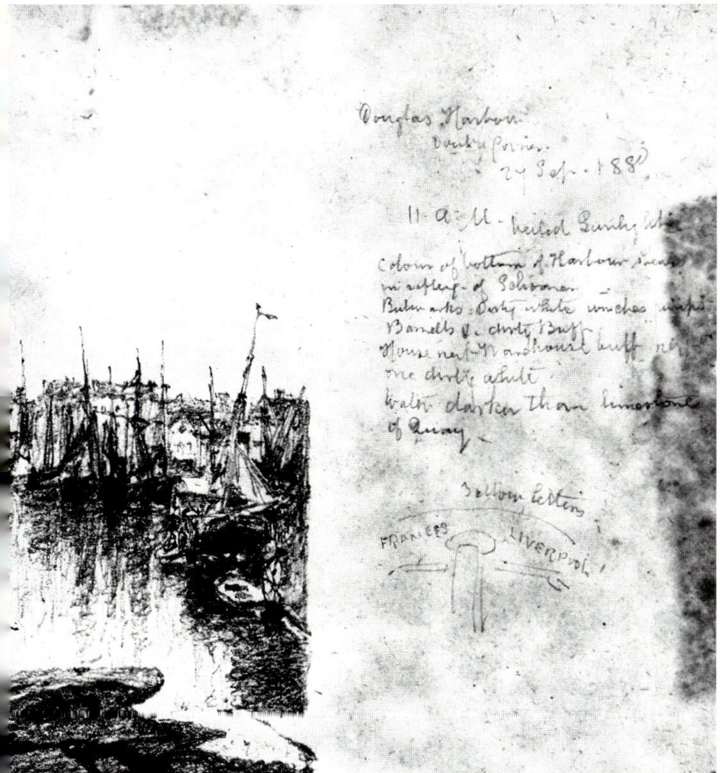

a number of pencil sketches for distribution to galleries outside the Island. He also corresponded with Nicholson and was quite prepared to offer constructive criticism of the artist's approach and technique. In 1880, one letter from Ruskin contained a piece of advice which was to have far reaching consequences for Nicholson's artistic development. In an attempt to enlarge the artist's horizons above his renowned attention to insular detail, Ruskin commented:

". . . you are cramped and chilled by Isle of Manishness – you ought to take knapsack on shoulder – a grey paper book – half a dozen colours and a bit of chalk – and so walk to Naples and back".

It was two years before Nicholson followed Ruskin's advice but it had a profound effect on his artistic style. Although while in Italy, Nicholson's pencil had been characteristically active in recording his new subjects, his subsequent paintings emphasise the Turnerian quality of his work where the effects of light rather than detail are the dominant features. Archibald Knox, a fellow but slightly junior Manx artist, later described the effect of this visit on Nicholson's art:

> *". . . (he) returned with a reservoir of memories that almost fixed his character as an artist . . . it supplied him with new subjects, subjects after his heart . . . the change from the severity of his early technique to a later loose and broad condition was slowly going on. He brought back with him a painter's Italy: architecture and its colour tanned and bleached by the strong light of the mildly blue sky . . ."*

The influence of the Impressionist school of art did indeed remain with him. Some of his detailed Italian pencil sketches of 1882 were used as a source for his increasingly impressionistic paintings many years later, as may be seen in *Santa Maria della Salute, Venice*, painted in 1909.

The Art Gallery of the Manx Museum is extremely fortunate in possessing the largest single collection of Nicholson's work covering all phases of his artistic development including pencil sketches, book illustrations, illuminated addresses, water-colours and oil paintings. Generously endowed in 1927 with the initial deposit by the Baume Trustees of the "studio collection" of Nicholson paintings which had been offered for public auction five years after the artist's death, the collection has since been considerably enlarged. A changing selection of Nicholson's work is a permanent feature in the Island's National Gallery but for the many visitors who view his work, it is clear that his artistic contribution extends far beyond the shores of his native Isle.

Santa Maria della Salute, Venice, sketched in pencil in 1882 and painted in oils in Nicholson's later style in 1909.

Old St. Matthew's, Douglas, oil, J. M. Nicholson 1882.

The Old Market Place, Douglas, oil, J. M. Nicholson 1889.

Archibald Knox: 1864 –1933

Archibald Knox at work in his studio.

In the Art Gallery of the Manx Museum there is a rich array of artistic skill, beauty and graphic interpretation in the works by Manx artists and there is often lively discussion as to their respective merits and consequent place in the hierarchy of artistic achievement. There is one artist however, whose work seems to side-step such critical comparison and stands apart from the work of others in the way the history, traditions and soul of the Isle of Man is embodied in a unique but timeless form.

Archibald Knox was born at Tromode on the outskirts of Douglas in 1864, the son of a Scottish father whose business was engineering and whose work designing and building machinery for fishing boats gained him wide recognition. His son, Archie, was educated at the Grammar School in Douglas before attending the Douglas School of Art. At an early stage in his education, Knox became aware of the rich historic backcloth to his developing artistic talent as epitomised by the Manx landscape and the corpus of ancient Celtic and Norse cross carvings. Encouraged by his headmaster at the Grammar School, the Rev. John Quine, a noted archaeologist, Knox acquired a large number of photographs of these carved designs and their complex interlacing patterns became the dominating source of inspiration for his later work as a designer.

For a number of years, Knox was a teacher of art at his old school but at the age of 33, he left the Island and held teaching posts at three art schools in Surrey, Kingston-on-Thames, Wimbledon and Redhill, at various times between 1897 and 1912. However, the fact that he never lost his ability to perceive the roots of art in nature and the work of man when he left his native island, is confirmed in a recollection by one of his pupils, Miss Winifred Tuckfield:

> *"Instead of insisting on the English method of art education by making laborious copies of scraps of museum specimens of style, he made at his own expense, three thousand lantern slides illustrating works of art from prehistoric times down to the gipsy caravans of today, showing how art was produced by the workmen in the joy of using chisel and hammer."*

It was perhaps a legacy of his father's craftsmanship in engineering coupled with his own developing appreciation of the continuity of art's application which led Knox to commence a uniquely significant association with Liberty & Co. of London. The commencement of the twentieth century saw Archibald Knox emerge as one of the foremost designers in the English Art Nouveau movement, gaining international repute through his designs for Liberty's range of jewellery, Cymric silver and Tudric pewter. The Manx Museum has for many years been collecting the range

Some examples of Knox's intricate designs for Liberty's range of Cymric silver.

Silver tea-service and tray designed by Knox for Liberty, featuring a contemporary re-working of the type of "interlace" decoration carved on the Manx crosses.

Left: Jewellery designed by Knox, the two necklaces featuring gold, amethysts, turquoise and blister pearls.

of Knox's designed wares produced by Liberty, ranging from silver napkin rings and tea-services to pewter clocks, exquisite jewelled necklaces and his designs for textiles and ceramics. Throughout these pieces, Knox applies his knowledge and appreciation of the traditional interlace designs of the Isle of Man which he had studied and absorbed in his youth, but expands and re-defines their flow into a new and vibrant form which is unmistakably Knox and unmistakably the product of a great artist who is also a master of inventive and original design.

"Tudric" pewter clock with enamel dial, designed by Knox for Liberty c. 1903.

Although Knox's work as a designer was internationally renowned, his work as a water-colour artist was much less well known and an intensely personal aspect of his contribution to Manx art. His paintings were for himself, for the satisfaction of his own soul and were therefore never sold and rarely signed.

Knox's water-colours are a product of his native Island, capturing the hilly slopes and valleys with broad sweeps of tertiary colours, providing unsuspected insights into the everchanging appearance of the Manx landscape. His paintings were not the result of confined development of an idea in the studio; they were the product of an acutely tuned observation in the countryside, capturing with broad sweeps of the brush a cloud formation, the latent colours within the shadow of a building or the tortured aspect of a windswept tree on the hillside; features which would only be apparent for a moment but which created a lasting image in the artist's mind.

In 1900 Knox lived for a time in a remote cottage in the Sulby valley and thereby provided himself with a marvellous tapestry of inspiration for his paintings. However, he never succumbed, as so many other Manx artists have, to the painting of "pretty" pictures, but always strived to capture and combine the essence of form, colour and spirit of the Manx countryside within his paintings. Of some of his pictures he said:

> *"The places painted are within short walks from my home, passed often; one day something never seen before: some new appearance of colour and the benison of the sky. It may not be seen again; shortly it will fade and disappear, and in an hour is forgotten. Such sights are they, as men over unimaginable centuries have looked at, and learned to know their land as beautiful."*

Knox left his teaching post in London in 1912 and after a brief and not entirely successful visit to America, where he was unable to find "suitable employment", he returned to live in the Isle of Man. From 1914 to 1918 he acted as a censor in the Alien's

Two of Knox's watercolours showing his typical use of muted colours and broad washes to recreate the effects of the Manx landscape.

Top: Lhergy Rhenny.

Bottom: Knockaloe.

Knox's title page for Sophia Morrison's *Manx Fairy Tales*.

Detention Camp at Knockaloe near Peel but was also in great demand as a book illustrator and designer of memorials and addresses. His contribution to Sophia Morrison's *Manx Fairy Tales* reveals the artist's sensitivity to his theme and his audience but the intricately interlaced lettering of these black and white illustrations indicate his unique talent for manuscript design which is given full exposition in illuminated form in *The Deer's Cry*.

Drawing inspiration from the Manx cross carvings and earlier examples of Celtic art such as the *Book of Kells*, Knox's artistic treatment of the well known prayer of the Deer's Cry (or St Patrick's Hymn) reveals a mastery of illuminated lettering and design while displaying his characteristic individuality in the use of subdued tertiary colours and complex interlacing. This work also reflects Knox's deep religious beliefs and is thus a unique expression of the complex personality of the man himself.

After the war, Knox remained in the Island, living in a house in Athol Street, Douglas, teaching art at Douglas High School and continuing to provide numerous designs for public monuments, including many war memorial and commemorative stones.

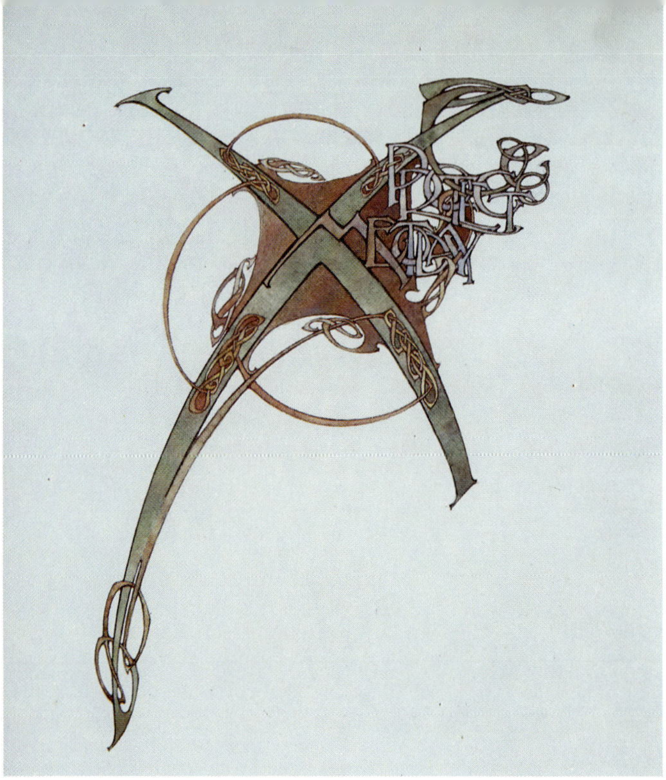

The "Chi Rho" page from Knox's large-scale illuminated manuscript, *The Deer's Cry*.

However, his reputation as an artist and designer continued to grow outside the Island and in 1926, the National Gallery of Ottawa in Canada opened an exhibition devoted to his work. Knox's own continuing search for the perfection of his art led him to visit Italy to study frescoes, but his main inspiration continued to be drawn from his own country.

In 1933, his sudden death from heart failure at the age of 69 robbed the Island of its most inventive and creative artistic talent. No Manx artist, before or since, has matched his ability to interpret the artistic essence of the countryside or to extend the boundaries of design technique in a revolutionary way while still maintaining a clear application of traditionally inspired forms. Knox was buried in Braddan cemetery, just outside Douglas where his tombstone, based on one of his own designs, bears an entirely appropriate epitaph:

"ARCHIBALD KNOX
ARTIST
A HUMBLE SERVANT OF GOD
IN THE MINISTRY OF THE BEAUTIFUL"

In 1946, the Knox family generously donated a large number of his paintings to the Manx Museum and this representative collection of his work was further enriched by a similar donation in 1959. The Museum now houses an important collection of Archibald Knox's work in all fields which provides a permanent reminder of his artistic achievement as well as a constant source of inspiration and pleasure to those who have inherited his legacy.

William Hoggatt: 1879

Mendelssohn's Spring Song, pastel by William Hoggatt.

Although perhaps lacking Knox's depth and subtlety of artistic creativity, William Hoggatt's paintings of the Manx landscape enjoyed a wider recognition outside the Island during the first half of the twentieth century, and his name today is increasingly mentioned as one of the trio of great Manx artists together with Knox and John Miller Nicholson.

However, Hoggatt was not a Manxman by birth. The son of a Cumbrian father and a Scottish mother, he was born in Lancaster in 1879, not coming to live in the Island until the age of 27. At school in Lancaster his artistic inclinations had surfaced with some vigour in his teenage years and he won, but did not take up, a scholarship to the Royal College of Art. Instead, he was apprenticed to a local firm of stained-glass manufacturers but he continued his artistic education at the School of Art in the Storey Institute, Lancaster. Thanks to H. L. Storey, son of the founder of the Institute and himself a local patron of the arts, Hoggatt was able to travel to Paris in 1901 to study at Julian's Academy under Paul Laurens, returning to England in 1905.

Shortly after his return, he was fortunate to obtain a commission which required him to work in the Tate Gallery, London, and it was here that a chance meeting was to profoundly affect the course of Manx art. While working at the Tate, Hoggatt was befriended by Leonard Archer, the manager of the great pianist Paderewski, and Archer invited Hoggatt to seek fresh inspiration at his parents' house in Chalfont St. Giles, Hoggatt struck an immediate rapport with Archer's sister, Dazine, and after a few weeks of acquaintance, they declared their intention to be married. The couple endured parental opposition on both sides. Perhaps in an effort to escape this family unrest, Hoggatt sailed to the Isle of Man in January 1906 and was immediately attracted by the qualities of light and landscape beauty. He quickly sent for his intended bride and they were married at Kirk Christ Rushen making their first home at Glen Down where they lived until 1920. By this time, Hoggatt's reputation was beginning to grow, particularly outside the Island, and the couple were able to purchase The Darragh at Port Erin, a traditional house they had both long admired. In subsequent years, The Darragh became a meeting place for intellectual discussion amongst the artistic community within the Island, and many of Hoggatt's finest works were drawn from subjects within walking distance from his home.

Hoggatt's artistic career was slow to develop and he had to wait until the age of 41 for his first one-man show in London entitled "Tone Poems". However, by the mid-1920s, he was achieving an international recognition, his pictures being reproduced in leading art journals such as *The Connoisseur* and *The Studio*. Hoggatt painted a majority of his pictures in water-colour or pastel, but he was also an accomplished artist in oils, as may be seen in his large canvas *East Baldwin* in the Manx Museum Art Gallery. He exhibited regularly at the Royal Academy from 1906 until his death. In 1925 he was elected to the Royal Institute of Painters in Watercolours and was also a member of the Liverpool Academy, the Manchester Academy and a Vice-President of the Lancaster Art Society. However,

East Baldwin, oil on canvas by William Hoggatt.

Stained glass window commemorating T. E. Brown's poetry, designed by William Hoggatt.

despite his recognition outside the Island, Hoggatt restricted his subjects almost exclusively to the Manx countryside he had come to love so dearly, and he was unstinting in the encouragement he offered to local artists, providing practical demonstration lectures at the Manx Museum and acting as President of the Manx Artists Group. From the time of his arrival in the Island, the artistic inspiration of its countryside sustained him completely. Persistent ill-health, resulting in his rejection for military service in both World Wars, allowed Hoggatt the opportunity to fully absorb the Manx backcloth, exploring fields and trackways and developing an enduring interest in and affection for the indigenous people who treasured and continued the traditional Manx way of life.

In view of the way he absorbed and was absorbed by the Manx community and remembering his early apprenticeship in Lancaster, it was fitting that Hoggatt's entry won the competition in 1934 to design a stained-glass window to commemorate the work of T. E. Brown, the Island's national poet. In his design, Hoggatt drew on his own deep love and knowledge of Brown's poems to assemble an array of famous characters from the poems providing an intriguing and amusing realization of the spirit and humour in Brown's works.

The high regard in which Hoggatt's work came to be held in the Island is indicated by the fact that two of his pictures were presented by Douglas Corporation to King George VI and Queen Elizabeth during their visit to the Isle of Man in 1945. He enjoyed further royal patronage when the Duke of Edinburgh purchased one of his water-colours *Ballaugh Curraghs*, from the Royal Institute's exhibition of 1949.

The work of this "adopted" Manx artist has continued to hold a pride of place in many Manx homes and the Island's National Gallery's large collection in all media provides the basis for a permanent exhibition of representative works.

Bryan Kneale

Ugo, a study in oil of a male figure, painted by Kneale in 1954.

Bryan Kneale is a Manxman whose talent and pioneering work in painting and sculpture has earned him acclaim in the international sphere of artistic achievement.

Kneale's grandparents were steeped in the traditional lifestyle of the Manx countryside, one as a farmer, the other as a saddler, and his father was at the very heart of the Island's community as editor of a local newspaper, *The Mona's Herald*.

Perhaps partly as a result of childhood hearing difficulties, Kneale pursued a solitary and accelerated course in the mastery of drawing techniques and by the time he attended Douglas High School painting had become his absorbing interest. He completed a number of portraits of his classmates which revealed his growing accomplishment as a painter and inevitably led him to a specialised year of study at Douglas School of Art in 1947. From here he was awarded a scholarship at the Royal Academy Schools in London and within a year had won the Rome Prize in Painting which enabled him to spend the next two years in Italy. Here, his developing artistic talent was exposed not only to the traditions of the old masters but also to the leading exponents of exciting and innovative modern artistic trends.

After his return to London in 1951, Kneale adopted a new style of painting, using the palette knife to achieve a "sculptural" quality in his work on canvas, but many of his paintings still drew on the inspirations of his native Island stored in his memory. He won first prize in the Daily Express Young Artists' Exhibition in 1954, exhibited regularly at the Royal Academy and held a number of one-man exhibitions at the Redfern Gallery in London. However, despite a growing reputation as a celebrity portrait painter, Kneale was experiencing increasing difficulty in expressing through such commissions the underlying artistic images of a more abstract nature which he was eager to explore.

In 1959 he stopped painting altogether and returned to the Isle of Man, living in a remote cottage in East

Baldwin in an attempt to recapture the essence of his artistic inspiration and to develop the latent creative images within him. During this retreat he found the rocks and caves of Santan Gorge to be an inexhaustible source for his intensive sketching and slowly, a new, more abstract and "primitive" style emerged.

In his search to expand the two-dimensional representation of his ideas, Kneale began experimenting with materials such as wood and plaster, but a dramatic breakthrough came in 1960 when he learnt the art of steel welding. With remarkable speed he created a number of large-scale metalwork pieces which provided the basis for his first exhibition of sculpture before the end of the year. This new direction for his artistic expression proved to be an overriding attraction and after acquiring a forge in Fulham, Kneale completed his transformation from painter to sculptor. From 1964, he worked as a tutor in the sculpture school of the Royal College of Art.

The Manx Museum holds a number of Bryan Kneale's paintings and sculptural pieces. Perhaps the most impressive of his later works is the giant sculpture *Yn Arreyder* ("The Watcher") which stands in the Museum grounds overlooking Douglas Bay. Constructed in 1977, it was originally exhibited at Battersea Park, London, as part of the Silver Jubilee Exhibition of Contemporary British Sculpture, during the Queen's Silver Jubilee celebrations. The Manx name of this metal sculpture and the fact that the sculptor himself has indicated that many of the traditional artefacts in the Museum provided him with an accumulative inspiration, provides a continuing assurance of Bryan Kneale's feeling for his native Island. As the artist himself admits, there is "a rich source of inspiration in the vigour and stylistic power which manifested itself in silver, iron and stone in a culture which still runs strongly when an artist grows from the same soil".

Yn Arreyder (The Watcher), constructed in 1977. Presented by the Royal Academy of Arts, through the Leighton Fund and mounted with assistance from the Museum's Archibald Knox memorial fund.

NATURAL HISTORY

L. S. GARRAD

P. M. C. Kermode, the first curator of the Manx Museum, did much to foster the study of the Island's wildlife. When the Isle of Man's own "learned society" was formed in 1879, largely at his instigation, it was christened the Isle of Man *Natural History* and Antiquarian Society. He encouraged its members to collect such things as lichens, stressing that anyone with time and patience to spare could collect for experts to identify later. As long as localities, dates and habitats were clearly recorded a future specialist would be happy with the specimen even if the work was long delayed.

This farsightedness was vindicated when, for example, a serious study of Manx lichens was done by P. M. Earland Bennett. He named for the first time specimens which were nearly a century old. Similarly, the Manx Museum's herbarium specimens of flowering plants – mainly collected by G. A. Holt, 1874–1918, the Reverend Theophilus Talbot, 1865–7 and 1880, and C. I. Paton, 1892–1949 among others – had their identities checked before the information was included in D. E. Allen's *Flora of the Isle of Man* (published 1986). Beetles from Dr. J. H. Bailey's collections of about 1896–1905, acquired by the Manx Museum in 1931–32, were studied by Dr. D. M. Luff in 1984–85. Data from all the Museum's insect collections and records has been supplied to the *Biological Records Centre* at Monks Wood for inclusion in the various *Atlases* showing the distribution of wildlife in the British Isles. None of this would be possible without Kermode's foundation of sound scholarship based on active field research.

There had, of course, been naturalists resident in the Isle of Man before the foundation of the Isle of Man Natural History and Antiquarian Society but to a large extent our earlier knowledge of Manx wildlife is dependent on fleeting visits by itinerant experts, or specimens collected almost by chance. For example, Francis Willoughby first described the Manx Shearwater from birds collected from the then vast Calf of Man colony in 1678. [The earliest "record" of this colony is believed to be a mention in a Norse Saga ("*Burnt Njal's*") recounting events which took place about 1014 A.D.] Similarly, a brief visit by the botanist, John Ray in 1666, resulted in an insignificant yellow crucifer being dubbed Isle of Man Cabbage (*Rhinchosinapis monensis*).

Puffinus puffinus, the scientific name of the Manx Shearwater, preserves the traditional vernacular name which is now reserved for another seabird. Over 10,000 shearwaters once bred on the Calf of Man where a colony, tiny in comparison, is now protected by the Manx National Trust.

Rhinchosinapis monensis Isle of Man Cabbage, one of the few plants named after the Island, is commonest on its northern shores, particularly on the Ayres *(photo: E. Huyton)*.

EDWARD FORBES 1815–1854

Edward Forbes 1815–54. This elegant white marble bust was carved by Neville Northey Burnard after the death of the great naturalist and "presented to the people of the Isle of Man by the subscribers" in 1858.

Edward Forbes, born in the Isle of Man on 12th February 1815, is deservedly famous as the greatest scientist the Island ever produced. He made a major contribution to our knowledge of the Manx flora, looking at it from an ecological viewpoint and attempting to correlate the plant life with the underlying geological strata, a concept somewhat in advance of contemporary thought.

He was a professor at King's College, London, and became a Fellow of the *Royal Society* before he was thirty. As a boy he had a private museum, housed in a specially built room in his parents' house, and is sometimes credited with being the first to undertake dredging for marine biological specimens, in 1830 off Ballaugh where his mother's family lived. One result of this early interest is *Malacologia Monensis*, a slim volume on Manx shells. During his vacation in 1832 he studied further the natural history of the Isle of Man and, probably then, prepared a *Hortus Siccus Monensis*, a small folio herbarium of pressed plants now in the British Museum. This *Hortus* includes the *Polygala oxyptera* (probably a "form" of *depressa*) which he described, but did not name, in a communication to the *Edinburgh Botanical Society*, 8th December 1836. Forbes was in the Island again 1834–36 and sent H. C. Watson a description of the geology and a list of 62 Manx plants for *New Botanists Guide, 1837.*

His dredging experience off Man was one of the factors which led to a grant from the *British Association for the Advancement of Science* for dredging in British seas in 1839 and then a post as naturalist on H.M.S. "Beacon" in the Levant. As well as some humorous pen and ink drawings, the Manx Museum has two examples of water-colours of fish executed by him at this time. They are of a *Young Ray in Navarino Bay* and a *Blenny at Serpho, July 1841.* His study of British Starfish was for long the definitive work.

Despite this weight of learning he never lost his sense of humour and is still remembered for his verse on the "Red Tape Worm":

> In Downing Street the tape worm thrive;
> In Somerset House they are all alive;
> And slimy tracks mark where they crawl
> In and out along Whitehall . . .

He was elected to the chair of Natural History in Edinburgh in April 1854 but died in November of that year. In his 40 years he had lived an unusually full life promoting science, arousing enthusiasm in others and endeavouring to connect together various branches of science, botany, geology and zoology.

GEOLOGY

The geology of the Isle of Man is quite diverse for an island of its size. Its main rocks are of the Manx Slate series, quite heavily mineralised with Iron, Lead often with a high Silver content, Zinc and Copper. Red Sandstone occurs in a limited area near Peel and round Castletown there is Limestone. The last is rich in fossils and the Manx Museum has the remains of an important collection made by the Reverend J. G. Cumming (1812–1868). Unfortunately the best examples were taken long ago by the *Geological Survey*. Those that remain have been studied and largely re-named by Lady Wilson, wife of the Director of the British Museum. Museum staff have tried to make the geological collections more comprehensive and most features of the rocks and their minerals are now represented.

The whole of the Northern Plain is the gift of the Ice Age. The Quaternary geology of the Island has been well studied and published with two visits by the *Quarternary Research Association* in recent years. One thing that is still desirable in this field is the creation of a collection of glacial erratics, named and with their source identified, which would be supplemented by the old Victorian collections of polished specimens.

Right: A geological trophy of the type usually known as a "miner's cabinet". They were made by miners from specimens found during their work for sale, or merely to commemorate special events such as royal births, weddings, or jubilees.

Below: An example of a modern geological specimen. Manganese dendrites in Manx slate from the Dreemskerry quarry, Maughold.

The Isle of Man is an area where a great deal of pollen analysis of Quarternary deposits has been undertaken but regrettably little has been done on the environmental background of the earlier part of Manx human history. Again work for dedicated professionals but in an area where the Museum has a history of fruitful and rewarding co-operation with them. There is a very real hope that there will be a continuation into 1986 of the study that Dr. W. R. Dackombe (and others from Wolverhampton Polytechnic) has commenced on recent exposures at Phurt, featuring both the "Forest Beds" and a habitation area of people who used similar pottery to that found in the unique Manx megalithic tomb on the Meayll Hill. This may well point the way for future studies.

RECORDING AND CONSERVATION

The Manx Museum also acts as the *Biological Records Centre* for the Isle of Man. The Island is "Watsonian Vice-County" 71 in the recording system which divides the British Isles up into more uniform land areas than the administrative counties. One of the *Centre's* roles is to help to disseminate information on conservation methods. It also collects records of the species present and their distribution and ensures that these appear in atlases of British wildlife, whether the species are rare or common.

Such records are presented on a ten kilometre square basis for computerised mapping to cover the whole of the British isles, or a fifty kilometre square for the whole of Europe. For its own purposes the Manx Centre prefers one kilometre squares. Another of its duties, for which it relies very heavily indeed on voluntary assistance and records supplied casually by members of the public, is the compilation of data files for all the sites listed on the Isle of Man Development Plan as being of ecological importance. This task started when the Manx Museum with the Isle of Man Local Government Board jointly funded an *Ecological Survey* of the Isle of Man. On the basis of recommendations made in the report of this survey, selected sites were designated on the Development Plan map. Since then the Museum has attempted, with its limited staff, to keep a watching brief over these sites, identify potential threats to their wildlife and publicise their existence.

The criteria for selecting the sites were varied and by no means all of the sites of wildlife importance were included. An attempt was made however to protect the main ecological groups, as well as the rarities, in the plant world. If, as on Langness, there was a rare insect and the area was an important landfall for migrant birds and insects, that was an important basis for reaching an assessment as to the site's inclusion on the list. Plants are the foundation of all other life. If the greatest possible range is protected then our wildlife heritage should retain its diversity.

The fauna and flora of the Isle of Man is somewhat restricted because of its island situation but it does have features of international interest. Some of its insects are very rare in Britain. The grasshopper *Stenobothrus stigmaticus* is apparently found on Langness and nowhere else in the British Isles. *Epitriptus cowinii*, a formidable inch-long fly, named in honour of W. S. Cowin, its finder, was new to science in 1940. New species are constantly being added to the Manx list; for example, the Dark Bush Cricket – found by Richard Barks in 1968 – and some fifty lepidoptera recorded between 1960 and 1980 by K. M. G. Bond. Dr. D. M. Luff added nearly as many beetles in 1984 and one (living near the summit of Snaefell) may be as rare as the Langness grasshopper. Such recording of seemingly insignificant creatures and research into their way of life forms the basis of advice given in connection with land development and may one day aid in the creation of reserves solely for the preservation of the whole of the Manx wildlife heritage. However, there is still a long way to go.

Bird protection is, in general, easier because there is rather more public sympathy than is aroused by slugs and snails, insects, or the apparently insignificant greenish flowers beloved by botanists. The obvious hazards, such as shooting Kingfishers or Terns to deck womens' hats, or caging wild-caught songbirds as pets, are much diminished. More stringent protection and ever-vigilant guardians are beginning to make egg collecting a thing of the past. Strict laws apply in the Isle of Man through some Chough, Kingfishers and Herons have fallen victim to the unsympathetic gun. In theory, however, the Victorian dictum that what is hit is history and what is missed is mystery, is dead. Birds are only shot on film.

Conservation is not, however, merely the protection of single species. It is the integrated network that ensures joint survival. In designating conservation areas as many aspects as possible were considered. The Billown quarries were given preference over those at Ballahot (now largely lost to "refuse disposal") not

Cowin's Fly *(Epitriptus cowinii)* a uniquely Manx creature named in honour of W. S. Cowin, the Manx naturalist, by Dr. B. M. Hobby.

merely because they held rarer plants. Their diversity of habitats (and therefore of species present) was greater. There was woodland mature enough to give a home to Rooks and, less often in recent years, Herons. The two lakes, large areas of freshwater in an area of the Island where it is scarce, also hold important freshwater plant life and creatures and the inland limestone grassland community is unique in Man.

Areas which it was hoped were typical of modern Manx vegetation were selected on hill and cliff tops. The latter are now well-protected by the Manx National Trust although it cannot afford to be complacent even where its holdings are strongest. For example, the upper shore communities featuring such plants as Sea Holly, Isle of Man Cabbage and Sea Kale are poorly represented on its properties. The *Manx Nature Conservation Trust* is doing fine work in managing its wooded glens and Lough Cranstal for wildlife but, as everywhere in Europe, our wetlands are in peril. Drainage for agricultural use and pollution are the chief hazards but building developments are an increasing threat. The peripheries of too many estates are scarred by dumped rubbish. The disposal of building rubbish is a problem which could well be taken out to sea. Scientists in the USA have found that bulky debris, like damaged pipes and sanitary fittings, large household appliances, old tyres chained together and even cars, the whole anchored to concrete blocks, can be converted into artificial reefs in shallow offshore waters. These are rapidly colonised by marine life and thus increase the number of sites available to tourist line-fishermen.

There have been some particular reasons for rejoicing recently. The find of Duck Mussels *Anadonta anatina* in the 1985 dredging of the Lhen augurs well for the health of the waterway. Some long lost plants, Beech Fern, Stagshorn Clubmoss and Sea Wormwood, for example, have been re-found to counterbalance the loss, due to natural causes, of the briefly returned Oyster Plant. A start has been made on managing the Ayres, partly for the benefit of the wildlife, following the spirit of the *Ecological Survey's* selection of the area as a proposed *Manx National Reserve*. It is to be hoped that the future will see further improvement in the conservation and preservation of our fragile natural heritage.

THE PEREGRINE FALCON
(Manx) *Shirragh ny Ree*

During the period of the Derby lordship, Peregrines were taken for hawking. So highly prized were the Manx birds that the fee paid by the Lords of Man to the English crown for the lordship was a pair of Peregrines taken from a Manx eyrie and trained by the Lord of Man's falconer. They were delivered at the English king's coronation.

Suitable food and nesting sites are still plentiful in the Isle of Man, with eyries on at least five of the Manx National Trust properties. Threats to our wildlife can be subtle. In the 1950s the Peregrine population diminished alarmingly throughout the British Isles and Man was not immune. Analysis of bodies showed that agricultural chemicals were to blame. So insidious was the hazard that a non-lethal dose could make egg shells unnaturally fragile, or destroy the complex nesting behaviour on which success depends. The more lethal chemicals are now banned but only constant vigilance can guard against similar future events in a developing and changing modern world.

Peregrine "habitat group" in the Natural History Gallery.

A modern Manxman's record of the Peregrine nest over which he kept protective watch: *Top:* from the time when the site was selected and the eggs were laid; *Above:* until the young hatched; and *Below right:* finally flew to safety *(photos: J. J. Callister)*.

THE GREAT DEER (or Irish Elk)

Megaceros giganteus

The Great Deer in the Manx Museum.

The Great Deer are popularly known as "Irish Elk" because of the many finds in Ireland. They lived in the British Isles before the islands had separated from mainland Europe, or each other, in the closing stages of the last Ice Age. They were essentially creatures of open countryside and withdrew eastwards and northwards as the climate improved and temperate forest became re-established. In England they have been shown to be contemporary with human Mesolithic hunters but they seem to have left Man before 10,000 B.C. and well prior to the arrival of its first post-glacial inhabitants. Enormous bones and spectacular antlers were found quite often when *Chara Marl* was dug to be spread on the fields as fertiliser. This marl was the remains of water plants which had grown in the many ponds which were a feature of the landscape as it emerged from under the ice sheet.

The bones attracted considerable attention. A complete skeleton was excavated near Ballaugh, 14th June 1819, and exhibited briefly in Douglas before being claimed by the Duke of Atholl. It is now in Edinburgh. P. M. C. Kermode, the first curator of the Manx Museum, initiated a search for another skeleton. After investigating a number of sites where oral traditions recorded finds, the "Elk Committee" found a promising one at Close y Garey, near St. John's. In 1897 a complete skeleton was dug out. The final work was done under the gaze of members of *The Isle of Man Natural History and Antiquarian Society* and *The British Association for the Advancement of Science* who had jointly sponsored the project. These bones were mounted and became a major feature of the newly-founded Manx Museum, then housed in Castle Rushen, and the skeleton still provides a dramatic focus of attention in today's new museum setting.

THE GREAT AUK
Alca impennis

The earliest known British picture of a Great Auk, now preserved in the British Museum *(photo: British Library)*.

Great Auks were familiar birds in the Irish Sea from prehistoric times. Daniel King drew this one, on shore and therefore almost certainly nesting, about 1645. The last bird seen in the British Isles was killed about 1840. In 1895, Bill Corlett told the young John Gawne of Fistard that the "Big Uig" used to come in summer to the flat rocks south of the Point at Port St. Mary. A few Great Auk bones, dug from a two thousand year old midden in a cave at Port St. Mary, are a further token of the once abundant bird's former presence in the Isle of Man.

RECORDING MOTHS & BUTTERFLIES

Some rare creatures are not always immediately attractive. They can also be very difficult for a layman, or even an expert, to identify. Nevertheless, they are all part of our rich wildlife heritage and we need to learn more about them. Our songbirds, who also dispose of many pests, can become very scarce if there are not sufficient insects for them at the time when they are feeding their young. It has been found that quite simple management, such as coppicing areas of willows in a curragh, or leaving unsprayed a strip six metres wide round two sides of an arable field, will increase the insect population and thus ensure that there will be birds to sing in the hedgerows of the future. The dissemination of information on such conservation measures is a vitally important task for the future, starting today. It is one of the responsibilities of the Manx Museum in its role as *Biological Records Centre* for the Isle of Man.

Some conspicuous Manx Moths and Caterpillars

Caterpillar of Grey Dagger – *Apatele psi* – they feed on Hawthorn; 32 mm long

Fox Moth Caterpillar – *Macrothylacia rubi* – very abundant on the hills in autumn – 70 mm long when mature

Herald – *Scoliopteryx libatrix* – the caterpillars, like those of the Buff Tip, often feed on willows – 22 mm head to wing tip

Angle Shades – *Phlogophora meticulosa* – 30 mm head to wing tip

The hunter's dictum applied in the past even to insects like these beautiful butterflies. They had to be killed before they could be studied. Now they can be shot on film. Rather few kinds of butterfly occur in the Island because of its early isolation and the absence of the preferred food plants, or suitable habitats, for many species. Those most commonly seen are listed below.

When trying to identify butterflies it should be remembered that often the male and female are not alike and the insects may also look different according to the time of year, or the locality. The Manx Museum collects wildlife records and is always grateful to hear of any sightings of unusual insects, preferably supported by careful field notes, or a photograph.

The modern Manx butterfly list comprises the four species illustrated together with those listed:

Clouded Yellow – *Colias croceus* – rare migrant
Common Blue – *Polyommatus icarus* – the only Manx blue apart from the Holly Blue
Dark-green Fritillary – *Mesoacidalia aglaja* – the only surviving Manx fritillary
Grayling – *Hipparchia semele*
Orange Tip – *Anthocharis cardamines*
Peacock – *Inachis io*
Red Admiral – *Vanessa atalanta*
Small Copper – *Lycaena phlaeas*
Small Heath – *Coenonympha pamphilus*
Small Tortoiseshell – *Aglais urticae*
Whites: Green-veined – *Pieris napi.*
Large (or Cabbage) – *P. brassicae.*
Small – *P. rapae.*

No other species has been *reliably* recorded more frequently than once in fifty years.

Some common Manx Butterflies

Meadow Brown – *Maniola jurtina*
22–25 mm

Holly Blue – *Celastrina argiolus*
13–17 mm

Wall – *Lasiommata megera*
22–25 mm

Painted Lady – *Vanessa cardui*
27–29 mm

Note: measurements are width across wings.

FLOWERS FOR THE FUTURE

Many people would say, "these plants are so common they are not at risk and too ordinary to be worth preserving", but even the common can be beautiful and interesting:

1. Red Campion *Silene dioica.* In the Isle of Man, the Fairies' flower, *Blaa ny Ferishyn*, which it is unlucky to pick. It is a common wayside plant and as such falls an easy victim to tidy-minded cutting and herbicide sprays.

2. Bog Bean *Menyanther trifoliata*. This attractive water plant, known in Manx as *Lubberlab* or *Luss ny tree diullagyn*, is quite common in the Curraghs and is found more rarely in wet places on the hills. However it is extremely vulnerable to pollution, or drainage, of is habitat.

These plants are already preserved:

3. Greater Butterfly Orchid *Plantanthera chlorantha.* Concerned lovers of Manx wildlife have already made private purchases of fields in the Isle of Man mainly to conserve their orchids.

4. Spring Squill *Scilla verna.* This tiny blue hyacinth is a feature of the fine turf of Manx cliff tops yet it is a comparatively rare plant in the British Isles. Miles of its habitat are now preserved by the Manx National Trust.

5. Sea Bindweed *Calystegia soldanella.* This attractive convolvulus is now somewhat local in the Isle of Man but it should survive human activity as much of its Ayres habitat is now protected.

These need preserving:

6. Autumn Lady's Tresses *Spiranthes spiralis.*

7. Dense-flowered Orchid *Neotinia maculata.*

These two insignificant greenish-white orchids both grow on the Ayres where the Autumn Lady's Tresses has its most northerly colony in the British Isles and probably the only surviving Manx one. It has not been seen at Chapel Hill, Balladoole for many years.

The Dense-flowered is otherwise known in the British Isles only in Clare, Galway and Mayo, although its wider distribution extends to Cyprus, Crete and the Canary Islands. There is only one tiny colony known and it has fared very badly in recent years, partly because thoughtless photographers removed the protection pegged over it and allowed rabbits to destroy the blooms. It is hoped to give it more effective protection in 1986.

Will this plant still be growing in the Isle of Man in ten years' time?

8. Bee Orchid *Ophryr apifera.* This lime-loving orchid has flowers that mimic a bee almost perfectly. It is near the northernmost part of its range in the Isle of Man and is known only from one inland exposure of limestone, there being no alternative site to which it could be transferred. A few years ago there were four patches of flowers but the making of tracks to facilitate refuse disposal reduced them to one on a site liable to be flooded for long periods. This could be fatal. A new second patch appeared in 1985. If these can be preserved there is hope for the future.

1

2

4

3

5

6

8

7

Photographs: J. J. Callister.

THE TALE OF THE WHALE

Balaenoptera borealis

The Rudolph's Rorqual, or Sei Whale, now on display in the Manx Museum, came ashore alive at the Horse Gullet, Langness, on the 8th May 1925. It could not turn in the gully to escape and was stranded when the tide fell. As so often happens with such large marine mammals, it was smothered by its own weight. Its body was towed by a boat to Derbyhaven and then dragged behind three steam traction engines to Douglas. Local tradition says its police escort's function included advising householders along its route to close their windows against the prodigious smell. The great body was buried in a pile of sand and nature was allowed to clean the skeleton. No existing part of the Museum could house it and plans were made for an appropriate extension but it was not until some ten years later that it was cleaned and mounted in the newly-built Natural History Gallery.

Below: The beached whale at Horse Gullet, Langness. This species of whale is now rare in British waters, only four being stranded 1913–29, for example, as against sixty-five Lesser Rorqual in the same period. This was a mature animal. Its one hundred and sixty bones weigh $3\frac{1}{2}$ tons and it was forty-eight feet long. The Manx Museum also acquired a Pygmy Shrew *Sorex minutus*, the smallest British mammal, in the same year.

Above: Transporting the whale to Douglas with the aid of steam traction.

Below: The cleaned skeleton on display in the Natural History Gallery.

THE MANX LOGHTAN

The loghtan sheep is the sole survivor of the earlier native breeds of farm animals that were kept in the Isle of Man. The story of their survival is one in which the Manx Museum and National Trust played a major part.

The history of the breed is ill-documented and remains obscure but they are thought to belong dominantly to the Northern short-tailed group rather than that of the most primitive breeds. Recent research by R. E. Roberts, in connection with the excavations on St. Patrick's Isle, has shown that the modern loghtans have two characteristics that occur in ancient bones from this archaeological site. The cores of their horns are D-shaped, not unlike those of a goat, and an opening in the leg bone where a blood vessel emerges (the *nutrient foramen*) is commonly found low down, whereas in modern breeds it lies above the middle of the bone shaft. Further work on archaeological finds and the genetics of the living animals may eventually make it possible to determine how long the breed has been present and more about its development.

A four-horned loghtan ram in the Manx Museum and National Trust's flock *(photo: A. Maddrell)*.

"The Isle of Man has also an indigenous breed of sheep, little and hardy, but of mean appearance, with high backs and narrow ribs, slow feeders, and long in coming to maturity. The ewes are sometimes polled, sometimes horned; the rams always horned. Their general colour is white; but many are grey, some black, and a few of a peculiar colour, approaching to that of an unblanched bitter almond, which in the language of the country is termed laughton. . . . Another peculiarity attaches to the breed in the conformation of the tail, which has some resemblance to that of a goat, thick at the root, and tapering to the extremity. The lamb is a remarkably sinewy active animal; playful like a fawn, and graceful in his movements. This breed appears to have been once widely dispersed."

This description by Thomas Quayle in 1812 is one of the earliest by a knowledgeable agriculturist, although James, the Seventh Earl of Derby, is said to have worn a loghtan wool suit, to encourage insular industries in about 1650, as did the tenth Earl a hundred years later. It should be noted that Quayle indicates that the "... peculiar colour, approaching to that of an unblanched bitter almond, ..." is only one of those present and he makes no mention of the additional horns that are now a feature.

From about the middle of the eighteenth century larger scale water-powered spinning and weaving and commercial dyeing grew in importance in the Isle of Man. This meant that coloured sheep lost their popularity. The natural darker wools had been valued to provide yarn from which to knit stockings and for the weaving of practical outerwear, particularly for the men. Used in weaving checks and plaids it could be over-dyed in the piece to give a subtle range of hues. With a commercial woollen industry this changed. The manufacturers disliked dark wools as they created problems in cleaning the machines after they had been processed and all the cards had to be replaced, as trapped dark fibres would contaminate white wool. William Kelly, proprietor of the Union Mills, "at the sign of the flail and the fleece", as his card-money stated, did much to accelerate the decline of the native dark-woolled strains by paying a premium for white fleeces. The white ones could be graded up towards a longer-stapled wool sheep, rather than a general purpose animal. The dark ones seemed doomed.

Robert Quirk of Abbeylands, Onchan, had one of the last pure flocks of Manx sheep. Some of these were sold to Colonel Anderson who kept them at Cooley Lodge, Michael. These, together with four ewes bred by Captain Windus, and other descendants of the Quirk flock, were acquired by Caesar Bacon of Seafield (Aragon) in Santon. His flock book of 1895–1907 is preserved in the library of the Manx Museum. He ran his sheep on the southern hills as three separate breeding groups. Seven Shetland ewes were imported to strengthen them in 1897 and he subsequently got Faeroese sheep from the Kirkjabour Farm, sending them three loghtans in exchange. This may explain, in part, why his sales mention sheep that were not uniformly "dark mouse coloured". However, they may have merely been descendants of the basic Manx sheep from which the brown loghtan was being segregated, the sale animals being his culls. He seems never to have kept more than thirty or so himself but always had at least one Manx-bred ram. The use of this he offered to a few other people he persuaded to keep small flocks, to yield what David Robertson, in *A Tour through the Isle of Man* in 1794, described as the most delicious mutton in the world. After Caesar Bacon's death and the consequent loss of the use of his ram, most of these flocks dwindled away.

Shearing the flock on the Calf *(photo: A. Maddrell)*.

Moved by the same impulse that made him a prime mover in the plan to acquire and preserve land at Spanish Head for the future, Sir Mark Collet then bought most of the remnants of Bacon's flock. It seems that it was at this point that the animals were culled so that the dominant strain in the survivors was a uniform brown colour. One, or more, of the founders of this flock also carried the secondary horn trait and subsequently four or more horns were a feature of rams preserved for breeding. The loghtans had now gone through two very severe reductions in numbers and when numbers were bred up again the animals selected for breeding conformed to an ideal set by one or two people. In consequence, the modern loghtans are not likely to be identical with all their ancestors, since they are a largely true-breeding segregate from the once large, and genetically more mixed, native Manx sheep stock.

Nevertheless, they are undoubtedly descendants of this ancient breed and consequently worthy of preservation.

After Sir Mark Collet's death his loghtan flock of thirty or so animals continued to graze peacefully on Peel Hill while an attempt was made to find them a permanent home. In 1945 they had been offered to the (English) National Trust, to be run on their Calf property, but they had to refuse because of the difficulty of shepherding them there. By this time there were few other survivors in the Island. Mrs. Lascelles had ten ewes and their lambs at St. Jude's, and Edward Christian fifteen or so at Northop. Those kept on the lowland pasture of the central valley by Edward Christian grew bigger than Bacon's. In pursuance of Sir Mark's wishes to perpetuate the breed, his flock were kept together on Peel Hill, under the watchful eyes of their shepherd, John Dale, the Isle of Man Board of Agriculture's Knockaloe Experimental Farm staff and the Manx Museum. Their numbers gradually increased and after the creation in 1951 of the Manx National Trust which took over responsibility for the Calf and Spanish Head, Lady Collet offered the flock as a gift. This was accepted with a sense of the deep gratitude that future generations must owe to Sir Mark and Lady Collet for making the preservation of the breed possible.

From 27th March 1953, the Manx Museum and National Trust took over all responsibility for the flock. The remaining loghtans were then transferred to Druidale where they remained for some years despite the problems of shepherding such agile and intelligent "unimproved" sheep. Their wool was spun into yarn for sale by the Museum by Howarth and Penrice's Sulby Mill. Their numbers were initially maintained at twelve pure-bred ewes and two rams, not without considerable difficulty because all located flocks were both close relatives and much inbred, so there was a serious decline in fertility. During the 1960s the situation slowly improved and in December 1968 plans could be made to at last fulfil Sir Mark Collet's wish and send part of the flock to the Calf. In July 1969, this comprised two shearling ewes, an older ewe with a ewe lamb and a ram who was as nearly as possible unrelated. By this time there were one or two small groups of loghtans in England and interest in

Loghtans on the Calf. *(Photo: A. Maddrell)*

preserving the genes of rare breeds was increasing. A Loghtan Breed Society was formed in March 1976 and there has been such a rise in loghtan-keeping that the gene pool is well spread, although loghtans are still officially listed as a rare breed.

The Trust had just over one hundred animals in its flock on the main island in 1972 and there were nineteen on the Calf: by November 1975, there were thirty-four healthy animals on the Calf. These were subject to minimal shepherding but not run as a truly feral flock. Their steady increase there has been allowed to continue, partly because their grazing is beneficial in providing good feeding for the Choughs. Thus the faith and hope of Caesar Bacon and Sir Mark and Lady Collet have continued to be fulfilled. In 1985, the Trust's two flocks comprised some two hundred animals, and it is now felt to be possible to "weed out" sub-standard animals each year.

The preservation of the native Manx sheep provides a further example of the extremely wide-ranging achievements of the Manx Museum and National Trust. In connection with this preservation project the Trust has been fortunate in being able to enlist expert assistance from local shepherds, Mr. Jack Quine in the north of the Island and Messrs Alec and Alexander Maddrell who make the regular shepherding trips to the Calf. Work continues on monitoring and recording the progress of the two flocks and the Trust remains vigilant with regard to preserving the true characteristics of this ancient breed for future generations to admire on the Manx fields and hillsides.

Loghtans being transported from the Calf to the mainland *(photo: A. Maddrell)*.

Breed Characteristics

Head – Light boned, long and narrow from ears to muzzle, straight nose.
Muzzle – Level jaws, neither protruding.
Eyes – Bright and alert.
Ears – Small, short and strong, carried at 45°.
Face – Clean, with minimum of wool.
Neck – Medium length, head carried well above the top line.
Shoulders – Ram showing strength, ewe light; in each case falling away slightly towards ribs.
Chest – Average to narrow, not outstanding or prominent.
Back – Straight, level and of even width.
Tailhead – Continuation of top line.
Tail – Well set in, not to reach the hocks nor to be below the bottom line, without wool for the greater part of its length.
Hind Quarters – Light and not too deeply fleshed.
Legs – Long with light flat bone without wool from hocks to feet.
Feet – Very small and neat, pasterns unobtrusive.
Horns – Very dominant in rams. Proportions to the size of the animal, two slightly curved primaries growing upwards and forward, two strong curved secondaries growing downward and forward; tertiaries are not unknown. Ewe has four finer curled horns, forward growing but not into the head.
Fleece – About 3 lbs.–5 lbs. in weight, staple 3″–5″, very soft, close textured and lustrous, heavily oiled and excellent for hand spinning. Colour at birth, black or "bitter chocolate" changing to lighter brown or coffee colour, bleaches in the sun. Loghtan is Manx Gaelic for mouse brown: lugh = mouse, dhoan = dark (or brown). The breed is named for its colour.

THE MANX MUSEUM LIBRARY

A. M. HARRISON

ESTABLISHMENT AND DEVELOPMENT

William Cubbon, Librarian and later Curator of the Manx Museum, and author of the *Bibliography of the Literature of the Isle of Man.*

In the seminal year of 1886 William Cubbon, son of James Cubbon, Master Mariner of Arbory, was already twenty-one years old and working as a compositor on the *Manx Sun* newspaper. His direct connection with the Museum institution started only in 1922 when at the age of fifty-seven he became the first Secretary and Librarian, yet his far-reaching vision of the purpose and development of the Manx Museum Library still sets the course for the Library today.

For in the beginning there was no library – antiquities and artefacts, the material relics of the Manx past, were the legally prescribed preoccupations of the first Trustees. It was only in 1906, twenty years on in our history, that the first nonchalant mention of documentary accessions occurred at the end of the Trustees' Annual Report – "for the storage of books, prints and papers [the Trustees] are indebted to Mr. McLaughlin, the custodian of Castle Rushen, for kindly keeping them in his house".

Significantly this year, 1906, marked the first Chairmanship of A. W. Moore, the great Manx scholar and Speaker of the House of Keys who learned his historian's craft from his contemporary avant-garde Cambridge teachers who were the great pioneers of administrative history. The Ordnance Survey Maps and Meredith's 1805 prints of Douglas were the start of an annual recorded accession of documentation which fortunately survived Moore's untimely death in 1909. The fundamental Manx language document, the Book of Common Prayer, in which the language was for the first time recorded and transliterated (tantalisingly by a Welshman, Bishop Phillips in his episcopate of the See of Sodor and Man, 1614–1633), was bought by the Trustees in the financial year of 1913 for £30. By 1914, a library section was an established part of the Annual Report.

Of course at this time, the Trustees had no home for their developing collections, stored and partly exhibited in Castle Rushen. When the Museum building was finally secured in 1922, the work of ordering the documentary sources, which by now included manuscripts, books, prints and maps, began in earnest.

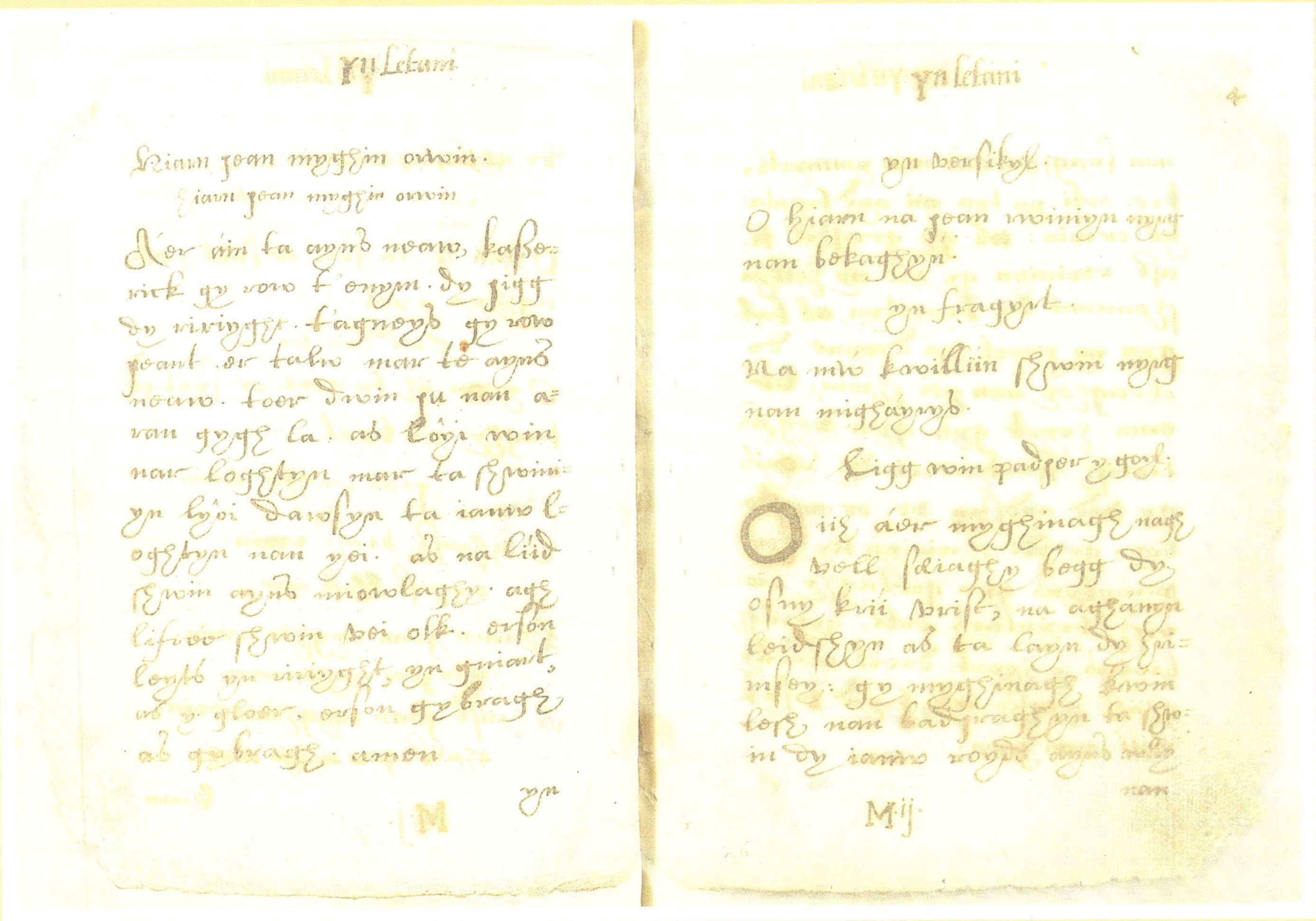

The *Lord's Prayer* from Bishop Phillip's translation of the book of Common Prayer into Manx. This part of the Prayer book helps to date the beautiful transcript: Petitions mention Charles I but not his son Charles II and therefore place its origin between 1625 and 1630.

William Cubbon began work in July 1922. Given rooms upstairs in the central block of the old hospital and with the special guidance of a Library Committee of seven Trustees, the new Librarian set about building the Museum's National Library.

At fifty-seven William Cubbon was a powerfully knowledgeable Manxman. He had worked in newspapers as editor of the *Isle of Man Examiner* and proprietor of the *Manx Sun*, been Douglas Town Librarian and a devoted antiquarian and was in touch with Manx culture and learning at all levels of society. He was uniquely able to build the National Library in the ways laid down in the 1922 Report. The aim of holding all publications relating to the Island was virtually achieved at one blow by his purchase of the G. W. Wood collection of Manx printed books in 1923. (Cubbon and Wood, an expatriate bibliophile, had been in correspondence as friends and Manx scholars since the 1890s). Cubbon had lived through and taken a part in the resurgence of Manx national scholarship, which found expression in historical and linguistic studies as well as antiquarian and archaeological studies, from the 1880s.

William Cubbon's central position in Manx studies reaped its rewards. None of his contemporaries were better placed for the implementation of the second collecting aim. After the comprehensive collection of Manx printed books to make the National Library, as it was already styled in the 1922 Report, came the collection of Manx manuscripts which in practice became the foundation of the collection of National Archives, which today occupy three out of five floors of the existing storage stack.

Certainly record collections flowed in to the Museum Library. In terms of official public records, the archives of the Diocese of Sodor and Man and the documents of the Government left behind at Castle Rushen when the Government moved to Douglas, accrued to the Library. The accessions of records of private persons and families kept pace with them to such an extent that in 1926, only four years after its official opening, the Library Sub-Committee had to report that:

> "it is a source of real pleasure to the Committee to possess so many valuable manuscripts. There comes with this pleasure, however, a decided feeling of depression when one realises that every shelf in the Library is occupied and that thousands of papers (many going back to the sixteenth century) have to be kept in the cellars of the building, which are unfortunately damp".

The need for more and better storage space and the lack of accommodation for students who were being increasingly drawn to the collections, became the twin themes of the inter-war years. The building of the new Library named after A. W. Moore, and opened to the public in 1936, served for a time to answer these two needs.

Public support and approval, fostered by the creation of a pleasant and spacious reading room, brought more and more books, maps, prints and documents to the Library. Its very success, the recognition of its fundamental position in all Manx studies, ensured the inevitability of its growth and its constant needs for expansion.

But the period of equilibrium in the thirties was extraordinarily productive. The years 1933 to 1939 saw Cubbon's publication of the *Bibliography of the Literature of the Isle of Man*. By 1936 as Director as well as Librarian of the Manx Museum, he had set the National Library firmly on a professional course and the National Archives, now rivalling the printed collections in bulk, had begun to take on real shape and significance.

The moment of balance passed. By the end of the war, both object and documentary collections, growing rapidly, could not be contained in the existing Museum building. The answer to the problem was the planning of a new National Library and Archives extension to the Museum, which was completed in 1960.

For the first time the precious books and manuscripts were housed in conditions specifically designed to ensure their security and their safety from the hazards of fire and the dangerous effects of the humid Manx climate. The storage stack with its controlled temperature and humidity levels and its ground floor reading room at the eastern end of the Museum site is a landmark at the centre of Douglas Bay.

Equally important in the Library's story was the appointment in 1956 of the first professional Archivist, W. R. Serjeant. William Cubbon's successor as Director and Librarian in 1940, Basil Megaw, who led the planning for the new up-to-date Library development, thus set the course leading to today's expanding institution.

We have moved ahead in both numbers of staff and building amenities, which were notably augmented by the construction of a new, enlarged reading room and, for the first time, associated work rooms in the 1971 extension. With the confidence that our premises are of the standard of the progressive County Record Offices in the U.K. and our professional links with the Public Record Office in London, we look forward to our second century role being enlarged to include a recognition of the Museum Library as the Public Record Office of the Isle of Man.

Below: The reading room of the Manx Museum's Library where modern technological aids such as microfiche and microfilm allow wide and safe access to the information contained in fragile original documents.

Right: The five floors of the Library storage stack, completed in 1960, dominate the seaward aspect of the Museum grounds.

Marshall Wane, in business as a photographer from 1865 to 1882 left a collection of 20,000 negatives in his Douglas Studio. His gifts as a portraitist bring our immediate ancestors vividly to life. The studies of Frederick Frith and his Company recorded the Island itself in its heyday as the premier resort of the British Isles. His topographical prints and negatives, presented by the Friends of the Manx Museum, capture the atmosphere and activities of by-gone holidays.

KEEP TO THE RIGHT
FRITH

Douglas Sands.
FRITH

SCOPE OF THE LIBRARY COLLECTIONS

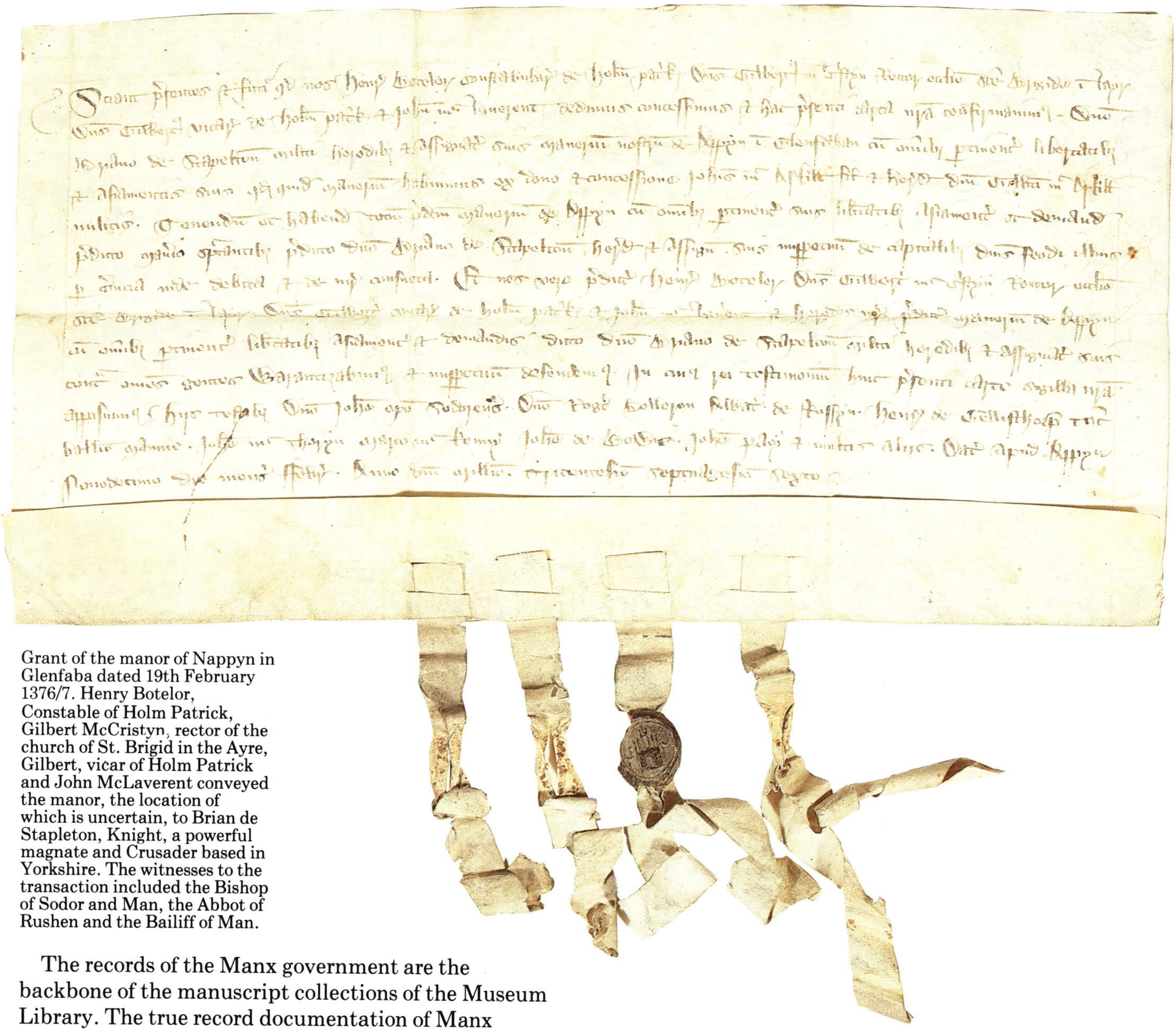

Grant of the manor of Nappyn in Glenfaba dated 19th February 1376/7. Henry Botelor, Constable of Holm Patrick, Gilbert McCristyn, rector of the church of St. Brigid in the Ayre, Gilbert, vicar of Holm Patrick and John McLaverent conveyed the manor, the location of which is uncertain, to Brian de Stapleton, Knight, a powerful magnate and Crusader based in Yorkshire. The witnesses to the transaction included the Bishop of Sodor and Man, the Abbot of Rushen and the Bailiff of Man.

The records of the Manx government are the backbone of the manuscript collections of the Museum Library. The true record documentation of Manx history begins only in 1377, in the period of the Montacute Lordship. There are no manuscripts to chronicle the life of the Manx in any earlier period – the fourteenth century Chronicle of Man and the Isles, which is in the British Library, is a literary work. The earliest document in the Library, a deed dated 1377, granting the manor of Nappyn in Glenfaba to Sir Brian Stapleton, Knight, was a survival from the public records of the Montacute family when they were Kings of Man. Apart from its date and its pride of place in our collections the grant has a special significance. The connection of the powerful Yorkshire landowner and Crusader with Peel Castle, the western centre of government, is a subject for investigation of great significance in the history of this most important Manx institution.

Continuous documentation dates from the period of the Lordship of the Stanley family of Lathom in Lancashire, later to become the Earls of Derby with a seat at Knowsley near Liverpool. They were granted the Lordship of Man in 1405 after their support for Henry IV at the battle of Bosworth and were quick to assert their new-found sovereignty. The earliest surviving court records, the Sheading Roll of 1417–18 and the Garrison Roll of 1428 mark their initiative in organising their forces in Man and in controlling the disposition of justice throughout the Island.

The Sheading Roll records the acts of the peripatetic Justices moving through the Island sheadings to administer justice – always a great profit to the Lord – throughout the parishes and is the first instance of the documentary emergence of individual Manx men and women in their historic roles, albeit as petty criminals and malefactors.

The Garrison Roll, remarkably a court record in Middle English rather than the customary Latin of the medieval period, lists the enquiries into the discipline of the two Stanley garrisons on Man, at Peel Castle and Castle Rushen. The life of the soldiers and officials from England, their internal squabbles and their interaction with the Manx people and the strangers in the land are all vividly portrayed in the twenty-two feet long parchment roll.

These are the notable survivals of the first century of Derby Rule. As Lords they laid the foundations of the organisation of the Island into the national state whose independent existence is so jealously guarded today. From the beginning of the fifteenth century the series of Court records, the Books of the Courts of Chancery, Common Pleas and Exchequer, which echo the structure of the English legal system, exist in continuous sequence, and provide the primary sources for our unique national history. Other records developed as the Lordship developed its administrative competence and ambitions.

The system of landholding, a blend of customary tenure at the will of the Lord, with certain jealously guarded tenant rights more usually springing from the possession of freehold land, is unique to the Island. It was of course, and this is not unique, a great profit to the Lord as chief landholder and the records of four hundred years, 1511–1911, immortalise the many tenants, and their many rents, who held land in the Island while the system flourished. A rich but complex archive of great potential for detailed local studies it includes Books of Rentals (*Liber Assedationum*), Books of Transactions (*Liber Vastarum*), and a series of original recorded deeds which start in the 1680s and continue to this day in the General Registry's Registered Deeds series.

Henry IV granted the Kingdom of Man to the Stanleys in 1405. From the start they ruled the Island firmly through a group of experienced and responsible officials. Their two bases of power were Castle Rushen and Peel Castle, both garrisoned with their soldiers.

The parchment roll *(right)* records the actions of the controllers of the garrisons in preserving the discipline and good order of the often unruly troops. Remarkably well preserved, the roll dates from 1428 and is unusual for its use of Middle English, rather than Latin, in a formal court document. Its free form and literal reporting makes it an extemely valuable source for our late medieval history.

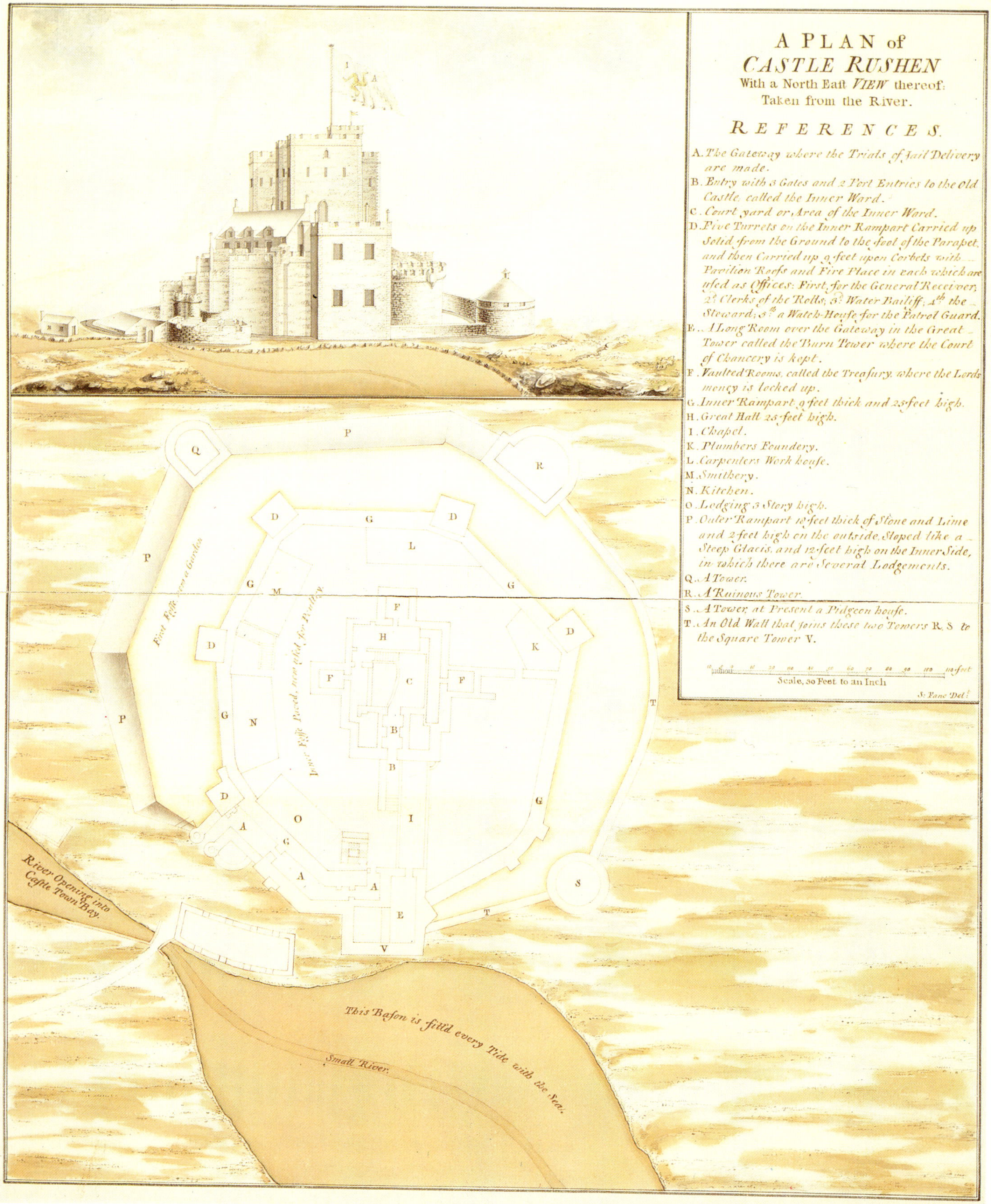

Fane's plan of Castle Rushen dates from the period of the Atholl Lordship, 1736–1765. It is difficult to date it more closely as the cypher 1 A on the standard flying over the castle could relate equally to James, the 2nd Duke, and John, the 3rd Duke.

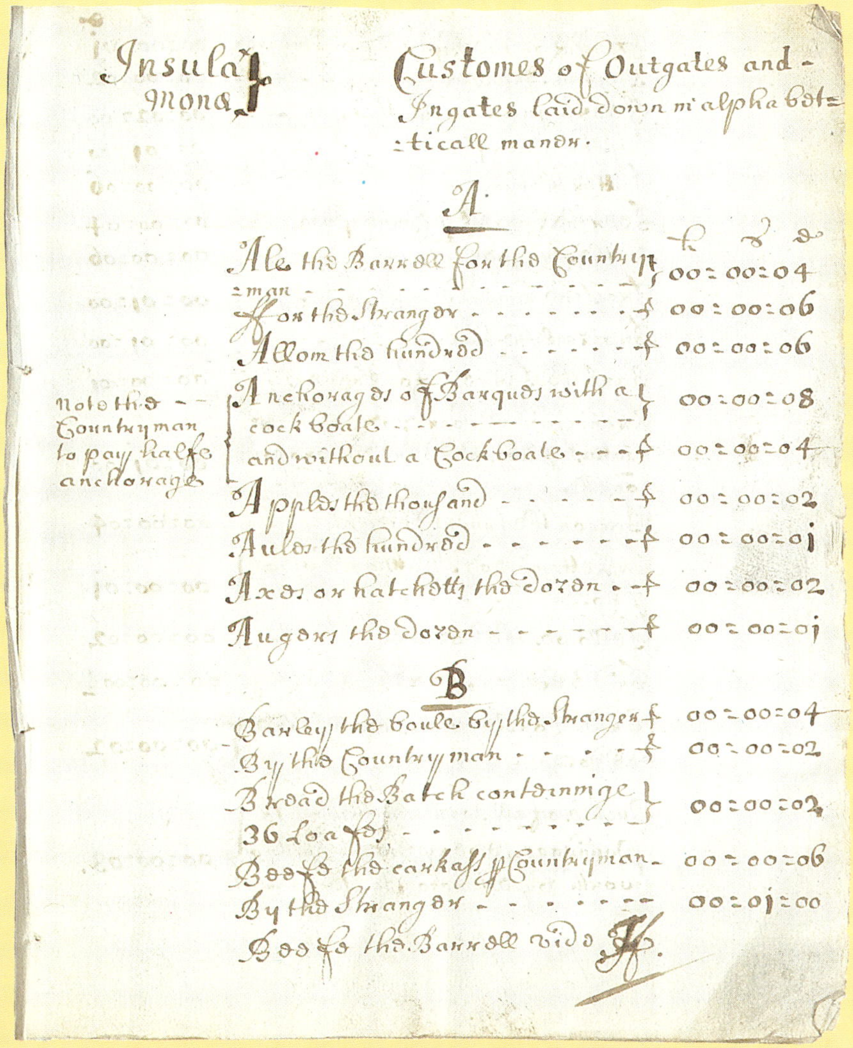

Insula Mona

Customes of Outgates and Ingates laid down in alphabeticall manner.

A

	£ s d
Ale the barrell for the Countryman	00:00:04
For the Stranger	00:00:06
Allom the hundred	00:00:06
Anchorages of Barques with a cock boate	00:00:08
and without a Cockboate	00:00:04
Apples the thousand	00:00:02
Awles the hundred	00:00:01
Axes or hatchetts the dozen	00:00:02
Augers the dozen	00:00:01

Note the Countryman to pay halfe anchorage

B

Barley the boule by the Stranger	00:00:04
By the Countryman	00:00:02
Bread the batch conteyninge 36 loaves	00:00:02
Beefe the carkass the Countryman	00:00:06
By the Stranger	00:01:00
Beefe the barrell vide F.	

The Book of Custom rates due to the Earl of Derby as Lord of Man on imports and exports to the Island for 1677. The native Islander has preferential rates: usually half the sum payable by "the stranger".

Left: Richard Wilson came to the Island from Whitehaven in 1768 to take up the post of Master of the Mathematical School in Peel. Ten of his beautiful and accurate maps survive in the Library Collections and he worked as a surveyor and mapmaker until his death in 1798, working even on Sundays, to the chagrin of the Vicar of German.

The two ruling families of the Island, the Earls of Derby who were Lords in Man from 1405 to 1736 and the Dukes of Atholl, who followed them in the Lordship up to 1765, have both deposited their family papers relating to their Manx period in the Library. The papers naturally reflect affairs of state and their scope has a range uncommon in the records of more private families. The customs rates books of 1677 and 1692 are both beautiful and informative records. The manuscript map of the Calf of Man in the Atholl papers, drawn by Richard Wilson, master of the Mathematical School at Peel, 1768–1798 is the earliest delineation of the island and is extremely decorative.

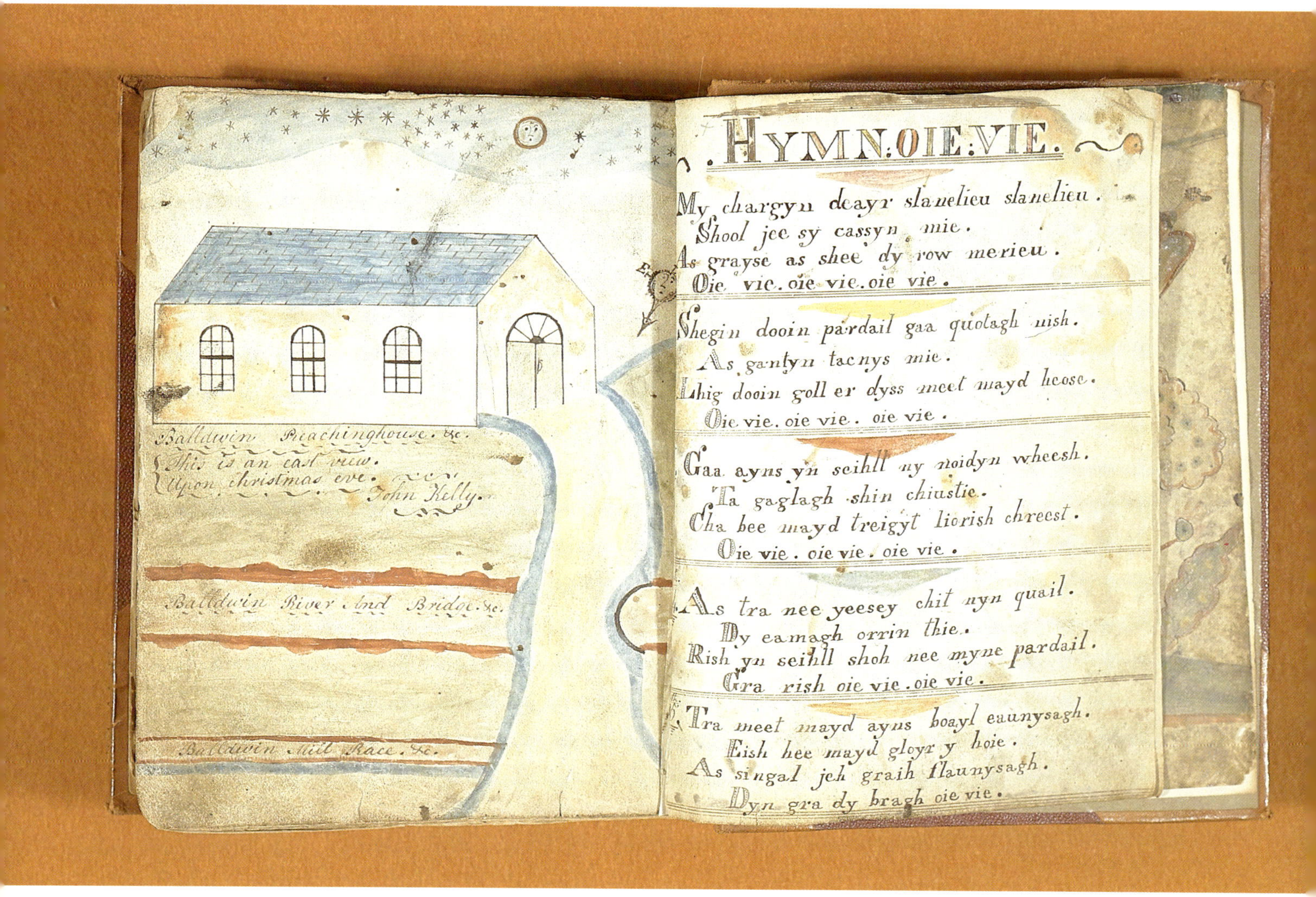

John Kelly of Ballaquine, Braddan, composed carvels, religious songs or carols in Manx and English, sermons and dialogues. He entered them between 1838 and 1846 in this beautifully illuminated book. The painting of Baldwin preaching house is particularly appealing.

These are family papers of great political importance, at the heart of Manx affairs. Other families, not of ruling status, produce equally important records – perhaps the accounts of trading ventures throughout the world, a commonplace of Manx merchant life, as written in the letter book of Sir George Moore of Ballamoore, Patrick, merchant and later statesman of Man. His archives also produce details of more private domestic concerns – the plants and seeds bought for his newly planted garden. The small accessions of documentation from individuals reveal for example, the day to day operations of a small-holding; the transcription and embellishment of the traditional Manx carols or carvals in the lovingly produced book of John Kelly of Ballaquine, Baldwin; the sermon writing, in Manx and English, of eighteenth century Manx parsons, a most important part of the corpus of written Manx held by the Library, the foundation of which is Bishop Phillip's manuscript of the Book of Common Prayer, written between 1614 and 1633 when the language was transliterated, by a Welshman, for the first time.

Societies and business concerns have deposited their records to add to our store of knowledge of the Manx people in their cultural pursuits and their working lives. The illustrated minute book of the *Dilettanti Debating Society* tells us much about the social concerns and issues exercising our minds in the 1960s. The records of the *Great Laxey Mining Company*, including the enigmatic entries documenting the building of the Great Laxey Wheel, and the many mining plans and prospectuses stemming from our nineteenth century commercial mining boom add greatly to our understanding of the industrial past.

The scene at the opening of the Great Laxey Wheel in 1854.

"The interesting ceremony of starting the immense waterwheel lately erected in Laxey Glen, for the purpose of keeping the mines there free from water took place on Wednesday last, September, 27. The day being beautifully fine, between 3,000 and 4,000 persons arrived from all parts of the Island, in the course of the morning, to witness so great an achievement for our Isle as the completion of the largest wheel in Europe. . . . Simultaneously with the first motion of the wheel, the ceremony of christening was performed by Mrs. Dumbell, lady of George W. Dumbell, Esq., who gracefully threw the bottle ornamented with lace and filled with champagne, and named the wheel *'Lady Isabella'*, in honour of the Governor's Lady. At the same moment a flag at the top of the wheel was unfurled and made known the title to the assembled crowds, who greeted it with loud cheers, while the shouts from the strong lungs of the workpeople vied with the booming of the cannon in proclaiming the satisfactory accomplishment of a great undertaking."

The Manx Sun, 30th September 1854.

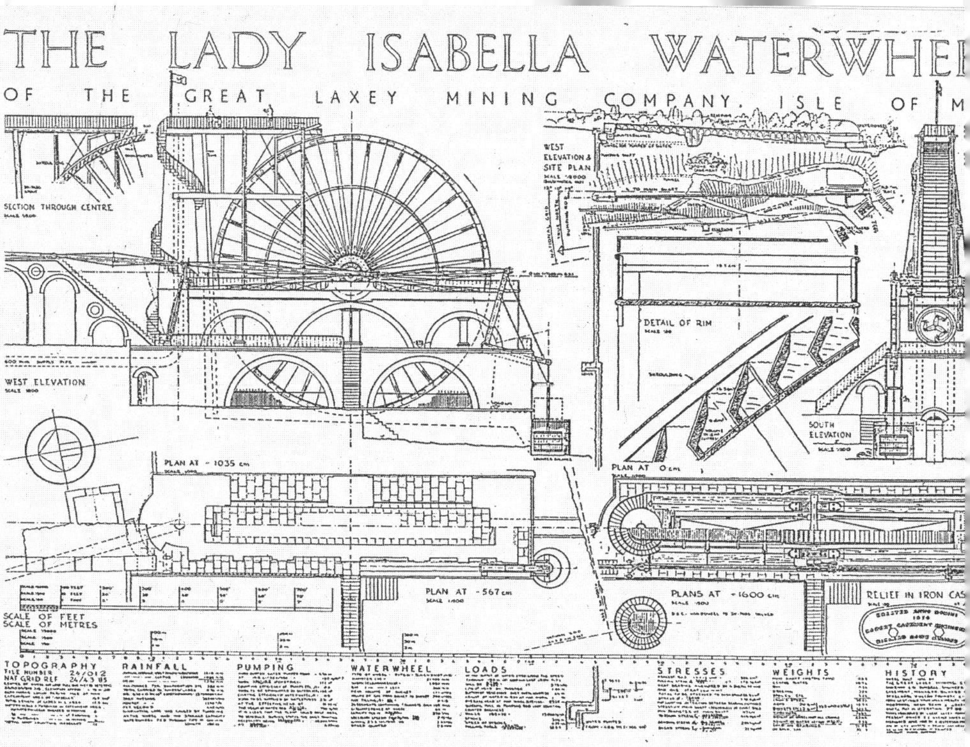

Plan of the Laxey Wheel.

This measured drawing of the Laxey Wheel was undertaken by Anders Jespersen in 1949 and reveals the truly grand scale of this feat of engineering skill.

Laxey lead miners c. 1910.

Thomas Wilson, Bishop of Sodor and Man from 1697 to his death in 1755 at the age of 92, was born at Burton in Cheshire.

His long episcopate was remarkable for his activities on behalf of the people "entrusted to his guardian care". He built churches, wrote works of piety, established schools and libraries, encouraged industry and agriculture and was noted for his works of charity and general benevolence. He defended the powers of the Church against the pretensions of the Earls of Derby and was a vigorous church administrator; his characteristic hand-writing is found throughout the records of the Diocese. He is depicted in a mezzotint after the Museum's 1732 portrait by Charles Phillips at the age of 69.

"His piety, beneficence, and charity will be remembered and recorded by the people of this Isle, with gratitude and affection, to the remotest generations."

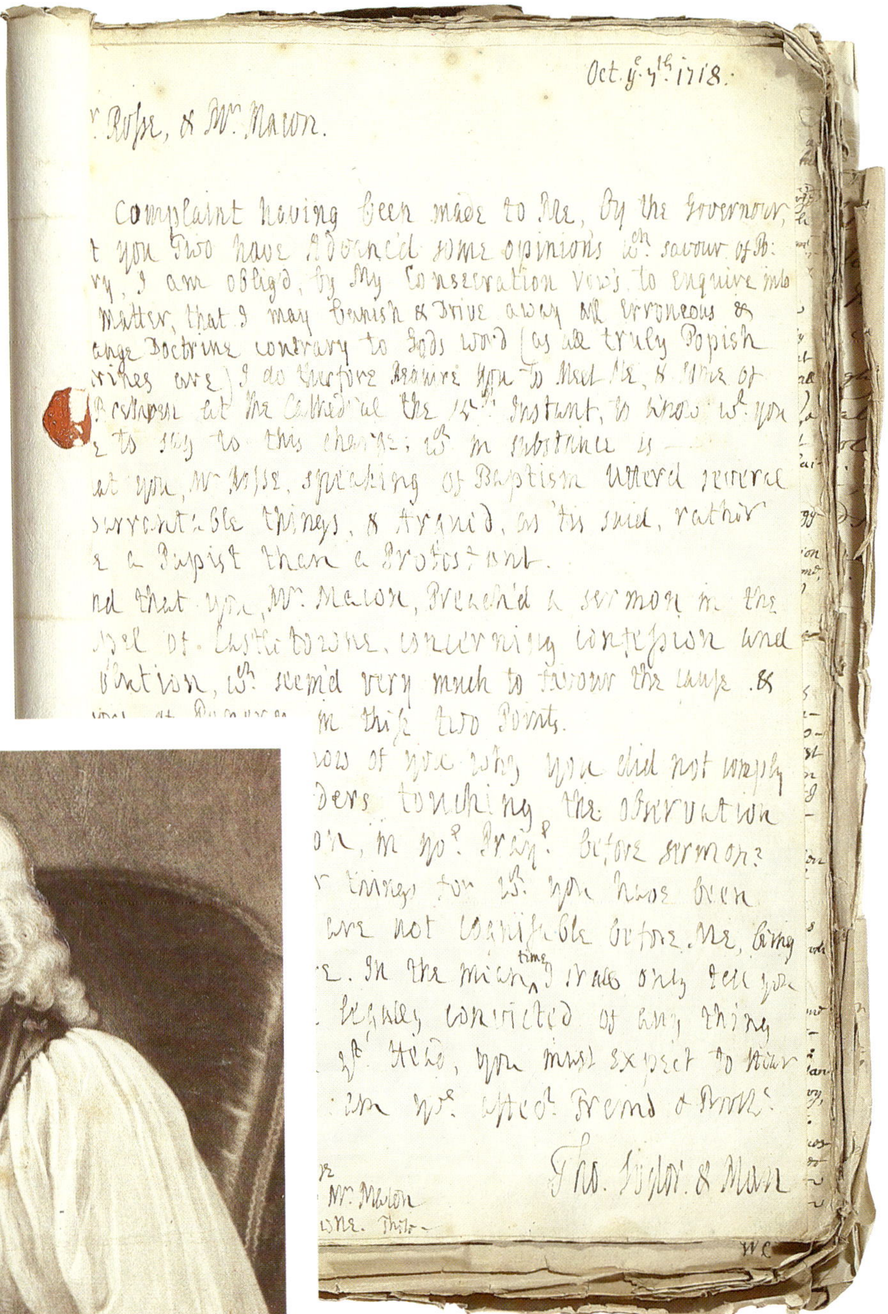
Oct. ye 7th 1718.

...Rosse, & Mr. Mason.

Complaint having been made to Me, by the Governour, ...t you two have advanced some opinions wch savour of Po-...ry, I am oblig'd, by my Consecration vows, to enquire into ... matter, that I may banish & drive away all erroneous & ...ange Doctrine contrary to Gods word (as all truly Popish ...rines are.) I do therefore require you to meet Me, & some of ... brethren at the Cathedral the 15th Instant, to know wt you ... to say to this charge; wch in substance is — ...at you, Mr Rosse, speaking of Baptism uttered several ...warrantable things, & argued, as tis said, rather ... a Papist than a Protestant.
...nd that you, Mr. Mason, Preach'd a sermon in the ...pel of Castletowne, concerning confession and ...lution, wch seem'd very much to favour the cause & ... in these two Points.

...ow of you who, you did not comply ...ders touching the observation ...on, in yr Pray. before sermon: ...r things for wch you have been ...are not cognizable before Me, being ...e. In the mean time I have only tell you ... legally convicted of any thing ... yt Head, you must expect to hear ... am yr affect. Friend & Brother

Tho. Sodor & Man

...r
... Mr. Mason
...wne. This

October 18th 1718: Bishop Wilson's autograph letter to Mr. Rosse, Academical Professor and Mr. Mason, Schoolmaster of Castletown complaining about their opinions "which savour popery". They are required to meet the Bishop and some of "his brethren" at the Cathedral on the 15th of the month to answer to the charge. From the Consistory Court papers.

The Church itself produces records of public importance. The pursuit of family history which has drawn so many people to an understanding of their cultural heritage through their search for ancestors leans on the records of baptisms, marriages and burials. Manx genealogy is based on copies of parish register transcripts made for the General Registry and broadened and fleshed out by the more personal records produced by the established church in the Isle of Man. The Church had jurisdiction over the probate of wills and the disposition of the goods of persons who died intestate. Parsons heard and wrote down affirmed wills, the verbal testaments of the illiterate, and exercised through the Courts of the Bishop and Archdeacon, profitable legal control of the large estates of the eminent and wealthy. Wills necessarily include details of family relationships so important to a pedigree, and the nature of goods handed down gives a marvellous insight into the intimate personal lives of our ancestors.

Nonconformity has been known in the Island since the seventeenth century. A congregation of Quakers existed in Maughold and the Callow Black Letter Quaker Bible and the printed Quaker marriage certificate dated 1683 are a striking record of their presence. Methodism was the second, and most powerful, religious movement known in the Island and the tangible evidence of the presence and progress of the people called Methodists on the Island is visible in the numerous remaining chapels. Their records, principally of their efficient and democratic organisation, vividly reflect the way, orderly and at once inspired, in which they revitalised the religious life of the Manx people. The early account book of the Wesleyans for the first Douglas Circuit shows the lives of their first ministers and the chapel account book of the Leodest Primitive Methodist Trustees details the expenses of a tiny Andreas chapel.

In the eighteenth century new responsibilities were assumed by the government as the life of the Islanders grew more complicated. The organisation of towns, and in particular their economic functions as depots and ports for the trading, free or illicit according to one's national standpoint, of that booming century was a matter of great concern and the development of committees or boards of government were a result of this expansion. From this arose the appointment of Harbour Commissioners, whose Minute Books, surviving from 1771, and now deposited in the Manx Museum Library, are the forerunners of the Boards of Tynwald, equivalent to English ministries.

1765 is a key date in Manx history, marking the revestment of the sovereignty of the Isle of Man in the Crown of England and the dispossession of the Lords,

The First Quakers came to the Island in the 1650's. The Callows of Ballafayle in Maughold were swiftly converted to the faith in spite of persecution by the Church, imprisonment in the Bishop's prison in Peel Castle and even banishment, and gave a portion of their lands to be "Rhullick ny Quakeryn", the Quaker Burial Ground. The marriage of Robert recorded in this certificate, notable for its early printed form, was not recognised by the Church and Elinor Stockdale suffered years of confinement on this account.

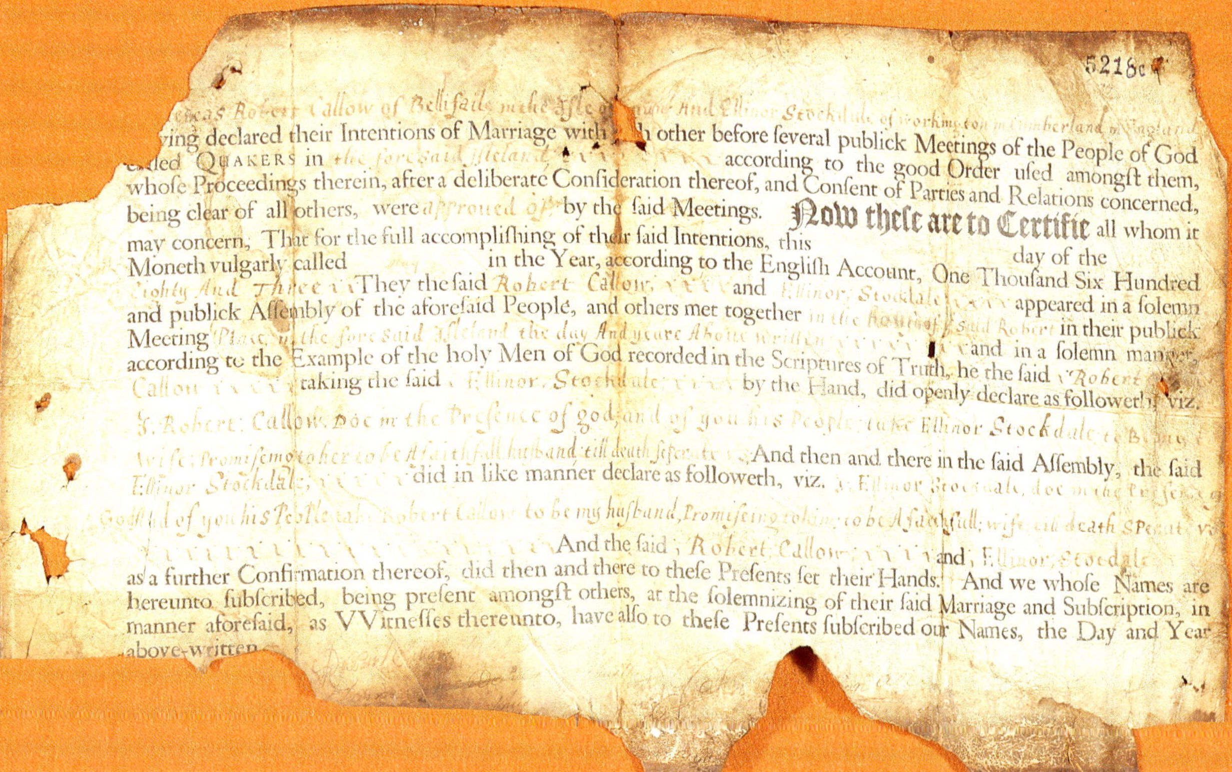
5218c

[illegible]eas Robert Callow of Bellifaile in the Isle of Man And Ellinor Stockdale of Workington in Cumberland in England
[illegible]ving declared their Intentions of Marriage with each other before ſeveral publick Meetings of the People of God called QUAKERS in the foresaid Isleland according to the good Order uſed amongſt them, whoſe Proceedings therein, after a deliberate Conſideration thereof, and Conſent of Parties and Relations concerned, being clear of all others, were approved of by the ſaid Meetings. **Now theſe are to Certifie** all whom it may concern, That for the full accompliſhing of their ſaid Intentions, this day of the Moneth vulgarly called in the Year, according to the Engliſh Account, One Thouſand Six Hundred Eighty And Three They the ſaid Robert Callow and Ellinor Stockdale appeared in a ſolemn and publick Aſſembly of the aforeſaid People, and others met together in the house of said Robert in their publick Meeting Place in the foresaid Isleland the day And yeare Above written and in a ſolemn manner, according to the Example of the holy Men of God recorded in the Scriptures of Truth, he the ſaid Robert Callow taking the ſaid Ellinor Stockdale by the Hand, did openly declare as followeth, viz. I Robert Callow Doe in the Presence of god and of you his People take Ellinor Stockdale to Be my wife: Promiseing to her to be A faithfull husband till death seperate us. And then and there in the ſaid Aſſembly, the ſaid Ellinor Stockdale did in like manner declare as followeth, viz. I Ellinor Stockdale doe in the Presence of God and of you his People take Robert Callow to be my husband, Promiseing to him to be A faithfull wife till death Seperate us. And the ſaid Robert Callow and Ellinor Stockdale as a further Confirmation thereof, did then and there to theſe Preſents ſet their Hands. And we whoſe Names are hereunto ſubſcribed, being preſent amongſt others, at the ſolemnizing of their ſaid Marriage and Subſcription, in manner aforeſaid, as VVitneſſes thereunto, have alſo to theſe Preſents ſubſcribed our Names, the Day and Year above-written.

Above: Douglas in 1805 by Edward Meredith. The town, the emerging capital of the Island lies pin-sharp and neat on the margin of a romantic bay backed by exaggerated hills. The new church of St. George's stands at a distance from the town on the left and the Red Pier recently built, with promenaders, is at the right hand margin.

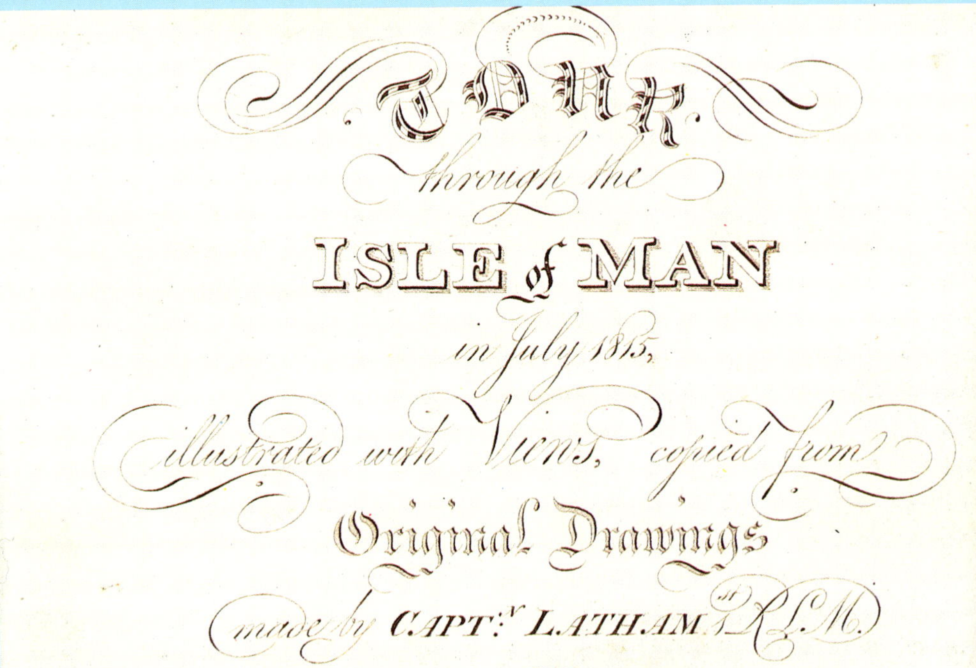

TOUR
through the
ISLE of MAN
in July 1815,
illustrated with Views, copied from
Original Drawings
made by CAPT.N LATHAM, R.L.M.
BY
S. D. SWARBRECK.

Right: "The tour through the Isle of Man was written by Captain Latham and W. Walmsley Esq. of Liverpool in the month of July 1815."

"The following remarks served to amuse and fill up the evening hours after the fatigues of a day's journey." There are two versions of this lively contemporary record. The text and the beautiful line and water colour illustrations bring the Island in 1815, discovered by the Tourist, vividly to life, and include this fine depiction of Tynwald Hill.

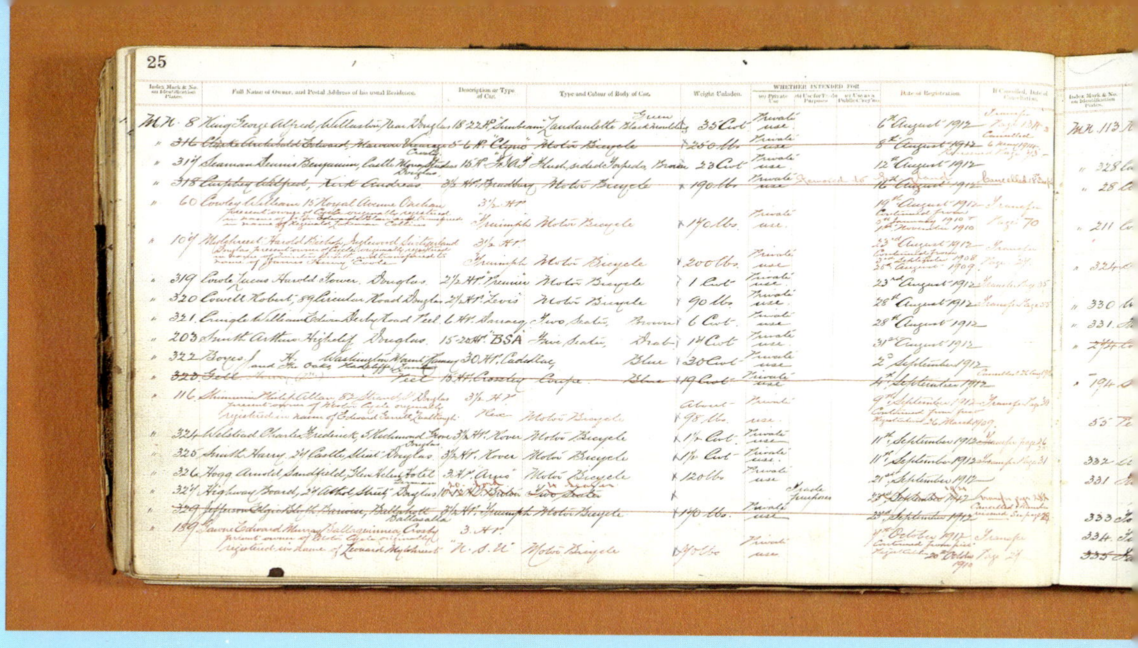

The car licensing registers of 1912, deposited in the Library by the Highway Board, record an interesting group of contemporary Manx-owned cars.

then the Dukes of Atholl, from their quasi-regal rights. The first consequences of revestment were a serious economic decline and the tight control of all Manx revenues by the English Crown. A powerful contrast to this situation was the emergence of the House of Keys, albeit still in their self-elected status, as a force in Manx affairs. The Journals of the House, in their legislative and judicial functions, date from 1764 and 1760 respectively and the development of this most ancient parliamentary body, from a relative eclipse and subservience to the Lord's Council under the Derby and Atholl Lordships to the modern democratically elected government of the Island, is reflected in the records held in the Museum Library.

Modern governmental records lack the romantic appeal of old parchments and vellum bound volumes but their preservation is essential for the administrative efficiency and political accountability of the official institutions which generate them. Their historical significance for future generations of Manx men and women is their second, and abiding, service to the community from which they arise. For these reasons the consolidation of public records in the collections of the Manx Museum Library and its progress towards its additional designation as the Public Record Office of the Isle of Man lays the long overdue foundations of a Records policy for the Island and is one of the significant events of our first hundred years.

V.  R.

BY THE LIEUTENANT-GOVERNOR.

A

PROCLAMATION

FOR

DISSOLVING

THE PRESENT

HOUSE OF KEYS

ISLE OF MAN TO WIT.

WHEREAS by the fifth section of "The House of Keys' Election Act 1866" it is enacted that within three months after the Promulgation of the said Act, the Governor shall dissolve the present House of Keys by Proclamation, and that thereupon the Members of the said House shall to all intents and purposes absolutely cease to be Members thereof, and that on the Dissolution of the present House of Keys the Governor shall within Fourteen Days thereafter issue Writsdirected to the Returning Officers of the several Sheadings and Towns within this Isle, for the Election in the manner provided by the said Act, of Members to serve in the House of Keys, which Writs shall be made returnable within Twenty One Days from the Day on which they shall bear date.

And whereas the said Act was Promulgated on the 20th day of December, 1866,---

Now I the said Lieutenant Governor in order to carry into effect the hereinbefore recited provisions of the said Act, do publish this my Proclamation, and I do hereby dissolve the said House of Keys; and I do hereby make known to all Her Majesty's Subjects within this Isle that I have given order, that there issue out forthwith Writs in due form and according to Law for the Election of Members who are to serve in a new House of Keys, which Writs together with the proceedings of the Returning Officers thereunder are to be returnable to the Rolls Office within Twenty-one Days from the date hereof.

Given under my Hand at Government House the 19th Day of March, 1867,

HENRY B. LOCH,

Lieutenant-Governor.

GOD SAVE THE QUEEN!

Printed by R. B. Fargher, "Herald" Office, Douglas.

The proclamation ordering the first elections for Members of the House of Keys, before 1867 a time-honoured but self-elected body, forced into reform by the Liberal Government of the day and the financial pressures of the bad state of Manx harbours.

CONSERVATION

Behind the scenes – the archive conservator at work.

The 1971 Library extension had one very important element – in the outmoded professional jargon of that period a "repair room". For the first time it was possible for a conservator to work on the mass of documentation which had accrued since the fifteenth century and which now faced not only the ravages of time itself but the perils of handling by students.

Damp, mildew, insect pests, flood and fire are the age-old enemies of books and manuscripts. Additionally the pressure of consultation which rises every year endangers the existence of the original archives. However careful the reader is in handling them, to fragile paper originals, use is eventually equivalent to destruction. There is therefore an ongoing programme of microfilming which provides increasing protection for the original documents and ease of access to information for the average daily user.

The backlog of work, which includes as well as fragile papers from the late medieval period, the woodpulp papers of the late Victorian era, requires the services of an expert craftsman, a conservator both scientifically and practically trained in highly specialised techniques.

Research into documentary conservation which also includes the care and preservation of photographs, a most powerful and evocative record source, is increasing and developing continually. The modern conservator has a chemistry background and is as familiar with the latest developments in control of moulds on paper by gamma-irradiation techniques as with the time-honoured craft of the book-binder.

While the first room designated for this purpose and indeed the first conservator appointed still make up our conservation centre, an increasingly sophisticated range of techniques are employed and, though necessarily the output can only be small, considered against the background of the size of the collections and our responsibilities, we are proud that they reflect the highest contemporary standards at a national level.

The Manx first knew the modern amenity benefits of local newspapers in 1782 when the *Manx Mercury* first appeared. Most of the adult population were unable to read but groups of men met regularly in the public houses to hear the news read out to them. The *Manks Advertiser* published by George Jefferson followed in 1801 and lasted until 1842 when he retired. *The Manx Sun* and *The Mona's Herald* lasted much longer. The *Sun*, a conservative organ, was first published in 1821 as *The Rising Sun*, or *Mona's Herald* and persisted throughout the nineteenth century with many changes of owners and editors, notably in the hands of the Museum's William Cubbon from 1900 to 1906 when it was taken over by *The Isle of Man Times*. The *Mona's Herald* was its radical rival. Robert Fargher, its first editor was a fearless controversialist and made the paper a considerable political force on the side of Liberalism. It celebrated its centenary in 1933 and was taken over by the Isle of Man Courier in 1975.

Manks Mercury

AND BRISCOE'S DOUGLAS ADVERTISER.

[PRICE TWO-PENCE, BRITISH.]

[Advertisements Ready Money.]

The Manks Advertifer.

No. 20. DOUGLAS, SATURDAY, DECEMBER 19, 1801. Price 3d. Britifh.

HOUSE OF LORDS.

HOUSE OF COMMONS.

WAYS AND MEANS.

PRINCE OF WALES' THEATRE,

ATHOLL STREET, DOUGLAS.

BY PERMISSION OF THE WORSHIPFUL THE HIGH-BAILIFF.

LESSEE, MR. BISSON.

LAST NIGHT BUT ONE

OF THE ENGAGEMENT OF

MISS CUTTRISS.

On TUESDAY Evening, July 17th, 1849,

The Performances will commence with SHERIDAN KNOWLES'S Play of the

HUNCHBACK!

Master Walter (the Hunchback) .. .. Mr. P. RAE.

Sir Thomas Clifford .. .. Mr. ROSIERE.

Lord Tinsel .. .. Mr. MUNGALL.

Master Wilford .. .. Mr. THOMPSON.

Modus .. .. Mr. G. EVERETT.

Master Heartwell .. .. Mr. BISSON.

Gaylove .. .. Mr. HOGAN.

Fathom .. .. Mr. J. WOOD

Thomas .. .. Mr. FIELDING.

Stephen .. .. Mr. CORKERRY.

Julia . . . . Miss CUTTRISS.

Helen .. .. Mrs. J. WOOD.

DANCE - - - - MISS ADA TAYLOR.

DANCE - - - - Mr. MUNGALL.

To conclude with the Laughable Farce of the

SERJEANT'S WEDDING

Frederick (King of Prussia) .. .. Mr. THOMPSON.

General Omelette (Commandant of the Fortress) .. .. Mr. FIELDING.

Sergeant Orloff (of the King's Body Guard) .. .. Mr. G. EVERETT.

Poomple (a young Farmer) .. .. Mr. MUNGALL.

Sergeant Krantz .. .. Mr. HOGAN.

Frow Dumnicks .. .. Mrs. BISSON.

Telzia (with a Song) .. .. Miss ADA TAYLOR.

Katrine .. .. Mrs. J. WOOD.

SEASON, or MONTHLY TICKETS, may be had of Mr. BISSON, at the Theatre.

It is so arranged that the Performances will conclude about 11 o'clock

Nights of Performing---Monday, Tuesday, Wednesday, Thursday, & Friday.

Acting Manager, Mr. BISSON. Stage Manager, Mr. G. EVERETT.

Prompter, ... Mr. FIELDING.

Boxes, 2s.; Half-price, 1s. Pit, 1s.; no Half-price. Gallery, 6d.; no Half-price.

Young Ladies and Gentlemen, under 12 years of age, half-price to the BOXES and PIT, from the commencement.

Doors open at Seven o'Clock, to commence at Half-past Seven.

M. A. QUIGGIN, PRINTER, 52, NORTH QUAY

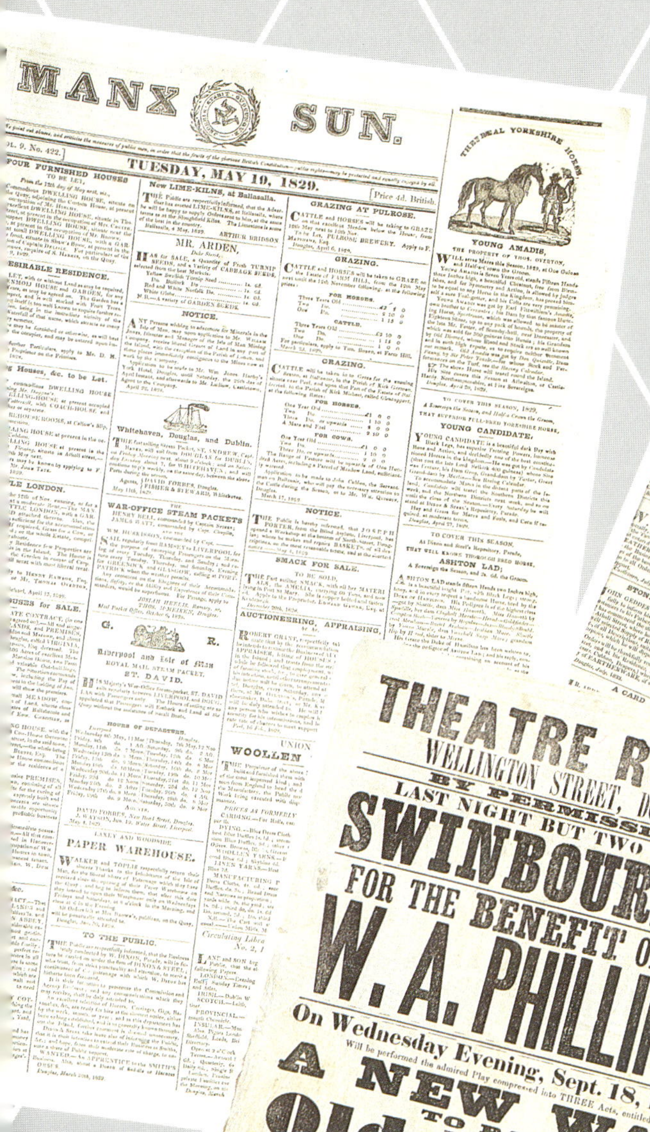

MANX SUN.

TUESDAY, MAY 19, 1829.

Mona's Herald AND GENERAL ADVERTISER.

No. 11.—Vol. I. DOUGLAS, FRIDAY, OCTOBER 11, 1833. Price 3d. British.

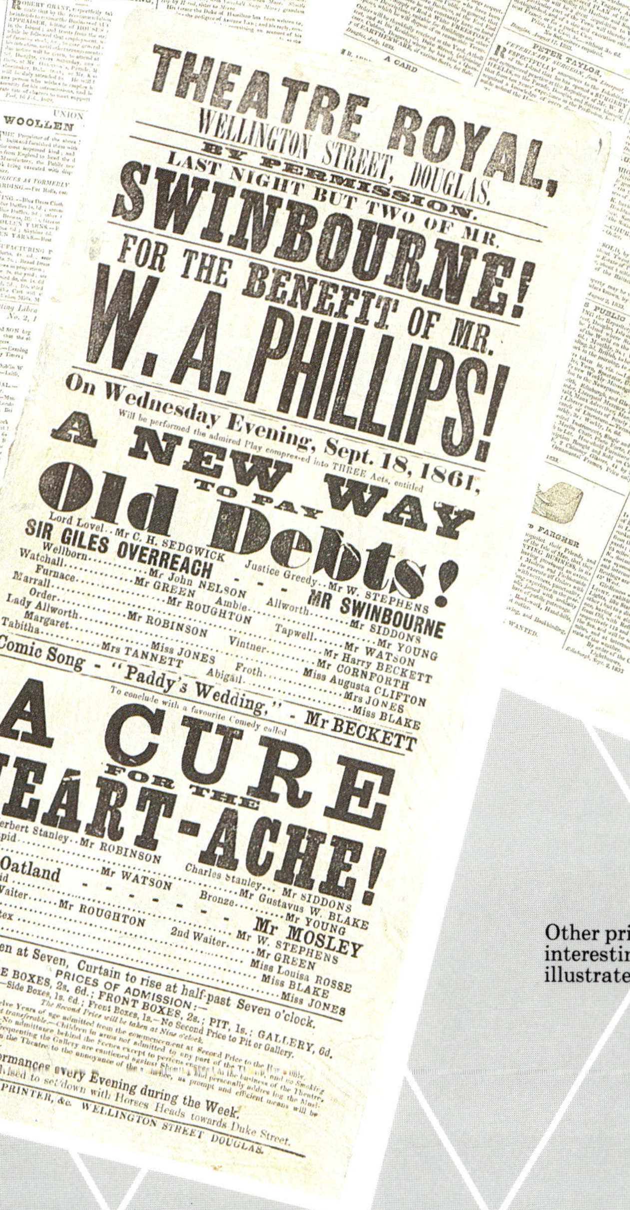

THEATRE ROYAL,
WELLINGTON STREET, DOUGLAS.
BY PERMISSION.
LAST NIGHT BUT TWO OF MR.
SWINBOURNE!
FOR THE BENEFIT OF MR.
W. A. PHILLIPS!
On Wednesday Evening, Sept. 18, 1861,
Will be performed the admired Play compressed into THREE Acts, entitled
A NEW WAY TO PAY Old Debts!

Lord Lovel...Mr C. H. SEDGWICK Justice Greedy...Mr W. STEPHENS
SIR GILES OVERREACH - - MR SWINBOURNE
Wellborn...Mr John NELSON Allworth...Mr SIDDONS
Watchall...Mr YOUNG
Furnace...Mr GREEN Amble...Mr WATSON
Marrall...Mr ROUGHTON Tapwell...Mr Harry BECKETT
Order...Mr ROBINSON Vintner...Mr CORNFORTH
Lady Allworth...Miss Augusta CLIFTON
Margaret...Miss JONES Froth...Mrs JONES
Tabitha...Mrs TANNETT Abigail...Miss BLAKE
Comic Song - "Paddy's Wedding," - Mr BECKETT

To conclude with a favourite Comedy called
A CURE FOR THE HEART-ACHE!

Sir Herbert Stanley...Mr ROBINSON Charles Stanley...Mr SIDDONS
Young Rapid...Mr Gustavus W. BLAKE
Vortex...Mr YOUNG
Frank Oatland - - Mr WATSON Bronze...
Old Rapid - - - - - Mr MOSLEY
1st Waiter...Mr W. STEPHENS
Miss Vortex...Mr ROUGHTON 2nd Waiter...Mr GREEN
Ellen Vortex...Miss Louisa ROSSE
Jessy Oatland...Miss BLAKE
Miss JONES

Doors open at Seven, Curtain to rise at half-past Seven o'clock.
PRICES OF ADMISSION:
First Price—SIDE BOXES, 2s. 6d.; FRONT BOXES, 2s.; PIT, 1s.; GALLERY, 6d.
Second Price—Side Boxes, 1s. 6d.; Front Boxes, 1s.—No Second Price to Pit or Gallery.

Performances every Evening during the Week.
Carriages ordered to set down with Horses Heads towards Duke Street.
W. WHITE, PRINTER, &c. WELLINGTON STREET DOUGLAS.

Other printed material in the Museum's archive includes an interesting collection of nineteenth century play-bills. The two illustrated here are typical in both style and content.

THE MAPPING OF MAN

Man is an island and islands have a very particular need of mapping. The representation of their extent and position is essential for isolated communities and this is reflected in the size of the Manx printed map collection of the Manx Museum Library.

Ordnance Survey Maps were the first Library accessions ever to be reported by the Museum Trustees. Since 1906 the map collection in all its various manifestations has become a particularly noteworthy part of the Museum collections.

Maps are not only historically informative and intrinsically fascinating, they are decorative objects of great appeal. There are many interesting and attractive manuscript maps in the documentary collections, but the collection of Manx printed maps which, like our collection of printed books, is virtually complete, attracts much popular attention. It includes sixteenth century original maps of the British Isles showing Man as a detail, through elaborate and stylish examples of Dutch and British cartography in the seventeenth century to the more scientific examples of the eighteenth century where the shape of the Island approaches the projection we know today.

The charm of the many small nineteenth century maps, often associated with the guides to the Island, contrasts with the accuracy of the Ordnance Survey Maps, of both large and small scale.

It is not quite true to say, as we do of the books and pamphlets, that our map collection is totally comprehensive. At the very earliest limits of map-making for the Western fringe of Europe, we rely on copies of the Portolan coastal charts of the fourteenth, fifteenth and sixteenth centuries, made by the sailors of the Mediterranean for practical use.

The sixteenth century saw the beginning of the scientific tradition of cartography, embodying the accuracy of the local practical Portolan charts with the academic tradition of the Renaissance map-makers and it is from this period that Mercator's maps of the British Isles date. They are the first maps which show the Island in reasonable detail.

It is in this period that the foundations of the map collection were laid. The earliest original printed map in the Library is Ptolemy's Map of the British Isles, reprinted at Basle in 1552, which shows the Island as Monaida a tiny speck off the North of Ireland. *Claudius Ptolemaeus, Ptolemy*, flourished in Alexandria, c. A.D. 150. His works as astronomer and geographer, were rediscovered in the Renaissance period and first printed in the late fifteenth century.

Ptolemy: 1552 edit.of A.D. 150.

BVLA EVROPAE I
Thyle ſeu Thule
Maleos
Epidion
Ricina
Nouãtum pmõt.
obogdiu
monaida
OCEANVS
Duecaledonius
Orcades inſulæ 30
Dumna
Ocetis
Epidiũ pmõt.
Longus
Caledonia ſylua
Itys fl.
Nabæus
Mertæ
Orcas promõt.
Loxa
Ila fl.
Vierue drũ pmõt.
Berubiũ promont.
Deus
Nouantæ
Nouius
Gadeni Otadeni
Tinna fl.
Diua fl.
Celnius
Alaunus
Dãmnij
Selgouæ
Brigantes
Vedra
Taizalum
Orduices
Parisi
ALBION
INSVLA BRITANNICA
Abos fl.
Ocellos pmõt.
Oceanus Germanicus
Cornabij
Idumania fl.
Dimetæ
Simeni
Trinoãtes
Atrebatij
Regni
Dobuni
Belgæ
Durotriges
Cantij
Counos
Toliapis
Cantiũ pmõt.
Victeſis
Britãnicus
Britanniæ populi.
Nouantæ, Selgouæ, Damnij, Gadeni Otadeni, Epidij, Cerones, Carnonacæ, Careni, Cornabij, Caledonij, Decantæ, Mertæ, Vacomagi, Venicontes, Texali, Orduices, Coritani, Catyeuchlani, Trinoantes, Demetæ, Sylires, Dobuni, Rutupiæ, Belgæ, Durotriges, Dumnonij. Reliqui ſunt in tabula. Ciuitates Alauna, Alata caſtra, Aquæ calidæ, Bremeniũ, Banatia, Brannogenium, Bullæum, Carbantorigum, Corda, Colania, Coria, Curia, Caturractoniũ, Culetũ, Camudolanũ, Camunlodunũ, Corinium, Caleua, Deuana, Deunana, Daruernũ, Dunium, Epiacum, Eboracũ, Iſurium, Iſchalis, Iſca, Lucopibia, Lindum, Luentium, Londinium, Mediolaniũ, Maridunũ, Næomagus, Orrea, Olicana, Petuaria, Ripa alta, Rhetigoniũ, Rigodunũ, Rhage, Salinæ, Tamia, Tamare, Tueſis, Trimontium, Viroconium, Victoria, Vrolanium, Venta, Voliba, Vinnouium, Vxela.
Albis
Viſurgus
Moſa fl.
Rhenus fl.
Amaſius fl.
BELGICAE PARS
GERMANIAE MAGNAE PARS

Later on in 1586. Ortelius' British Isles map shows the Island in greater detail and more accurately placed. *Abraham Ortel* (1527–1598), otherwise *Ortelius*, was born in Antwerp and after a classical and mathematical education set up in business at the age of twenty as a map colourer and salesman. His greatest work as a map-maker is the *Theatrum Orbis Terrarum* published in 1570, effectively the first modern atlas.

Ortelius: 1586.

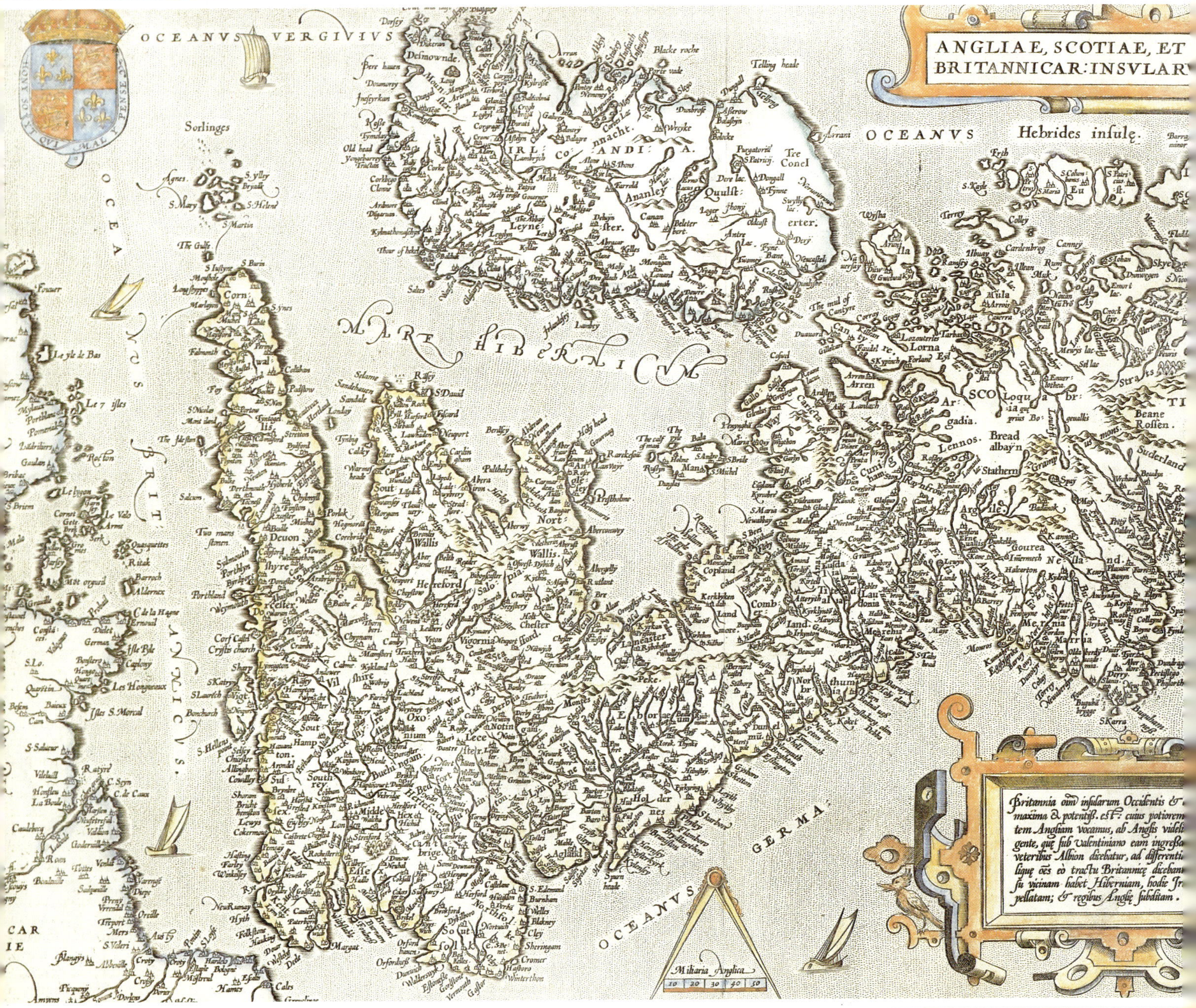

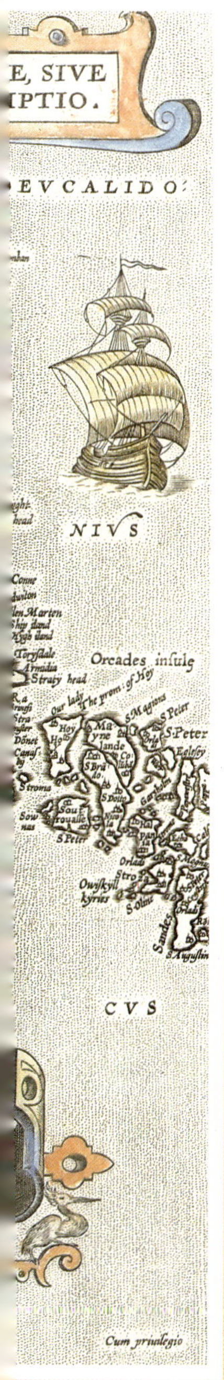

Humphrey Lluyd: 1573.

Humphrey Lluyd's illustrated map, the earliest engraved map of England and Wales, was completed in 1568 but published in 1573 as an addition to Ortelius *Theatrum*. Lluyd was born in Denbigh in 1527. He studied medicine and practised as a physician but he devoted much time to music and the arts and became a "person of great eloquence, an excellent rhetorician, a sound philosopher, and a most noted antiquary". He was in touch with Ortelius and impressed him with his nobility and erudition.

From this period the collection grows in comprehensiveness and importance, boosted in the 1920s by major accessions from the G. F. Clucas collection.

Blaeu: 1645.

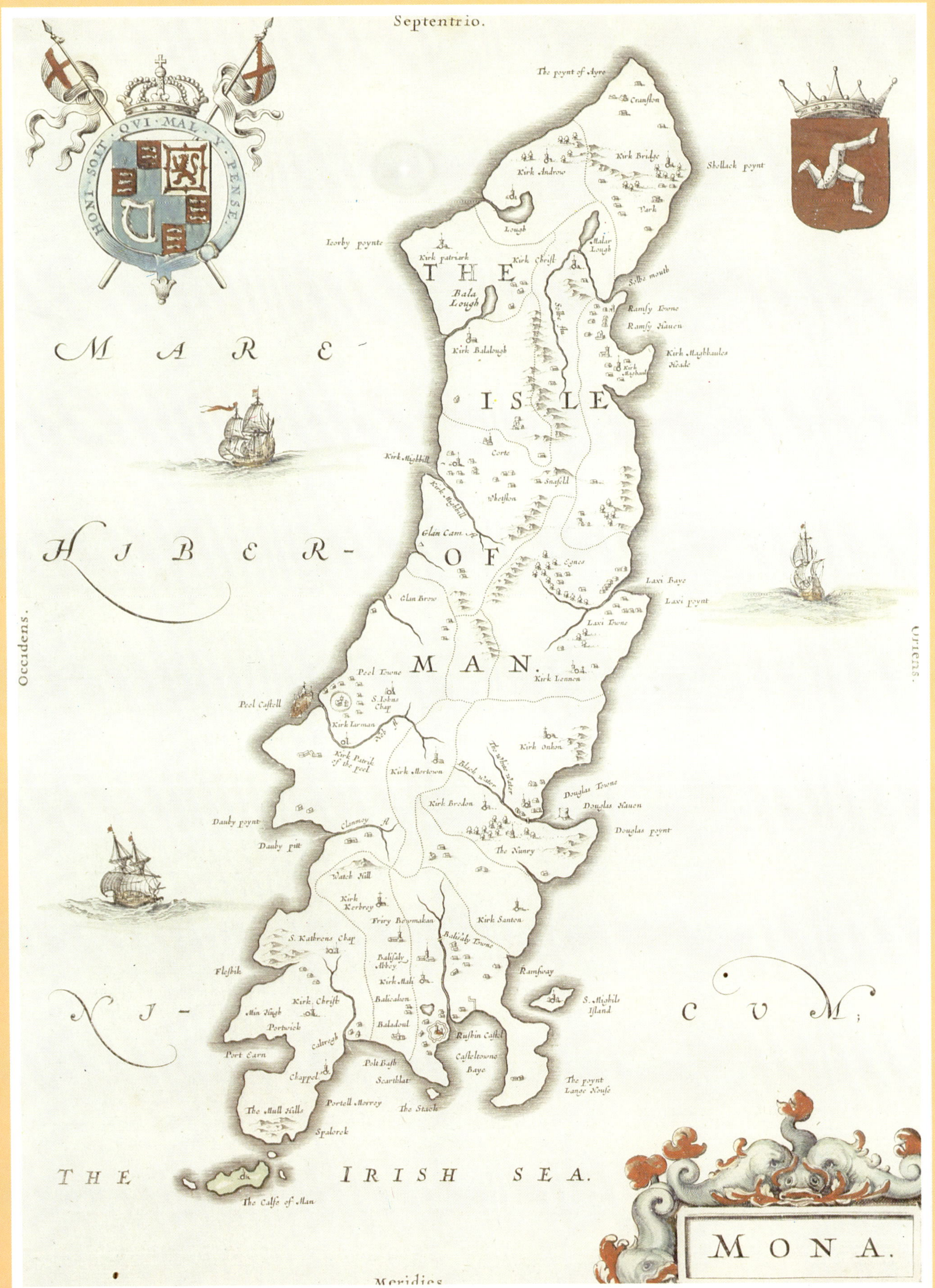
Septentrio.
HONI SOIT QUI MAL Y PENSE.
The poynt of Ayre
Cranston
Kirk Bridge
Kirk Andrew
Skollack poynt
Park
Lough
Malar Lough
Jeorby poynte
Kirk patriark
Kirk Christ
THE
Bala Lough
Solbe mouth
Ramsy Towne
Ramsy Hauen
Kirk Balalough
Kirk Maghhauls Heade
MARE
ISLE
Kirk Mighhill
Corte
Snafell
Whetston
Glan Cam
HIBER-
OF
Egnes
Laxi Baye
Laxi poynt
Glan Brow
Laxi Towne
Occidens.
Oriens.
MAN.
Kirk Lennon
Peel Towne
S. Iohns Chap
Peel Castell
Kirk Larman
Kirk Onkon
Kirk Patrik of the Peel
Kirk Mortown
Black Water
Douglas Towne
Douglas Hauen
Kirk Brodon
Dauby poynt
Glanmoy fl
Douglas poynt
Dauby pitt
The Nunry
Watch Hill
Kirk Kerbrey
Friry Bewmakan
Kirk Santon
S. Kathrens Chap
Balisaly Towne
Balisaly Abbey
Flesbik
Ramsway
Kirk Mali
S. Mighils Island
NI-
CUM;
Kirk Christ
Balicahen
Min Hugh
Portwick
Baladoul
Rushin Castel
Port Earn
Castletowne Baye
Polt Bash
Scarthlat
Chappel
The poynt Lange Noyse
Portell Morrey
The Mull Hills
The Stack
Spalorck
THE IRISH SEA.
The Calfe of Man
MONA.
Meridies

Some of the most decorative and efficient maps were printed in the Netherlands in the seventeenth century. For accuracy according to the knowledge of their time, magnificence of presentation and richness of decoration, the Dutch maps of this period have never been surpassed. *William Janszoon Blaeu* who died in Amsterdam in 1638 at the age of 67 worked with his two sons Johann and Cornelius. The works of the family firm were remarkable in scope, taking in both the terrestrial globe and the Universe. Their contemporary and rival, *Jan Jansson*, died in Amsterdam in 1664, at the age of 68. The maps of Blaeu (1645) and Jansson (1646) are singularly attractive both in colour and design.

Jansson: 1646.

The work of British cartographers was however more significant in the development of the mapping of the Island. Because of its strategic importance Man was of interest to the British Crown and the first detailed survey of the Island, "described by Thomas Durham anno 1595, performed by John Speed" may have been made for military and defensive reasons.

John Speed was born in Cheshire in 1552 and published his *Theatre of the Empire of Great Britain* in 1611. The map of the Isle of Man included in this Atlas bears the date 1610, though an earlier plain sea version is dated 1595. As a Cheshireman, the Island would perhaps be fairly well-known to him and his informative, well-engraved and beautifully designed map is in any edition much sought after by Manx collectors. Our earliest version of the map has considerable detail. There is an attempt to delineate the parish boundaries and the Castles and two early bridges are shown as well as some of the churches and chapels. The large scale of the Island dwarfs the surrounding coasts of England, Scotland, Ireland and Wales.

John Speed: 1610.

MAN by Cæsar Called Mona, by plini Monabia, by ptol. Monoeda, and by Gildas Eubonia, is an Island seated in the Ocean be: twixt the kingdomes of England, Scotland and Ireland, it formerly bare the name of a kingdome, and hathbene populous and well inhabited very plentyfull of Cattell, Foule and Fyshe, it is nowe deuided into seauentene parishes, many Villages, and de: fended by twoe Castells.
PERFORMED BY. IOHN SPEED Anno. 1610
Are to be sold by Tho: Baßett in Fleetstreet, and Ric: Chiswell in St Pauls Churchyard.
5. 10. 15. 20.
THIS SCALE is to be measured from the Compasse in the midst of the Island vnto the bordring Coasts of England, Scotland, Ireland, and Wales.
The poynt of Ayre
Shellack poynt
Kirk Andrew
Kirk Bridge
Icorby poynte
Kirk patrick
Kirk Christ
Balalough
Lough
Ramsy Hauen
Kirk Maghhaules Heade
Kirk Balalough
Workinton
PART OF CUMBERLAND
Egremonde
Glan Cam
Laxi Baye
Laxi poynt
Laxi Towne
Miltum cast.
Peel Towne
St Iohns Chap.
Kirk lemnon
Kirk onkon
Kirk Mertown
Part of Lancashire
De pole of Foodray
Douglas Towne
Dowglas hauen
Dowglas poynt
Kirk Bredon
The Nunry
Watch Hill
Kirk Kerbrey
Kirk Santon
Ballsaly Towne
Lerpoole water
St. Kathrens chap.
Ramsway
St Mighils Island
Rushin Castel
Castellto wne Baye
The poynt Lange noise
Hillbre Island
PART OF CHESSHIRE
The Stack
DEE FLUD
Part of Flint shire
PART OF DENBIGHSHIRE
PART OF CAERNARVANSHIR
Calfe of Man
Presthholme Island
ANGLESEY
Bewmaris
N.B.W. NORTH. N.B.E. N.N.E. N.B.E.N.
N.E. NB.EE. E.NE. E.BN. EAST. E.B.S. E.S.E. S.B.EE. S.E.
S.B.W. SOVTH. S.B.E. S.S.E. S.E.B.S.

Captain *Greenvile Collins* was engaged by the British Admiralty in 1681 to chart the coasts of the British Isles. His small scale chart of the Eastern Irish Sea published in 1689, shows the Isle of Man, and is the first representation of the Island to break away from that of Speed. His 1693 large scale map of the Island was dedicated to the Earl of Derby. It considerably improved the representation of the Island's shape and provided the basis of many later maps. Little is known of Captain Collins apart from his service in the Navy, that he was a younger brother of Trinity House, and that his work for *Great Britains Coasting Pilot* was a great advance on previous work in this field.

Capt. Greenvile Collins: 1693.

Latitude
Peel Castel
Dauby P.t
Knockaly
Watchill
St. Patrick of Peele
Peel Castle
Peele
St. Sarmane
L E O F
St. Iohn
Glanbro
9 foot Sand
Heward
St. Michael
Michael R.
M A N.
Ballough R.
St. Ballough
Ierby Point
St. Patrick
St. Concan
Suawble Snawble
Christ Church
St. Lomon
St. Andew
Laxsey
Laxsey Bay
Selby R.
Bourn
Ramsey
St. Bridget
Point of Aire
Shellack P.t
St. Maughold
Ramsey Bay
Maughold Head
5 foot 5 foot
H. Moll Sculp

These and following charts of the eighteenth century naturally concentrated on coastal detail of nautical importance. *John Senex*, cartographer, engraver, and bookseller in London, issued an English Atlas in 1714. His 1728 map of the Irish Sea showing the Isle of Man, based on Collins, was published as part of *The General Coasting Pilot*.

A map-maker resident in Douglas, *Peter Fannin*, was the first to add considerable detail to the interior of the Island. Fannin, himself a "Master in the Royal Navy", sailed with Captain Cook in his second voyage of discovery and later settled in Douglas where he ran a navigation school. In 1789 he published his map of the Island, which, fittingly, indicated safe anchorages around the coast. The map at the scale of approximately 1″ to 1 mile, showed the Island's roads for the first time and the first published Douglas town plan.

The growing fame of the Island as a resort produced many interesting and decorative maps. At the start of the nineteenth century, John Cary's map of the Island in the *New British Atlas* (1805) provided a new interpretation of the features mapped by Speed. Although beautifully drawn and tinted, it is antiquarian in its adherence to the inaccurate projection of the Island. This is not typical of Cary's usual high standards.

Below: Peter Fannin: 1789.

Right: John Senex: 1728.

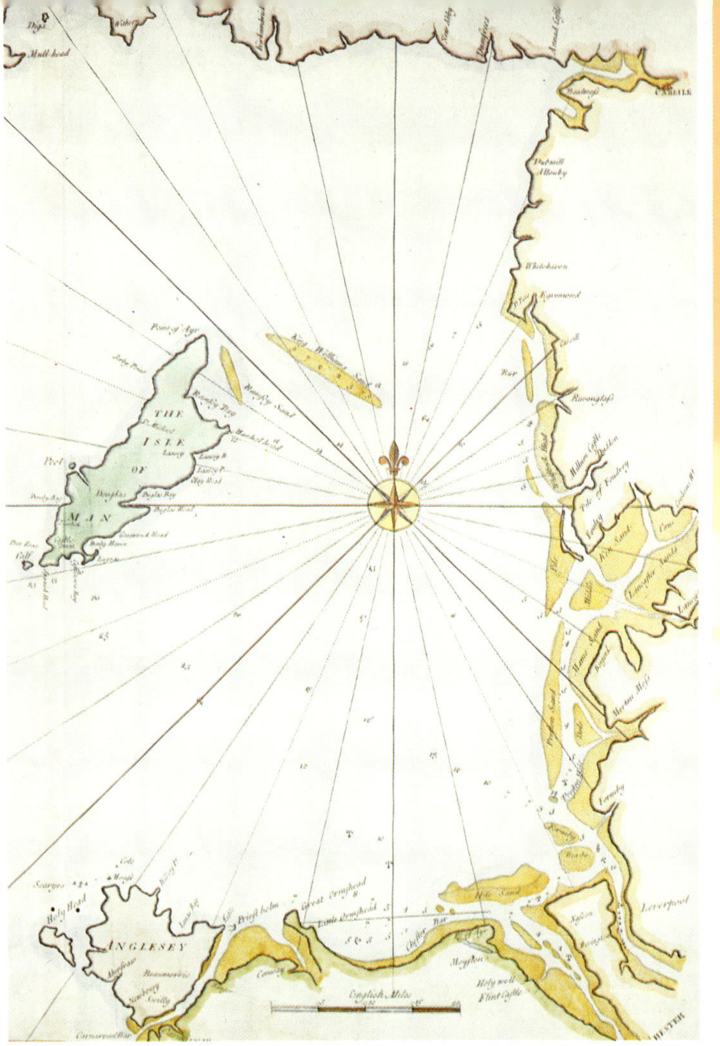

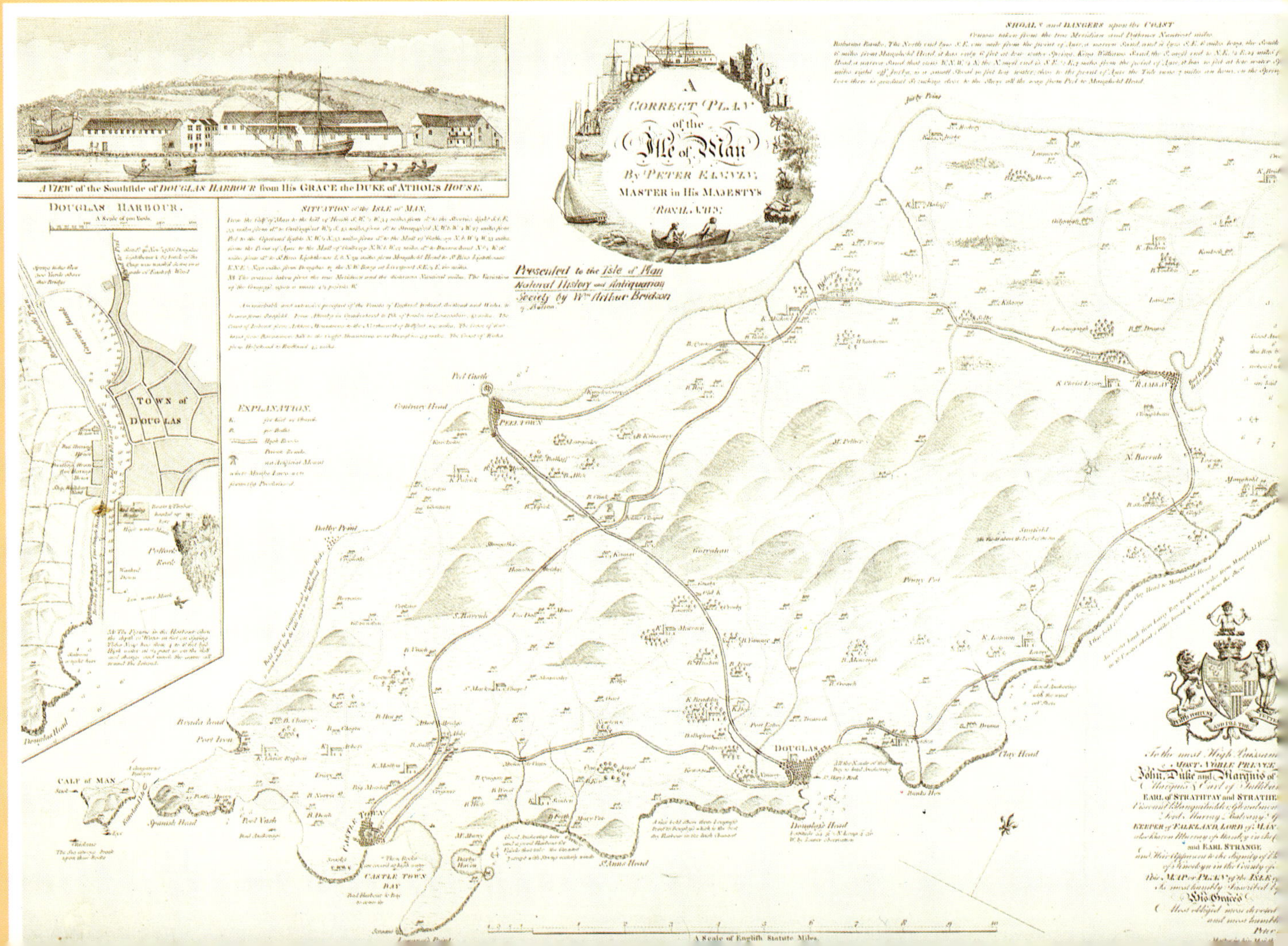

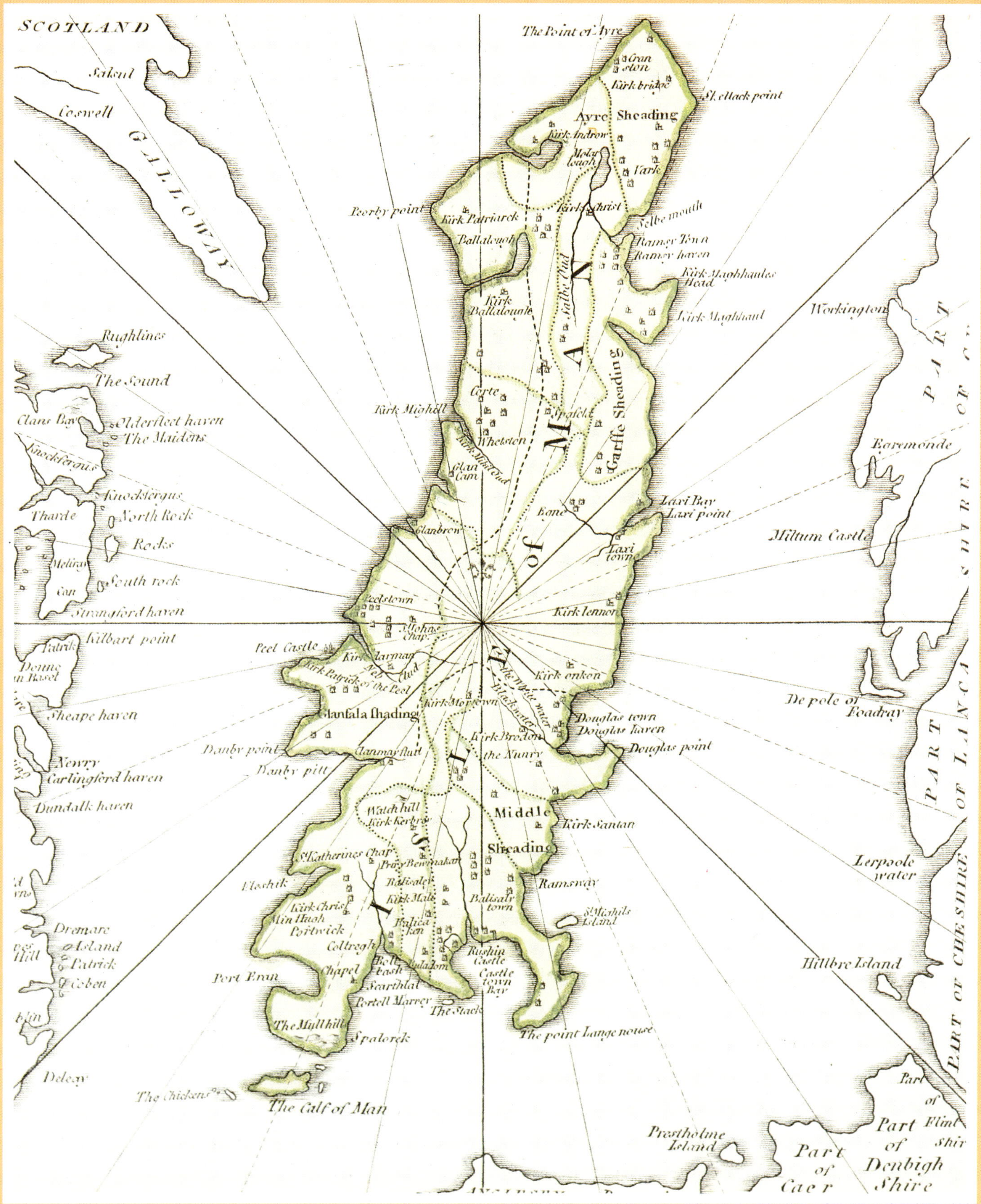

John Cary: 1805.

Benjamin Smyth's map of the Island, published by John Drinkwater in 1826 was a great step forward in the accurate mapping of the Island. Here, for the first time, there is significant plotting of roads and buildings and the mountain land is well represented by hachures. It stands as the best Island survey until the work of the Ordnance Survey in 1869 laid the foundations of modern scientific cartography in the Island.

Benjamin Smyth. Pub. by Drinkwater: 1826

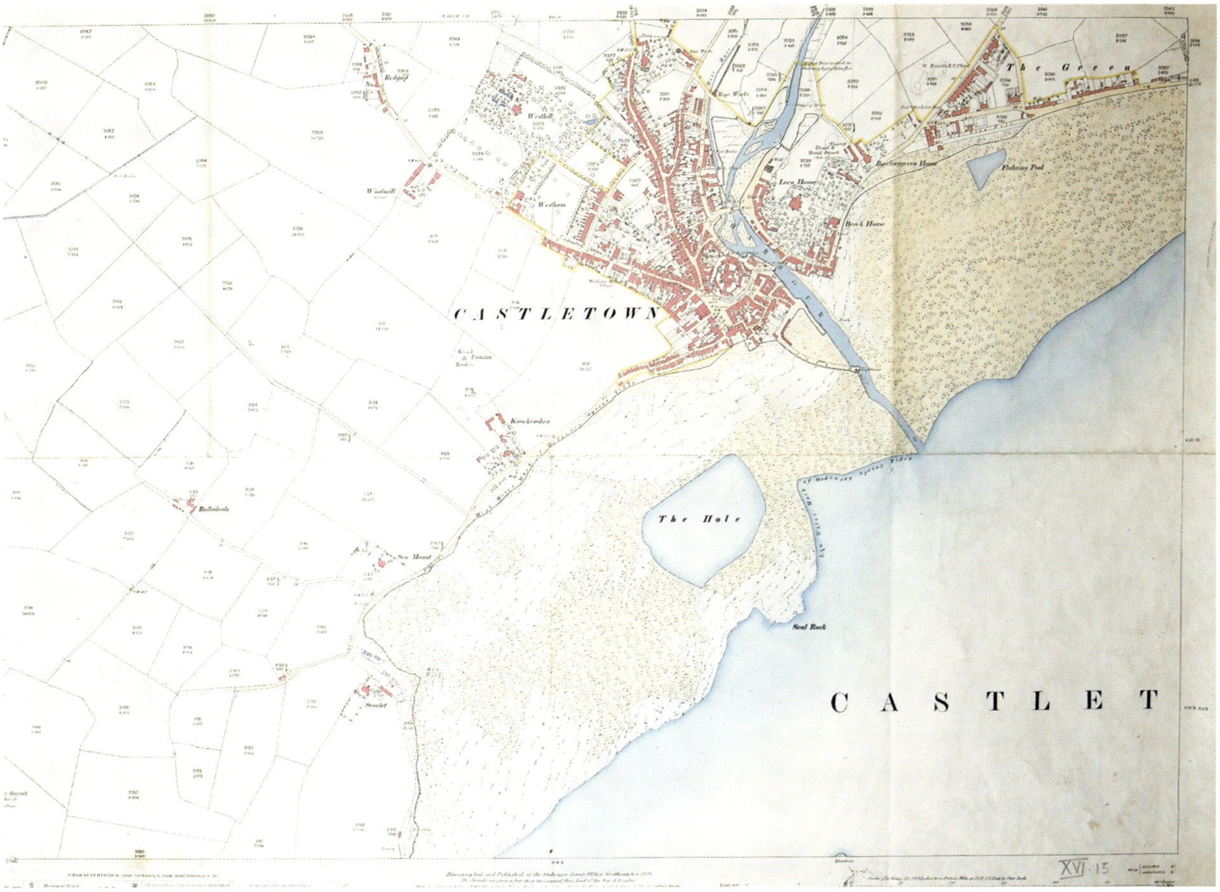

The first Ordnance Survey team visited the Island in 1868. These two illustrations based on their scientific survey of the Island, the 1869 maps at the scale of 25 inches and 50 inches to the mile, show the old and new capitals of the Island, Castletown and Douglas in accurate detail.

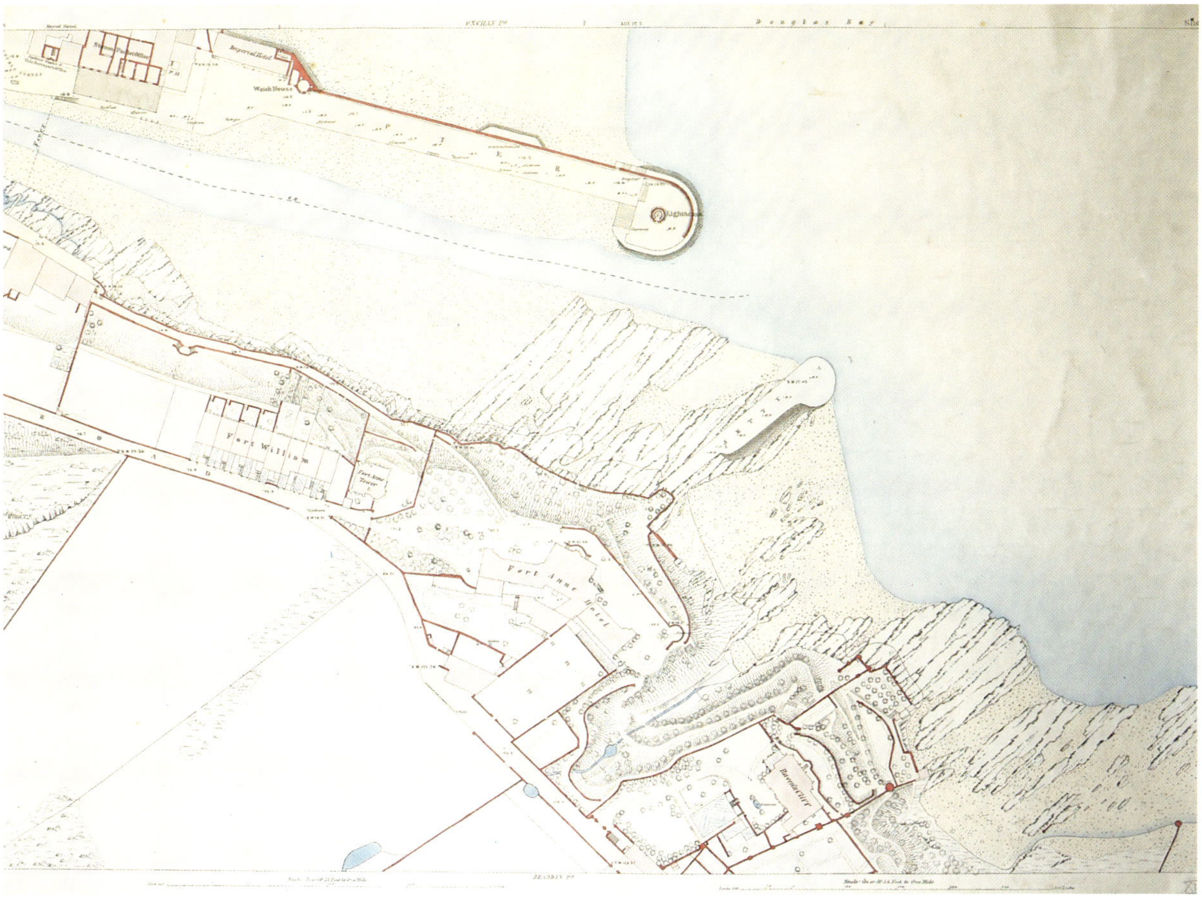

THE COUNTRYSIDE IN TRUST

L. S. GARRAD

The Manx National Trust was created by Act of Tynwald in 1951 largely as the result of the initiative of Deemster Sir Percy Cowley, Kt., C.B.E., J.P. (1886–1968). The infant Trust at once took control of a sizeable area of coastline at Spanish Head. This had previously been acquired by Sir Mark Collet and others, almost as an act of faith that a body dedicated to preserving at least some part of the Island's heritage of beauty would one day come into being. The new Trust was quickly granted a long lease of the Calf of Man by its owners, the National Trust for England and Wales, who had acquired it in 1937. In consequence, this voluntary body has a representative among the Manx Trustees which affords the insular trust a most valuable opportunity of drawing on the English Trust's acquired skills and experience.

Further coastline was acquired at Maughold and Eary Cushlin in 1953 and other properties have steadily been added over the years to consolidate the Trust's existing holdings, particularly with regard to the preservation of the natural setting of the village folk museum at Cregneash.

Small portions of the Ayres and the Curraghs have been acquired as a foundation for Man's two proposed *National Nature Reserves*. St. Michael's (or Fort) Island off Langness, a more recent and highly prized acquisition, was purchased in 1984.

The memorial to Deemster Sir Percy Cowley stands above the swirling currents of the Sound, with a superb view across Kitterland to the Calf of Man, both islets in trust for the future.

CALF OF MAN

The Calf of Man is a 616½ acres (249.46 ha) islet isolated from the main Isle of Man to its north by the swirling waters of the Sound. This channel is only about a quarter of a mile wide but its tidal currents are so fierce that a full knowledge of the state of the tide is needed for a safe crossing. The Calf islet is covered with heath and bracken with rough grassland on the former arable. It is now nearly treeless but must have retained part of its ancient woodland until quite late, since on 4th October 1417 John Shirlock (of the family that gave its name to Ballersherlogue on the Arbory boundary with Rushen) was accused of cutting brushwood there. The most notable tree now is the Ash above the mill.

The Calf has long been noted for its seabird colonies, particularly for the vast numbers of Manx Shearwaters – the bird was first named scientifically from a specimen from here in 1676. The strategic importance of the islet and the value of the Shearwaters were such that in the period of the Norse Kingship it is likely to have remained in royal hands. By the beginning of the sixteenth century it was held by the Stevenson family, being taken back in 1644 when a defence was being prepared against the Parliamentary forces. After the

The Calf of Man looking northwards to the main Island. The pattern of the old farmland stands out against a background of purple heath.

Restoration, the Earl of Derby, Lord of Man, retained the islet in his own hands for a while and attempted to establish there the Red Deer gathered from the main island. Fallow Deer were tried in 1754.

The islet remained in the possession of the Lords of Man until, in 1773, the Duke and Duchess of Atholl granted it to John Quayle of the Creggans. The Calf passed to the Crown on the Revestment in 1765 and was subsequently sold to William Leece Drinkwater in 1832 and through his descendants reached the Carey family of Castletown. Under its various occupiers, the islet was farmed, its wild-life was exploited for profit and it was used as a holiday retreat.

The Calf's wildlife was increasingly admired and Manx bird watchers began to dream of the day when it would be a sanctuary with its birds scientifically studied and fully protected. Their dream was ultimately realised when F. J. Dickens bought the Calf in 1937 and gave it to the National Trust for England and Wales who employed a resident warden. It was leased to the Manx National Trust soon after that body's creation in 1951 and formally joined the ranks of British Bird Observatories in 1962. Ownership of the Calf of Man was finally transferred to the Manx National Trust in 1986.

There are a number of structures on the islet, including a complex of harbour works at the Sound and an improved jetty at South Harbour. The oldest

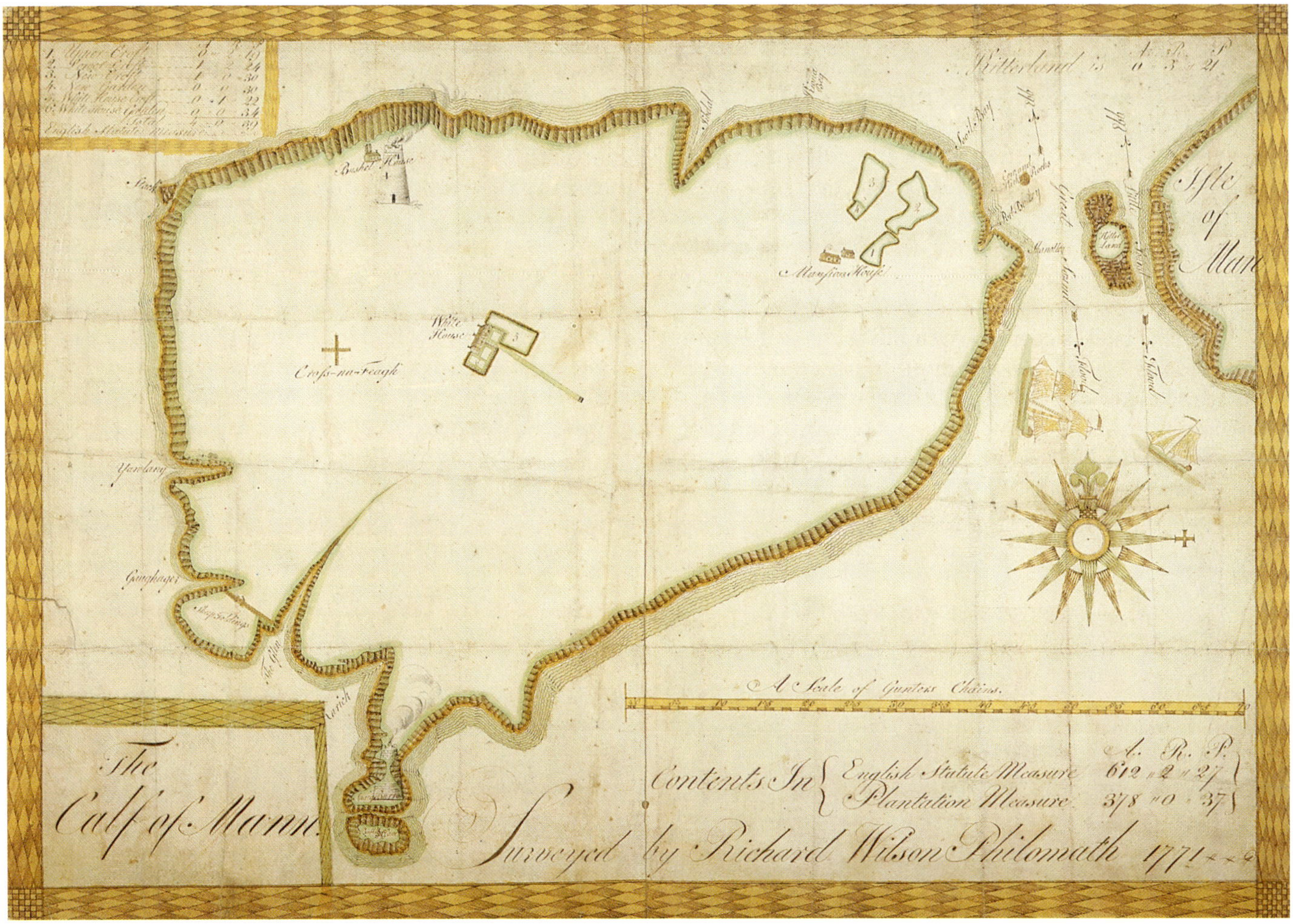

surviving house was probably part of that on the site now called "Jane's House" where the Mansion House is shown on Richard Wilson's map of 1771. Its water supply came from a trickle draining a little wet hollow which was led down in a deep gully beside the small fields which are a relic of the first modern farmers. It was last lived in by workmen building a new dock at the beginning of the twentieth century but the roof remained fairly sound until 1950 and it would appear to have been used occasionally up to that time.

During the eighteenth century, walls had been built across the islet and what was to become the main farmhouse was built. It was then called the White House. Like Jane's house, it is a solidly stone-built dwelling with a slate roof and so superbly sited (a south-west gale can rage above its chimneys, and its fields and garden lie open to the sun) that it is impossible to believe that it did not have precursors. It has several springs, one of which was used to feed a header tank for domestic water supply, making it at one time the only British bird observatory with an indoor W.C. and running water. The farm's extensive buildings include a windmill-like stone-built tower silo, only the second Manx example to be erected. The protective railing beside its upper door was once the base of a sewing machine and an artistic warden has

The Calf of Man as mapped by Richard Wilson in 1771, "scale 1 inch to ½ chain". The map is preserved in the Library of the Manx Museum.

Below: The "White House", formerly the main farm and now the Calf of Man Bird Observatory. On the hill above is the structure traditionally called "Bushel's House" which may have been the site of an Early Christian chapel, or *keeill*.

topped it with a weather vane carrying the outline of the islet's most notable bird inhabitant, a Manx Shearwater. In the eighteenth century, a single pair of mill stones were powered by the islet's main stream – one is now the garden table at the Observatory, the other lies broken beside the shell of the mill which gave its name to Mill Giau. Wood for various purposes, including firing, was gathered on the shore. Turf dug on Caigher helped to keep the fire in over-night. The little pool created by this digging was deepened, and like the mill-pond, is now maintained for the birds.

Most of the islet is covered with heath, with a notable absence of the Dwarf Gorse *Ulex gallii* which makes its presence so clearly felt on the main island. On the deeper soils, abundant Bluebells cast a mantle of blue over large areas in the late spring. As on Skomer, a rather similar island off the Welsh coast, these are followed by a dense growth of bracken which is spreading considerably now that farming has virtually ceased. The tops of the coastal cliffs have typical maritime heath, with the paler blue stars of the Spring Squill to accompany the Bluebells. Thrift, Scurvy Grass, Sea Campion and Sea Scentless Mayweed are also abundant and Royal Fern occurs in one or two places on ledges on the cliff faces. Lichens are common on the coastal rocks and, because of the high humidity, on the walls and shrubs. The willows behind Jane's House, although under five feet high, are clothed in *Usnea subfloridana. Ramalina siliquosa* furs the walls about the mill fields.

A number of boggy areas and seepage springs add considerably to the attractiveness and variety of the Calf's plants and are particularly interesting in that a number of species survive that have become decidedly rare and local on the main island. Thus the Primrose-fringed seepage below the track at Gibbdale has Adder's Tongue Fern and that below Jane's House has Common Sundew and Bog St Johnswort. All-seed *Radiola liniodes* is also much commoner on the Calf than on the main island. Brookweed *Samolus valerandii* grows on some of the wetter rocks, such as the little seepage between the silo and the South Harbour track.

The mill has a pond, less than a hundred years old, which has been planted with a pondweed *Potamogeton natans*, a white waterlily and willows. The last have spread to form quite a dense scrub. Two water snails *Ancylus fluviatilis* and *Potomopyrgos jenkinsii* are present. The first may well have come in with plants but the second has been known for so short a time in Man that it is likely to have been carried in by birds in the last few years. If it did arrive with the introduced waterlily it may be that this pond is the source from which the species spread to be detected at several southern stream-mouths in the early 1940s. Small though this pond is, Mallard and Moorhens breed in most years and it is attractive to birds at all seasons.

A number of garden plants have been naturalised round the farm, Rose of Sharon and Elecampane, for example. The roots of the latter were once candied and the plant was used herbally; it is fairly common as a relic of cultivation in cottage gardens and hedgerows, particularly in the south of the Island. It was also used to treat galled horses. It seems to have been a plant favoured by the Irish monks and survives on other isolated islands they visited, such as Rathlin, off the north of Ireland, and Raasay, next to Skye. Other cultivated species have spread further afield on the Calf, including the incredibly invasive (*Helixine*) *Soleirolia soleirolii*, known variously as "wandering sailor", "mind your own business" or "hell", which has appeared on the cliffs after being unsuccessfully evicted from the Observatory garden.

Pygmy Shrews and Wood Mice are plentiful, particularly in the Bluebell and Bracken areas. Rabbits thrive, including a fair number of melanistic variants. Despite waves of myxomatosis, possibly spread by gulls carrying infected bodies, the population seems to maintain itself. It is uncertain when rabbits were first introduced to the Calf. They may have been brought in to provide additional nest sites for the highly valued Shearwaters, or imported to the main island by the monks of Rushen Abbey and taken to the islet only after the start of the Derby Lordship. When rats from a wrecked ship virtually eliminated the Shearwaters the rabbits went some way to replace them as a "crop". Both rodent populations were a pest to the farmers and remain so. The only other mammals now present are Grey Seals which apparently breed off the islet since the bulls may be heard calling in autumn and young seals have been seen. In the past there have been small numbers of feral goats. Deer were kept intermittently prior to the Revestment but the Red Deer tended to swim the Sound to raid the farmers' crops on the main island.

Grey Seals hauled out on rocks off the Calf of Man. There is a small breeding colony and their haunting cries can be heard from the Observatory on warm, still nights in August and September. *(Photo: D. Wood)*

The islet is almost completely cliff-bound and the breeding seabirds are therefore well distributed. The most abundant are the Herring Gulls with some 1,000 pairs. Great Black-backed Gulls have a 40 or so pair colony on Kitterland, the rock between the Calf and the main island, and about 100 pairs breed on the Calf itself. The main Lesser Black-backed gullery, now down to about 25 pairs, is inland near South Harbour. There are now no more than 140 (down from 500–1,000) pairs of Kittiwakes. A colony was established on Caigher in 1955 but lost 19 nests to storm waves in 1984. An indication of the origin of some of the birds was provided by the recovery, as a nesting adult at Caigher, of a bird ringed at the other end of Man at Maughold Head, also a Manx National Trust property. These population fluctuations are not yet such as to give rise to anxiety since seabirds generally live twenty years or more.

The first modern Fulmar colony in Man was that on the Calf where breeding was proved in 1936 but many of the mainland colonies are now much larger than those on the Calf. Shags have large rookeries between Kione ny Halbey and Kione Roauyr and below the lighthouses but were down to about 250 nests in 1984 from about 400 in 1982–83. The eastern cliff birds can be seen from the mainland, the rows of long snaky necks topped by curved crests producing the impression of rows of wrought-iron brackets, or gargoyles, ornamenting the ledges. Shags may also be frequently seen feeding in the Sound but Cormorants are much less plentiful and have also decreased in recent years, as is general in Britain. Puffins, however, may have incresed slightly with about 30 pairs in 1984. About 120 pairs of Razorbills and rather more Common Guillemots, recovering now from the adverse effects of "Torrey Canyon" (the great oil spillage of 1967) and subsequent "auk deaths", are present. The Black Guillemot does not nest on the Calf but there were signs of birds moving in, in 1984–5. The returned Manx Shearwaters now frequent the Gibbdale area. Recently it has been suspected that Storm Petrels are also now numbered among the Calf's breeding birds. They have been recorded at night and 72 birds were caught and ringed in 1984. Three had previously been ringed on the

The Kittiwake colony on Caigher, Calf of Man. They first bred here in 1955 but recently their numbers have decreased, although they are still quite numerous elsewhere in the Isle of Man. *(Photo: D. J. Slinn)*

Nesting Fulmars flanked by flowering Thrift. They were first proved to breed on the Calf in 1936 and are now very abundant there and on the main island. *(Photo: D. J. Slinn)*

A Puffin in breeding plumage, a bird known to have bred on the Calf of Man for at least four hundred years and one which has usurped the original common name of the Manx Shearwater. *(Photo: D. J. Slinn)*

Calf and another two had come from Sanday Island.

Manx Shearwaters nest in holes and burrow. They feed their young at night and when they are mature abandon them. The over-plump young birds fast in the burrow for a while until they are light enough to make their way to the cliff edge and fly down to the sea. While they are alone in their burrows they are easily caught and traditionally were culled then for the benefit of the Lord of Man. Their flesh was esteemed both fresh and preserved and their feathers were also utilised. The oil that could be extracted from their plump bodies served many purposes, including preventing armour from rusting, and lighting. Great numbers were taken. Long-lived seabirds such as these can normally sustain such culls. Each pair has only to be followed by two young for the overall population to remain static. However, rats got onto the Calf from a wrecked ship and nearly wiped out the ground- and hole-nesting birds. When the Manx National Trust took over the Calf a determined war on the "longtails", as rats are called in Man, so reduced their numbers that the equilibrium was restored and small numbers of both Manx Shearwaters and Storm Petrels now breed.

Choughs build on the cliffs although they also favour window ledges and similar niches in the semi-derelict buildings. The old lighthouses are walled off for their benefit. They seem to require short grass to feed in during the rearing period and this was becoming scarce on the Calf until the Loghtan sheep were established. The Choughs' breeding success has been good in recent years.

Above left: A desirable avian residence in a kitchen fireplace on the Calf of Man where the old lighthouses are kept secure so that Choughs may nest in peace. *(Photo: A. del Nevo)*

Above: These young Choughs on the Calf carry lightweight, durable metal rings so that their origin can be proved if they are caught by ornithologists, or found dead. *(Photo: A. del Nevo)*

Left: An adult "Red-legged King of the Crows", the name by which that handsome bird, the Chough, was traditionally lauded. *(Photo: A. del Nevo)*

Ringing a bird at the Calf Observatory. The rings are closed very carefully with specially-shaped pliers, so there can be no injury to the bird. *(Photo: D. Walker)*

One of the main duties of the wardens of the Calf Observatory is the ringing of birds. The placing of a light metal ring on one of the bird's legs is a simple research method which is of enormous value. It is designed to be painless to the bird, causing an annoyance on a human level of being kept waiting at a supermarket checkout, or in a traffic jam. Ringing recoveries map out the routes taken by birds and the destinations of migrants, so that conservationists know what areas to protect. They may pin-point a particular hazard, from a major one, such as an area where human beings traditionally hunt even tiny birds for food, to such relatively minor ones as a lighthouse, or awkwardly placed high-tension wires. In great disasters, such as the pollution caused by the "Torrey Canyon", they show the source of the affected birds. Ringing monitors longevity (Razorbill 3076074 ringed as a nestling on the Calf in June 1959, and controlled on its nest there a quarter of a century later is the oldest yet provenly recorded), causes of death, changes in population numbers and breeding success, the conditions required for successful migration, etc. It provides facts which it is hoped will alert bird lovers to declines in a particular species *before* it becomes endangered.

Measuring a captured bird at the Calf Observatory. *(Photo: D. Walker)*

Birds are caught by a variety of means. One of the first pieces of equipment installed at the new Observatory was a Heligoland trap. This type is named after the German islet where much scientific ornithology was pioneered. A large tunnel of fine mesh wire netting is erected in a place attractive to smaller birds, over scrubby vegetation near a source of water for drinking and bathing, for example. The tunnel narrows and finishes in a "catching box", the end of which is glass so that birds think it is a route to freedom. When the trap is used, the ornithologist walks quietly towards the mouth of the tunnel. The "driver" taps the vegetation lightly with a cane when the mouth of the trap is reached and the drive is completed with calls and arm waving. When the last bird has fled into the catching box, the door flap on the tunnel side is closed. The trapped birds are then removed one at a time from the catching box and carried back to the Observatory (separately, in soft cloth bags) for ringing.

A Heligoland trap on the Calf. *(Photo: A. del Nevo)*

Each bird is identified as to species. Its weight is recorded. As far as the evidence allows, its age, sex, degree of moult or wear in the plumage, etc., are noted and some measurements are taken. Parasites may be collected for study. Only trained and licensed ringers and, under their supervision, those they are training, may ring birds. (A prospective trainee may be allowed to ring one or two birds to determine aptitude, under the eye of a vigilant master ringer, but thereafter must also be licensed.) The rings are put on with special pliers with holes for each size of ring, so that they will close that size perfectly. The size of ring is selected according to that of the bird, from featherweight Goldcrest, to Goose or Gannet.

The original Heligoland trap on the Calf was that nearest the Observatory and therefore known as the *House Trap*. At various times others were built but because of the fineness of the wire mesh of which they are made they are liable to be damaged by lying snow, or high winds in winter. Different wardens have had their favourite ways of catching and varied ideas as to the spots most attractive to birds. There was a cunning

Studying the birds of the Calf – a warden completing a field record sheet, 1983. *(Photo: A. del Nevo)*

"double Heligoland" which worked two ways, on the line of the wall beside the footpath from the silo to the South Harbour road and a large funnel suspended in the Mill Giau. Peter Bennett built a *Crow Trap*, in which birds are attracted down a vertical wire mesh funnel by a container of water and, on the principle of a lobster pot, cannot then escape. Various somewhat "Heath Robinson" devices catch the waterfowl on the mill pond. The gull chicks are ringed before they can fly. Young Shags are eased from their nest holes with a "Shag hook", ringed on the spot and returned – swearing! The young resident songbirds may also be ringed as nestlings, *pulli* in the reports, but the most important modern catching device is the mist net.

These very fine synthetic nets are erected between poles. Only very experienced ringers are permitted to use them. They are virtually invisible to the birds against a background of vegetation and are so fine that bats fly into them – Pipistrelle, Natterer's and Long-Eared and, a species not recorded from the main island, Daubenton's (Water) Bat. It takes great patience and skill to extract uninjured a furiously pecking tit – pecked ringer *au naturel* is often on their menu. The nets have to be constantly patrolled when in use. When it is too misty, or windy, or there are few birds about, they are collapsed to guard against accidental captures. One reason why visitors during the migration season see no sign of the Observatory's inhabitants is that they are indoors recovering from working the nets from first light and (sometimes) ringing hundreds of birds in a very few hours, or getting cold but catching little. Dawn is preferred because if the weather deteriorates sharply, or the light goes, birds have to be kept until they can safely be released. If this has to be overnight it might unduly disrupt their activities.

A full description of Calf birdlife has not been given as only a visit can show how rich it is. 99,042 birds of 134 species have been ringed since the Observatory opened and 11,280 recovered. It is abundantly clear that it was worth establishing this observatory and that the presence of resident trained observers has ensured, and will continue to ensure, that the presence of outstanding rarities does not pass unnoticed. However, it is the accumulation of data on the movements, fluctuations in numbers and origins of residents, summer visitors and passage migrants that will demonstrate the value of the Calf of Man as part of the chain of observatories in the British Isles.

Calf of Man Conservationists

F. J. Dickens who purchased the Calf and gave it to The National Trust for England and Wales in 1937.

Kenneth Williamson (once Museum Assistant at the Manx Museum, Douglas, and later on the staff at The British Trust for Ornithology) who campaigned unremittingly for Observatory status for the islet.

R. M. Mitchell Warden for The National Trust for England and Wales 1939–51.

Resident Observers for the Manx National Trust

F. J. Faragher	1952–54
Lt. Commander Frank Williams	1954–58

Wardens of the Calf of Man Observatory

Einar Brun	April 1959–1960
	(First Warden – 3,282 birds ringed.)

(Gordon Craine acted as warden during autumn migration 1961.)

The Calf attains official Observatory status

Alan H. Morley	1962–early 1964
Rodney Rayment	from June 1964
Peter Bennett	1965 & 1966
Michael Alexander	1967
Malcolm Wright	1968–74
Bob Haycock	1975–77
Pete Jennings	1978–81
Adrian del Nevo	1982–83
David Walker	1984–86

All the volunteers, boatmen, light-house keepers and others who over the years have done so much to assist in the work of conservation and ornithology on the Calf.

An *Observatory Report*, including such items as ringing and ringing recovery records and a summary of breeding results and migration observations, is published annually by the Manx Museum and National Trust.

KITTERLAND, SPANISH HEAD AND THE CHASMS

Spanish Head – the spectacular Manx Slate cliffs rise to unspoilt open heath. This gives way to the little fields about the Cregneash Folk Museum. All are now preserved because a few had faith that there would one day be a Manx national trust and that Trust has kept faith with their dreams.

Left: Common Guillemots on Spanish Head, 1966, another reason for preserving this magnificent coastal scenery.
Right: The Chasms and the Sugar Loaf. *(Photo: D. J. Slinn)*

The area of unspoilt landscape acquired in the faith that there would one day be a Manx National Trust to preserve it extended to just over 212½ acres. This has since been augmented by gifts from C. F. Watterson (1956), A. H. Karran (1967) and Dr. A. W. Kelly (1970) and small purchases. These helped to consolidate the main Spanish Head holding and preserve the environs of Cregneash, the first publicly administered outdoor folk museum to be opened in the British Isles. H. G. Maddrell and the Clague family gave their respective half interests in Kitterland in 1971 and the Trust's acquisitions in the area were crowned with the Chasms.

This superlative scenery is, like the Trust's cliffs at Maughold, among the most important breeding areas for seabirds in Man. Together with the Calf, they help to explain why the Isle of Man provides such an important southerly extension to the distribution of major sea bird colonies on the western side of Britain.

ST. MICHAEL'S ISLE

The Manx National Trust was fortunate enough to be able to acquire this very important islet in 1984. Its human associations start early – a stone axe, with the roughened butt that is characteristic of the tools of the farmers who lived in a rectangular house at Ronaldsway (now under the main runway of the Airport). The axe was found on the edge of the channel separating St. Michael's Isle from Langness in 1971. Another axe made of stone from the Lake District, is also recorded from "near the landmark" indicating that this is not an isolated find. Langness had extensive Iron Age and Medieval defensive earth works. Scuba divers recovered a Medieval mortar (grinding basin), probably an import from Germany and a relic of this defensive occupation from the bed of the gully in 1968.

St. Michael's Chapel

"The chapel on St. Michael's Isle is an example of the type of building erected by the Norse–Celtic Christian community, probably in the earlier part of the 12th century, prior to the establishment of the parishes and their churches, but differing from the earlier keeills in that they were intended for congregational worship. Despite quite extensive repairs to the walls and the probable re-setting of some openings, the church retains the ground-plan and several structural features of its 12th century origin. Considering that it has been roofless for at least three hundred years, the building may owe its comparatively good preservation to the fact that, standing as it does on a bare and windswept islet, it has been spared the deliberate dilapidation which has befallen many buildings on good agricultural land. In more recent times, the use of its precincts as a burial-ground has been an added factor in its preservation."

(J.R.Bruce: *Manx Archaeological Survey VI*)

St. Michael's Isle, with the calm waters of Derbyhaven and, in the distance, Castletown, former capital of the Isle of Man.

Inset right: The Derby Fort which houses most of the Museum's collection of iron cannon assembled from the Island's former coastal defences.

Inset left: St. Michael's Chapel – probably twelfth century – which gave its name to the islet.

The Derby Fort

Fortifications on St. Michael's Isle long played an important part in the defence of Derbyhaven, the secondary harbour of Man's capital, Castletown. The development of "great guns" made it possible to deny entry to intruders rather than, as hitherto, be forced to retreat to a safe refuge when invaded. These smooth bore cannon were developed in the fifteenth and early sixteenth centuries and fired solid, non-explosive, round shot to an effective range of about four hundred yards. A round stone tower with eight gun ports and walls eight feet thick was erected to house them on St. Michael's Isle. It has been compared with one of the defences of Calais built about 1541 and is probably of a similar date. It was later supplemented by an earthwork battery to the south-west, the whole being named the Derby Fort in 1645, when restored to withstand the

forces of Parliament during the English Civil War.

The Derby Fort was again in use at the end of the eighteenth century. About this period it also functioned as a lighthouse, a light being shown from a little turret built on its walls, when the herring fleet was at sea. The round stone building now serves as a home for a small collection of cannon, among them a pre-eighteenth century demi-culverin which once formed part of the armament for the defence of the northern plain and two guns from Ramsey quay which are probably the pivot guns from the town's nineteenth century battery. This assembly of historic remains in a picturesque setting is surpassed in Man only by St. Patrick's Isle, Peel.

Unlike most of the Trust's coastal properties, St. Michael's Isle is not a home for many breeding seabirds but it affords a vantage point for bird watchers studying the waders and waterfowl of Derbyhaven. A Little Egret was the great rarity of 1985. Its shore rocks are rich in lichens. Now that the erosion by motor vehicles can be controlled, the locally uncommon Sea Purslane *Halimione portulacoides* may spread from the causeway and the caterpillars of the rare Thrift Clearwing moth can tunnel unthreatened in the roots of the Sea Pinks.

SILVERDALE GLEN

"On 25th May 1966, members of the Trust, with members of the Quine family, attended a short informal ceremony at which a small plaque was unveiled marking the gift of the lower portion of Silverdale Glen (downstream from the Creg Mill and the pleasure gardens) to the Manx Museum and National Trust in memory of William Quine, M.H.K. by the family of his son Dr. Richard Henry Quine. This generous gift provides the Trust with a delightful stretch of wooded glen – a most typical and characteristic aspect of the Manx countryside not previously represented in the Trust's holdings. Perhaps particularly when the fresh greens of spring mix with the shimmer of the banks of bluebells, and again in the autumn when the russets and golden browns glint in the declining sun this glen holds a special enchantment, a part of the magic and the beauty of the Manx glens."

(Editorial *Journal of the Manx Museum* VII: 83, 1967)

Silverdale Glen – the fall over the weir of cut limstone that creates a head of water in the Silverburn to feed the dam which is now merely a feature of the Trust's glen. The mill it once served was built in 1767 to process flax and later ground ochre and umber for paint and polishing powders.

The Monks' Bridge, Ballasalla – believed to have been built in the fourteenth century by the monks of Rushen Abbey and now a protected monument.

The glen is now managed by the I.O.M. Forestry Board as an extension to the National Glen. It offers a woodland footpath on the route to the railway station and 'bus stop at Ballasalla, by way of the fourteenth century Monks' Bridge (a protected monument).

Trees include fine Hornbeams, a species now extremely rare in Man although they were extensively planted in the eighteenth century. The little glen encapsulates the history of the area from the tranquillity of the well, so lovingly restored by William Quine (who believed that it was of considerable antiquity and had, perhaps, served the monks of an earlier monastery that preceded Rushen Abbey) to industrialisation, represented by the dam of the Ochre and Umber mill which he had converted into a dwelling.

This mill had been built about 1767 to break flax when this was a crop fostered by the Lord of Man. It was converted to grind colour by the nabob newspaper proprietor, James Grellier. His failure to pay dues on the Umber from the pit near the Billown quarries and Red Ochre (iron-stained slate) from Maughold, led to a dispute. One of the more resounding salvos in the battle was a letter from the Crown Receiver (13.VI.1836) to the banker father and namesake of Edward Forbes, the great Manx Naturalist, requesting that, when the newspaper owner ". . . could spare as much time, from raking up the ashes of the dead and defaming the living . . ." he would send in an account of the quantities of coloured earths that had been ground and sold. One wonders that so so vituperative a letter was ever sent at a time when the necessity to copy it in longhand into a letter book would give time for reflection. However, the mill is now a house, the glen no longer echoes to the hammer of the watewheel and the groans of stone grinding stones over a stone floor. Future generations will be able to take pleasure in the spill of water over the handsome dressed stone weir and the reflections in the now ornamental dam.

THE DHOON

Land at the Dhoon was purchased in 1973 and 1975, together with a two thirds interest in the Bulgham brooghs. This area is now the main haunt in Man of the larger feral goat flock. These animals are of particular significance because they preserve the genes of older strains of domestic goats, some going back at least two hundred years. A viewpoint for ornithologists and photographers has been provided to the south of Bulgham Bay and a footpath runs along the southern edge of the Dhoon Glen to its shore. These cliffs are also the haunt of the Chough, Raven and Peregrine. The coastal properties of the Trust now afford additional protection to a significant number of these most attractive birds.

The superb display of the geology of the Manx Slate Series in the cliffs at the Dhoon where the beautiful landscape is jointly protected by the Manx National Trust and as a Manx National Glen, administered by the Isle of Man Forestry Board.

Inset: The path to the shore on the National Trust's property, photographed in 1977. This is also the easiest route back to the top!

Land Seaward of The Marine Drive

As a result of the conversion of the Old Douglas Head to Port Soderick tramway track into a motor road, the Isle of Man Highway Board was in a position to assist the Manx National Trust's work of preserving as much as possible of the Island's unspoiled coastline, by donating land seaward of the new road. This is a typical maritime heath, with heathers and gorse, Thrift and Sea Campion, Spring Squill and Ladies Bedstraw. Its Manx plant rarity is Portland Spurge. The area is also important to nature conservation in the British Isles as a whole, since it is the home of the Grey Moth, otherwise known only in limited areas in Ireland and the Scottish island of Canna. This creature is very exacting in its habitat requirements, being virtually confined to a narrow strip along the shoreline where the sea maintains an equable temperature.

MAUGHOLD HEAD

1953 saw the Trust acquire its first land at Maughold. Part was a gift from Mrs. Halahan, a rather larger area was given by Mrs. Kee and Mrs. Sutton and the latter two ladies also sold a smaller piece to round out the holdings. Again it was a coastal property but one important for its ancient history. The iron ore exposure on the summit is guarded by a fortification, probably of Iron Age date. Analysis of ore excavated from the smelting site at Kiondroghad, beside the Lhen in Andreas, has shown that the sixth–seventh century iron workers were processing Maughold ore, conceivably from this precise exposure but more probably from the coastal cliffs.

The iron workers were not the first to roam these cliffs; a Mesolithic flint missile head was found on the Head a few years ago and a bronze axehead was recovered from the upper shore when a boat was being snugged for the winter at Port Mooar in 1921. A stone burial cist just south of the head and a burial site on its summit are probably also Bronze Age in date and traces of prehistoric burials were found in the churchyard itself. A Christian monastery was established here. Perhaps, a Lord of Man granted the derelict fortification to a missionary monk, just as King Daire gave the old rath at Armagh to St. Patrick. Little is known of this monastery save that legend credited it with a never-failing spring. A stone-lined conduit and a unique inscription recording how "*Branhui led off water to this place*" show the origin of the tradition. The unique assembly of Christian monuments of this period, mainly found in or near the churchyard, are now preserved in the "cross shelter" erected by the Museum Trustees.

> "The acquisition of the Maughold brooghs represents in a sense the completion of the earlier generous gift of Maughold Head itself and the adjoining Glebe brooghs. The new land has been purchased with funds from the Miss Kate Morrison bequest, and consists of thirty-six acres of seaward-sloping brooghs, with some rough ridge-top land on Ballaterson, and a strip of land linking the western end of the brooghs, at Ago, back to the main Ramsey to Maughold road near Port y Vullen. . . . A good footpath for rough walking has been opened up through this property, commanding splendid views over Ramsey Bay and away to the hills of Scotland and the Lake District. . . . A special word of thanks should be recorded to the two local farmers, Mr. J. R. S. Corkill of Ballaterson and Mr. R. E. Quayle of the White House, not only for their agreement to sell the land, but for their much appreciated help and co-operation while the fencing and clearing work was going on to prepare the property for its opening to the public in the spring of 1966."

(Editorial *Journal of the Manx Museum* VII: 83, 1967)

A young Cormorant, a species much rarer than its look-alike, the Shag, on its Maughold Head nest, July, 1965. *(Photo D. J. Slinn)*

Maughold Head from the sea. The tiny remnant of the village green, the carved cross slabs in their shelter, the slightly more modern standing cross and the Early Christian keeills – all in the churchyard, the ancient hillfort and the burial mound on the Head itself, St. Maughold's well and the footpath along the top of the northern cliffs, like the breeding birds below, are all protected.

Like most of the Trust's coastal properties, its vegetation is dominantly maritime heath kept short by a combination of grazing, often by Loghtan sheep, and sea spray. The cliffs provide homes for sea birds including Kittiwakes and Puffins, Shags, the ubiquitous Fulmars, Herring Gulls, Razorbills and Guillemots. Choughs, Ravens, Kestrels and occasionally Cormorants are to be seen and may breed in most years, as may the Grey, or Atlantic Seals, so

frequently seen offshore. Unusual features of the bird life are the colonies of cliff-nesting Swifts and House Martins, still using the ancestral homes that they favoured before human beings first created artificial cliffs, in the form of dwellings, shrines and store houses. Their future is now assured.

Inset above: A detail of the carved stone cross-slab commemorating Branhui's 'leading off water' to the Early Christian monastery at Maughold about 800 A.D.

GOB NY RONA

The little peninsula of Gob ny Rona was acquired in 1964, mainly as the gift of Mrs. W. Cunningham but with half an acre from the Trustees of Groves Estate. It gets its name from the Manx for a seal but it is a long time since the area was sufficiently undisturbed by men for any numbers to haul out on its shore. It seems probable that it was already fortified during the Norse period (and possibly earlier) but the present form of the earthworks reflects more the exigencies of the Civil War.

As with the Maughold Brooghs, the vegetation is mainly maritime heath. The low cliffs offer no nest sites to seabirds but the coastal footpath provides a very pleasant diversion on the route between Ramsey and the Maughold Brooghs. It can also prove unexpectedly rich as a place for watching birds, ranging in size from the Great Northern Diver feeding offshore to the Stonechat scolding from bush, or fence post, along the path.

Above: Gob ny Rona (the Headland of the Seals), an often-fortified promontory that extends the National Trust's holdings from Maughold towards Ramsey.

THE AYRES

The Manx National Trust unfortunately holds little more than token, albeit representative, areas in the two Manx National Nature Reserves proposed in the Island's *Development Plan*, the Ayres and the Curraghs. The Ayres are a unique maritime heath that has developed on a series of shingle ridges created by the sea. The only building on the unfenced four-and-a-half miles between Blue Point and the western edge of the area currently despoiled by gravel working, is the interpretation centre, provided by the Manx Nature Conservation Trust which functions as the Isle of Man's "County Naturalists Trust". This windswept beauty is available for public ramblage but vehicles have to be restricted to preserve the fragile vegetation cover.

The shingle ridges which underlie the heath grew over a long period of time. On the National Trust's Ballakesh property given by the Aston estate in 1973, the early Neolithic shoreline would have crossed the road about one third of the distance seaward from its inland car park to that containing the Visitor Centre. Any worked flints found seaward of this line have been rolled by the sea. The shore ran nearly parallel to its present line, since unworn flints were found in the early 1980s at the gravel quarry used as a tip. Bronze Age hunters later roamed the Ayres – one of their barbed and tanged arrowheads was found in 1942. Later still the Vikings landed here. "Ayre" is a Norse term for a shingle ridge, usually one with a lagoon behind it.

The vegetation is most varied between the conifer plantation and the depression into which the drain from Lough Cranstal discharges. The Trust's Ballakesh area is central to this. Heath is dominant, with Marram grass on the dunes near the shore. On the rear slope of the fixed dunes there are orchids of kinds rare in Man, such as Pyramidal and Early Purple. A feature of this area are the many tiny flowers – cranesbills and storksbills, forget-me-nots, Birdsfoot and other trefoils, Mouse Ear and Cats Ear. At one spot there is an insignificant whitish orchid, the Dense-flowered, found nowhere else in the British Isles save Clare, Galway and Mayo. Lichens are the commonest plants over large areas. One, *Usnea articulata*, normally grows on trees and the change of habit seems to be unique within the British Isles to this area of Ayres. Fungi are plentiful and insect life abounds – the heath near the road to the Point of Ayre lighthouse is said to be one of the best habitats for solitary wasps and their kin in the British Isles.

Top right: The Ayres – a wilderness area with surprisingly varied wildlife, including unique lichen-dominated maritime heath, ponds with frogs and damselflies and tern colonies. The only building on nearly four-and-a-half miles of unfenced coastal heath houses a visitor centre provided by the Island's own naturalists' trust.

Despite human disturbance there are still many ground-nesting birds. Arctic, Common and Little Terns still breed; the first two sometimes on the Ballakesh property. The wet areas and ponds behind the Ballakesh Ayre were the first places in the Isle of Man where Shoveller and Black-headed Gulls were proved to nest. One of the fields here was purchased in 1975. Surprisingly, to fastidious human beings, the birds do not dislike the modern gravel pits near the Point of Ayre. Mute Swans nest and possibly also Tufted Duck (if so, a new addition to the list of birds breeding in Man.) A start has been made on a joint management plan devised with representatives of the local commissioners and all landowners in the area (mainly the Trust and the Isle of Man Forestry Board) to protect wildlife and preserve the Ayres as a wilderness area for the benefit of all.

THE CURRAGHS

The Curraghs are an area of willow carr that has grown on the peat that has accumulated in the former bed of Lake Andreas. Geologists have given this name to a lake which, at the end of the last Ice Age, lay in the hollow between the retreating ice and the slate hills. Initially it is thought to have drained to Port Mooar. The channel now occupied by the Lhen once drained water from the melting ice front into the lake. Its vegetation has a longer continuous history than that of any area of the Island, save perhaps the summit of Snaefell, the same water-loving plants having grown here for more than ten thousand years. Human activity has, of course, had considerable effect. The great numbers of waterfowl that once lived here, including such now-rare species as Bittern – called *Ushag ny boob* in Manx – and Garganey, have dwindled. Only archaeological finds of the bones of the latter show it once was present.

A deep drain was cut along the lines of the Lhen valley about 1750. For some hundreds of years peat was dug and the willows were kept cut down until about 1900. Now willow scrub is replacing the sheets of open water seen by P. G. Ralfe in the 1880s. Skilful management could still further enhance the wildlife potential of the Curraghs but until this can be put into practice the Trust's eighteen acres, given by J. C. Clucas in 1978, will help to preserve this uniquely ancient landscape of reed and willow, dragonfly and duck. Nature herself preserves – only birds can fully explore this wilderness of reed and water.

EARY CUSHLIN

The now-remote buildings of Eary Cushlin farmstead, successor to the shieling which gave the place its name, is now an activities centre.

The Eary Cushlin farm was acquired in 1957. The original property extended from the Patrick–Rushen parish boundary at Lag ny Keeilley to the little stream feeding the beautiful and sometimes spectacular mare's tail waterfall at Gob ny Ushtey. A subsequent gift from L. H. Mayall in 1982 and small purchases have now provided for a footpath continuing as far as the Traie Vane. The shell of the farm's former water-powered threshing mill was re-roofed and the house was put in good order, so that it is now used as a wardened activity centre run through the Isle of Man Board of Education.

Most of the land is grassy heath with its Dwarf Gorse sculptured into fantastic shapes by Rabbits and the sea wind and much Bracken on the steep slopes at the southern end. A single oak tree high on the Cronk ny Irree Laa cliff may be a relic of native woodland. A few trees at Glen Maye probably have a similar status but such survivors are commoner on Man's east coast. Plants less common in the Island but found here include Dodder and Common Sundew.

The latter grows at the *Chibbyr ny Vashtey* (Well of Baptism), on the track to Lag ny Keeilley. Common Bugle in the stream gully may be a further indication that woodland survived late here. Some of it is unusual in having white flowers instead of the normal blue.

On the cliff tops Pigmy Shrews quarrel and hunt in tunnels in the dense turf. The caterpillars of the tiny Dew Moth feed on the lichens. It may be seen displaying its gauzy, black-dotted, yellow ochre wings at the same season (June) as the Green Tiger Beetle. Royal Fern grows on the rock ledges, as it does on the Calf. Birds are not particularly numerous on the cliffs but can include Choughs and Ravens. Hen Harriers and Short-eared Owls have also bred within the boundaries and rafts of duck may be seen on the sea. Scaup may lurk among the more plentiful Mallard and Wigeon. The cliffs also provide a fine vantage point for sea-watching ornithologists.

LAG NY KEEILLEY

"This most interesting of our ancient Keeills, set on a ledge forming a small natural platform near the foot of a lag, or hollow, torn out of the almost perpendicular western face of Cronk-ny-Irree-laa, can be reached by boat, but the landing – a mile-and-three-quarters south of Dalby beach – can only be effected within about an hour of high water on a calm day, and the upward climb of about 200 ft. is steep and not easy. The proper mode of access is by the old pack-horse road through Eary Cushlin, which passes on to the Sloc by foot tracks and so to the south of the Island. This roadway in itself is of great interest as the best existing survival of our pack-horse ways before the modern system of highroads, and a walk along it, about three-quarters of a mile from the farmland, calls up a picture of the condition of our Island in the centuries long ago."

(P. M. C. Kermode *Manx Archaeology Survey: First Report 1909.)*

The site of an Early Christian *keeill* and priest's cell, excavated by the Manx Archaeological Survey, in Lag ny Keeilley at the southern end of the property. The whole length of unspoilt cliff-top coastal path offers superb views southwards as far as the Calf and innumerable close-ups of wildlife.

If Kermode is correct in indicating that the pack-horse track is contemporary with the keeill and its cell, then it will in antiquity have been much less isolated than it is now that most visitors drive to the Eary Cushlin car park. Innumerable white pebbles found in and near the keeil hint that this was the case. As well as being associated with remembrance of the dead, these pebbles seem also to have symbolised a prayer, or a vow, and to have been left at places of pilgrimage. The keeill, in the hollow of the church or Lag ny Keeilley – its dedication is long forgotten – has walls over a yard thick and measured about thirteen × eight feet eight inches internally. There were remains of the altar at the east end. Part of the head of the window above it was found outside the gable and is now preserved in the Manx Museum. The lower socket for the door was still in position against the inside of the wall on its south side and its lintel, with a corresponding perforation, was also recovered.

The Keeill stands within a small enclosure used as a graveyard. Grave markers with simple incised crosses have been found from time to time but the plain markers now visible were placed over graves excavated during the 1908–09 research. On the northern side of the enclosure is a tiny cell for a priest, or other guardian, with a small garden plot opening from the graveyard. A piece of granite quern found near the keeill may have been used by the cell's occupant. In Ireland, however, the querns of those caught grinding grain on a Sunday were broken at the church where they did penance. The same may have been true in Man, since quern fragments are quite common on keeill sites. The broken pieces are sometimes built into lintel graves, or serve to support grave markers, and they may even have had a sacred association older than Christianity. Like some other keeill graveyards this was used for burials into the nineteenth century and the site was always respected. Most lovers of the Manx country-side will rejoice that this lovely, remote, spot is preserved for future generations.

VOICE OF THE PEOPLE: The work of the Folk Life Survey

S. HARRISON

However old and fragile objects in a museum may appear, they have inevitably outlasted their original owners in whose lives they played an intrinsic part. It is one of the duties of a Museum to attempt to reconstruct the context in which these objects were used to give a rounded picture of a vanished lifestyle and the most vital aspect of this picture is the people themselves.

The importance of recording the contemporary social setting was recognised by early writers on the Island. In their "Tours" and "Descriptions" we are given vivid glimpses of aspects of the contemporary domestic scene, agriculture and fishing, traditional crafts, customs and beliefs of the Manx people. William Blundell describing the typical Manx home in 1657 hovers between admiration and pity when he observes that:

> "These men's habitations are mere hovels compacted of stones and clay for the walls, thatched with broom, most commonly containing one room only . . . yet in this smoking hut . . . doth the man, his wife and children cohabit, and in many places with the geese and ducks under the bed, the cocks and hens over his head, the cow and calf at the bed's foot."

Above: Mary Gilrea's cottage c.1900, clearly showing the sod-wall construction of the gable, such dwellings being mistakenly described as "hovels" by some writers.

Bottom: A Manx Family – a posed photograph but nonetheless a fairly typical crofter's cottage. Note the *mollag* (dog-skin float) hanging outside the doorway.

Drawing of Kissack's Cottage, Jurby by W. H. Gill who played a valuable role in collecting the folksong and folklore of the Island.

Mrs. Morrison, Ballaugh Glen, eyes "twinkling".

The foreigner describing a strange country and a strange people is always prone to difficulties as George Waldron discovered in the eighteenth century. Waldron performed a great service for the Manx nation by commencing the recording of its folklore and traditions but his dificulty on occasions is indicated by his own recollection:

> "The Manxman would not trust the foreigner with his secrets; his eyes twinkled suspiciously, and his hand seemed unconsciously to grasp his mouth, as if to keep all fast."

However, for those that were fully integrated into this society came an understanding and appreciation of the people which penetrated beyond the initial impression. Thomas Wilson, Bishop of Sodor and Man throughout the first half of the eighteenth century was one such man and his assessment of the native people's disposition is perhaps closer to the truth:

> "The inhabitants are an orderly, civilised people, and courteous enough to strangers; and if they have been otherwise represented, it has been by those that knew them not, or perhaps it is because they have sense enough to see when strangers (who are apt to have a mean opinion of them) would go about to impose upon them, which they are not willing to suffer if they can help it."

Towards the end of the nineteenth century a small number of Manx patriots, scholars and enthusiasts became increasingly aware that the traditional patterns of life were slowly but irrevocably changing and that the people who were the bearers of the old traditions of custom and belief were rapidly disappearing. Valuable information on the folklore of the Island was collected by Speaker of the House of Keys, A. W. Moore, Sophia Morrison and William Cashen of Peel and Charles Roeder, while Dr. John Clague and W. H. Gill did sterling work rescuing a fine corpus of traditional songs from the remaining singers. A number of other distinguished contributions were made to the collection of such material into the present century but no thorough or systematic plan of collection was devised and much information was being lost forever.

Dr. John Clague, pioneer collector of Manx folk-music and song.

A. W. Moore, Speaker of the House of Keys, historian, and writer on the Island's folklore.

It was a recognition of the gradual disappearance of this unique information which prompted T. E. Brown, held by many to be the Island's national poet, to compose the short dedication, *Dear Countrymen*:

"Dear Countrymen, what'er is left to us
of ancient heritage –
of manners, speech, of humours, polity,
The limited horizon of our stage –
All this I fain would fix upon the page;
That so the coming age,
Lost in the Empire's mass,
Yet haply longing for their fathers, here
May see as in a glass
What they held dear:
May say, ' 'Twas thus and thus,
They lived'; and, as the time-flood onward rolls,
Secure an anchor for their Keltic souls."

Individuals continued their attempts to stem the tide of loss by collecting information from the old people. Notable contributions were made by W. Walter Gill

Top: A page from Dr. Clague's manuscript book where he noted down the songs and tunes he discovered.

Above right: Boys taking part in a house to house procession on St. Stephen's Day as part of the *Hunt the Wren* tradition, Ramsey, 1904. The garland of ribbons, flowers and evergreens also holds the dead bird.

Above left: The Doctor from a group of adult performers of the traditional *White Boys* play, a version of the Mummer's play of St. George, Ramsey, c.1900.

Below left: The White Boys at Port Erin, Christmas 1926. Back row: the Doctor, the Turkish Champion, Samson. Front row: St. George, Devil Doubt.

with his "Manx Scrap Books", by C.I. Paton in describing traditional Manx calendar customs, the Norwegian Professor Carl Marstrander who made wax-cylinder recordings of the Manx language, Miss Mona Douglas, particularly in the field of music and dance and the field section of the Natural History and Antiquarian Society which was active in recording the world of "bygones".

However, in 1938, the opening of Harry Kelly's cottage at Cregneash gave a new impetus to the collection of memories of traditional life in the Island. At the opening ceremony, the Director of the Museum, William Cubbon, learned from the invited Irish delegation of the work of the Irish Folklore Commission in collecting the "folk-memory" of Ireland. William Cubbon discussed the possibilities of undertaking a similar "folk-life survey" in the Isle of Man with his deputy, Basil Megaw. Unfortunately, Basil Megaw's plans to commence the Manx Folk-Life Survey were interrupted by the outbreak of war, but on his return from war-service, he realised that the need to collect this "unwritten history" was now even more urgent.

The final impetus to commence the Survey again came from Ireland. In 1947, Eamon De Valera, Taoiseach of Ireland, visited Harry Kelly's cottage at Cregneash in the course of an unofficial visit to Man and was most impressed by the wealth of the Manx cultural heritage. On hearing of the declining numbers of native Manx speakers and the Museum's lack of any suitable recording equipment to preserve this fragile aspect of the Island's heritage, De Valera offered to make available the mobile recording equipment used by the Irish Folklore Commission. This offer was eagerly accepted and in 1948 Basil Megaw, with the new secretary of the Manx Museum Eric Cregeen, visited the Commission's headquarters in Dublin where they were given much valuable advice by the Director Professor J. H. Delargy and the senior field-collector Kevin Danaher.

Eamon De Valera (*third from left*), Taoiseach of Ireland, visiting Harry Kelly's cottage in 1947, prior to the visit of the Irish Folklore Commission's mobile recording unit.

PRESERVING THE LANGUAGE: Some native Manx speakers and collectors

Professor Carl Marstrander (collector), Thomas Christian and Jon Killey (collector), Ramsey 1929.

Mr. and Mrs. Kneale, Ballagarrett, Bride.

Harry Kelly, Cregneash, c.1932.

Thomas Callister *(The Perkin)* of Peel and Harry Boyde of Ballaugh, 1948.

Mrs. Eleanor Karran of Cregneash, aged 80.

Ned Maddrell of Glen Chass and Tommy Leece of Kerrookeeil.

Walter Clarke (collector) with John Kneen blacksmith of Ballaugh and Bill Radcliffe (collector).

John Kneen (aged 95) and Harry Boyde (aged 78) being recorded by Bill Radcliffe and Mark Braide with the assistance of the Irish Folklore Commission's recording van, 1948.

Right page: John Thomas Kaighen of Bride enjoying listening to a recording of his own voice, 1949.

In the same year the Irish Folklore Commission's "mobile" recording van came to the Isle of Man as De Valera had suggested. However, as Kevin Danaher vividly recalled on a recent (1984) visit to the Island, the Taoiseach's promise of assistance was not easily fulfilled:

". . . And when he [De Valera] returned to Ireland he applied to the Irish Folklore Commission as a body engaged in similar work to go to the Isle of Man with recording apparatus and make the required recordings. And the good man was astonished and indeed horrified to find out that the Irish Folklore Commission didn't have any such apparatus because they hadn't interested themselves hitherto in it, although some of us had been experimenting with this and waiting and praying for the day when we would get the financial support required for it. Well, when the head of a Government is interested in something, usually something happens! And wheels turned and wheels perhaps within wheels turned and before very long money was available so that we set up a recording unit.

"It was a disc-cutting unit – you cut 16 inch discs each of which had 15 minutes on each side . . . We were using all sorts of peculiar methods. One had to work from batteries and convertors because one was working outside the scope of the normal electric grid usually . . . you had to balance your turntable so that your record was running absolutely level – we used to use a carpenter's spirit level for doing that. And you used pieces of rock and driftwood and things like that to prop up the apparatus . . .

"And we brought the thing over to the Isle of Man; this was our first (project). Oh in those days it was an adventure! I drove down at about 11 o'clock in the evening and had the recording van slung from a crane and dropped into the hold of a cattle boat which was coming over to Douglas. And then the cattle came in and they occupied the upper deck and, what should I say, the 'effluent' descended upon the lower deck, so that in the morning it was rather difficult to see where the van was, especially as the van was a sort of dark green colour and was more or less camouflaged completely. So I succeeded in getting into the van without too much disturbance and then drove it from the harbour in Douglas . . . and drove up to the Manx Museum to be greeted with horror by the Director thereof, Basil Megaw, a gentle soul who was somewhat perturbed to see the state in which we were. And he called to me from a distance – a safe distance – and he said, 'Don't get out and close the windows!'. And he summoned a stout fellow with a strong hose who hosed the thing down and succeeded in washing it fairly clean. And then we were ready to go ahead.

"And we spent some weeks going up and down the Island, meeting people and working with them. I have very happy memories of the people who helped us at the time. Of John Gell down in Port St. Mary and of Bill Radcliffe from Ramsey, of Leslie Quirk from Peel, Arthur Karran and Charles Craine, and Mark Braide and Tom Braide and the rest of them who worked with us. Eric Cregeen and his sister Sheila who helped us.

"And the old people we went to – I've very happy memories of those, such friendly people. Ned Maddrell probably was the chief one but there also was *Yn Gaaue Doo*, John Kneen from Ballaugh, and John Tom Kaighin who was a blind man from the north side of the Island, a very nice and gentle person. And Harry Boyde who was a tremendously fluent speaker of Manx . . . in fact the difficulty was to get him to stop talking! And several others. I mean we had a delightful meeting [at the Kinvigs' house] close to South Barrule where half a dozen of the old people got together and had a tremendous evening there talking. And also on another occasion, we brought *Yn Gaaue Doo* over to meet John Tom Kaighin and the two of them sat down and conversed in Manx because the old people at the time didn't have very much opportunity to speak to their contemporaries with difficulties of travel and so on, . . . and to get into the same natural fluency which they had. And, of course, when you got these two old boys going it certainly was worth listening to. We recorded at least part of their conversation . . . They were the first good voice recordings made in the Isle of Man."

[extracted from a tape-recorded interview in the Manx Museum's Folk-Life Survey archive]

MANX COTTAGES

Some of the cottages recorded by the Folk-Life Survey.

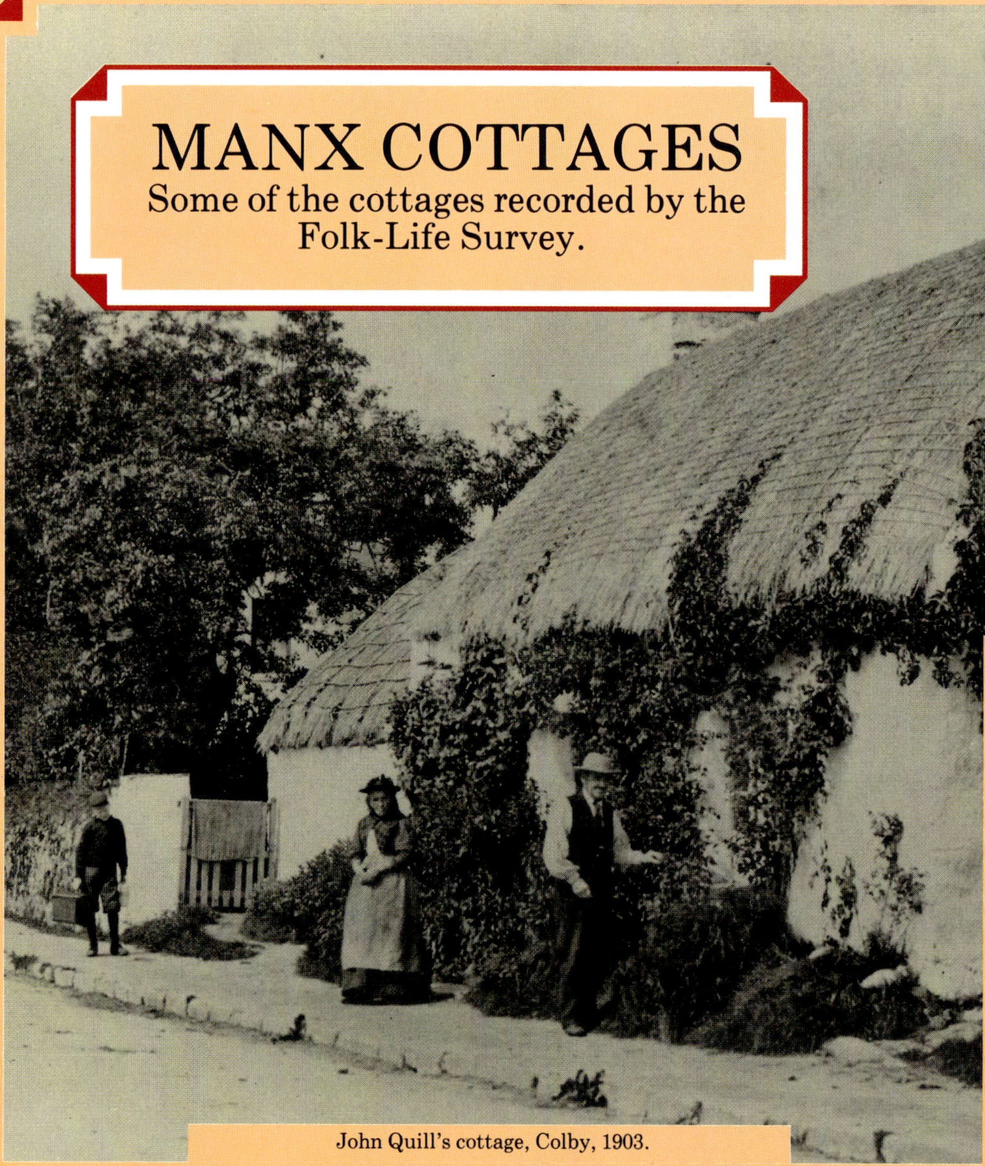

John Quill's cottage, Colby, 1903.

Carmodil Cottage, Ballaugh, c.1910.

Mrs. Morrison outside her cottage in Ballaugh Glen c.1900.

Stone and mud-walled house at West Craig, Andreas, 1939.

Farm buildings at Fleshwick, c.1920.

Mrs. Lace with spinning wheel outside her cottage c.1890.

Mud-walled cottage or *steam* at Ballaglass, c.1890.

Kevin Danaher's visit therefore proved to be of mutual benefit to the Irish Folklore Commission and the Manx Museum and resulted in the presentation to the Museum of twenty-six double-sided discs containing conversations, samples of dialect, hymn-reading and recitations from more than a dozen native Manx speakers.

Although these early recordings concentrated primarily on the Manx language, they also revealed the rich supply of informants who were still able to impart a treasury of information concerning all aspects of the traditional folk-life of the Isle of Man; from the daily routine of cooking and ploughing, to the most metaphysical flights of custom, belief and magic.

The Irish Folklore Commission's visit revealed how much valuable information could be collected in a short period when it was planned systematically and undertaken by a group of knowledgeable and enthusiastic field-workers. Recognising that no further opportunities should be missed, the Trustees of the Manx Museum appointed Mr. Leslie Quirk of Peel as the first full-time collector for the Manx Folk-Life Survey for an initial three-month period. Leslie Quirk began collecting in the Island after a two-week intensive training period with Séan O'Haughey, the Irish Folklore Commission's field-worker in Donegal, and using a borrowed Ediphone recording machine.

Meanwhile, Eric Cregeen as Secretary to the Manx Museum had taken on the task of organising a number of support groups in strategic parts of the Island to supply information on local informants and to do some initial collecting of information. It should be remembered that these were difficult times for organising such a large-scale project throughout the country, and special dispensation was sought from the post-war rationing committees to allow the project to advance. While transportation of the Ediphone recording machine to the remoter homes of the Island prompted an early agreement to an increased petrol allowance for Leslie Quirk's Austin Seven van, other requests proved more difficult for Government Office to deal with, as the following letter from the "Food Control Division" dated 13th December, 1948 implies:

"Sir,

Manx Folk Life Survey

I refer to your application for a permit to obtain ration commodities to enable you to supply refreshments to persons attending meetings in connection with the above subject, and I have been directed to inform you that, although there are no Ministry of Food instructions covering this type of application, it has been decided, after taking into consideration all the circumstances, to treat the application as an exceptional case. Permits will therefore be granted to obtain ration commodities of tea, sugar, and margarine for a limited period of 12 months . . ."

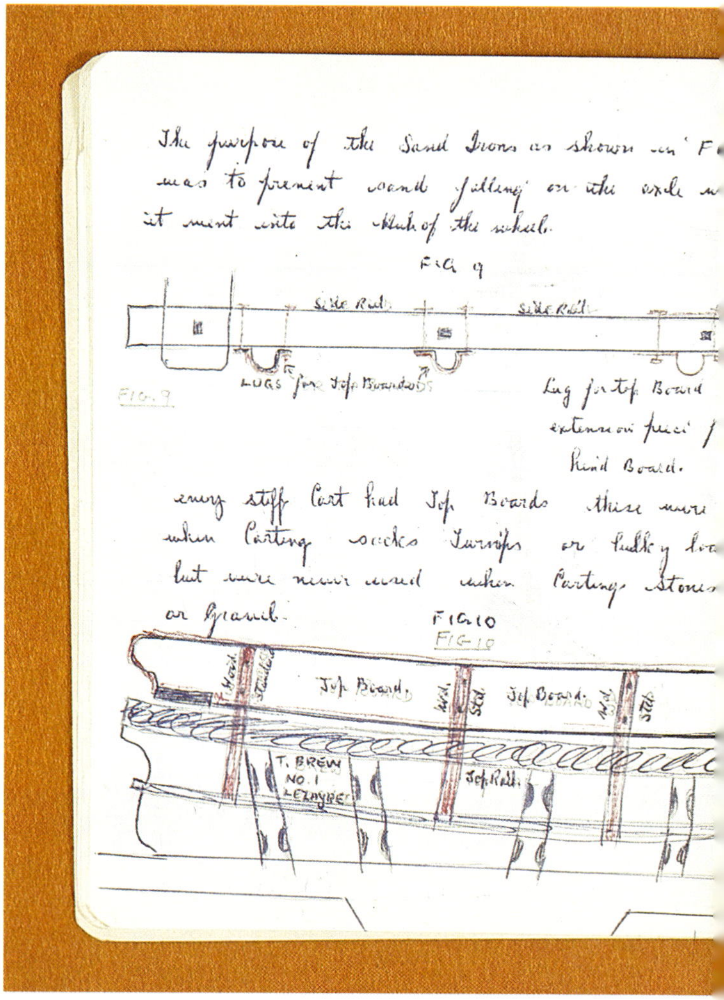

A number of Folk-Life Survey informants recorded their memories in note-books provided by the Museum. Mr. T. A. Brew of the Kella Mills in Sulby came from a family of joiners who were also cart builders and mill wrights and the pages from one of his many note-books reproduced above gives an indication of the quality of information which was being collected by the Survey.

The important work of the collection continued apace and attracted considerable interest from outside institutions. Professor Carmody from the University of California visited the Island in June–July 1949 to make a further fifteen valuable disc recordings, and the BBC featured a number of the older Manx people in its "Roundabout" programme in the same year.

However, although sound recordings were, and continue to be of prime historical and linguistic importance, an additional mass of information was obtained by supplying informants with blank "exercise books", to record in written form the memories of a lifetime's experience. These little notebooks were filled with fascinating and often unexpected detail and returned to the Manx Museum which issued the informant with a replacement blank book in the hope of collecting further expansive responses to the questions of the Survey's voluntary collectors and to its formal questionnaires.

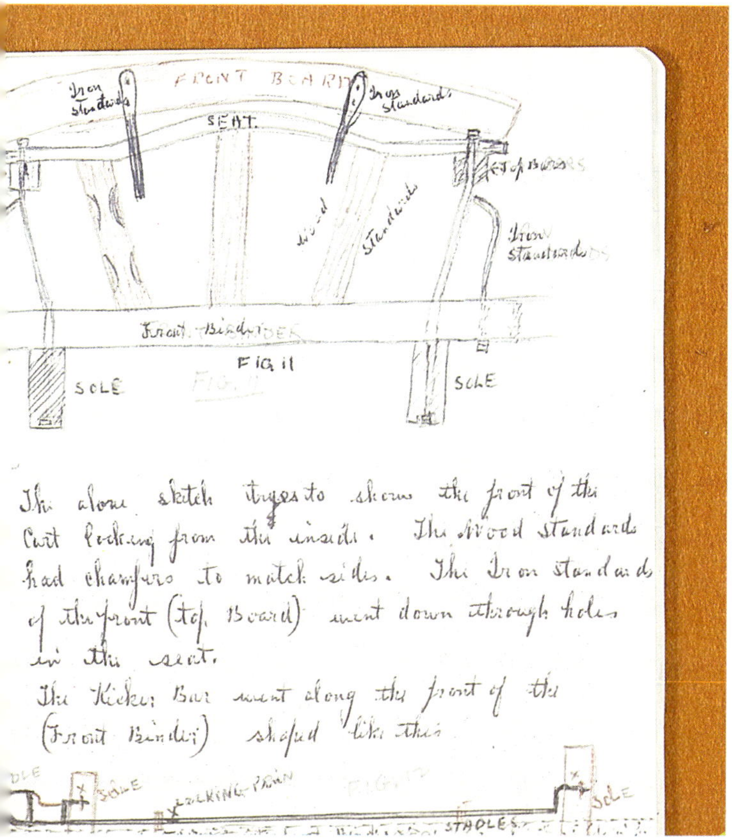

The energetic group of voluntary workers, particularly Mrs. G. M. Quilliam, E. Flanagan, M. Stevenson and Messrs Harry Rogers and Walter Clarke, in addition to those who originally assisted Kevin Danaher during his visit, proved a constant stimulus to the memories of the old people. The list of potential informants grew as more people became familiar with the aims of the survey, often through small exhibitions of old photographs mounted by the Museum and exhibited at village and church halls throughout the Island by the local volunteer groups. New avenues of information were explored as collectors were supplied with large scale Ordnance Survey maps to mark the traditional names of the small fields which characterise the Manx landscape, and the names of old tracks, roads and wells. The work of the Folk-Life Survey also extended (by post) to England and America, much useful information being collected about the nineteenth century Manxmen who emigrated to various parts of the world. In addition, collectors were always on the look-out for long forgotten objects of the previous age which could be rescued from destruction and preserved in the Museum, together with large numbers of evocative photographs either donated or loaned for copying by informants.

The enquiries of the Folk-Life Survey also unearthed a number of fascinating objects. *Quine the Forester's Book* (left) is a record left by Caesar Quine of the private marks of every owner who had sheep grazing on the mountain lands under his control in the second half of the nineteenth century. Each leaf of Quine's book has been cut to form the exact distinguishing ear-marks cut into the sheep's left and right ears with a note of the person, farm and parish to which they belong.

FARMING AND FISHING

Two binders at work in the harvest field c.1920.

Gutting herring at Port St. Mary c.1940.

Baiting the long-lines aboard the *Master Frank* of Ramsey c.1955.

A well earned break before the turf is loaded into the cart at the turbury, c.1900.

Cecil Kelly of Sulby c.1920.

Mr. Crebbin of Port St. Mary, mending the nets, c.1890.

Harvesting at Shenvalley, overlooking the Calf of Man, c.1890.

Sayle Corlett's "presser" in action c.1910.

VIEWS FROM THE ARCHIVE

Cowley and Joughin's bread delivery cart on the streets of Ramsey c.1920. (The cart is now in the Museum's collection.)

J. J. Christian's steam engine providing the power to this belt-driven plank-saw.

John Henry Teare on the bicycle he made himself c.1867 at Smeale smithy, Andreas.

Mrs. Teare, The Loughan, Jurby, one of the singers from whom Dr. Clague collected folk-songs.

Tom Taggart of Grenaby aged 83, 1930. (The cello is now in the Museum's collection).

The Two Sisters and her crew – the first Ramsey lifeboat.

Construction workers at the Laxey mine washing floors.

By 1950, large in-roads had been made. Although many people had doubted at first whether much of value could be found, as the months passed and interest grew, all doubts were quickly dispelled. It became clear that a mine of hitherto unrecorded information was still available to be collected. Work continued steadily and allied organizations such as the Manx Language Society, made major contributions to the recorded sound archive through an active programme of collection in the 1950s.

Of course, for all this collected information to be of use, there was a mammoth task of cataloguing and indexing to be tackled. This less glamorous side of the Survey's work was undertaken by Neil Mathieson and later by Grace Mary Quilliam who, from 1950, succeeded Leslie Quirk as the permanent collector on a purely voluntary basis. Ably assisted by Ethel Flanagan, the Survey's work continued apace and through careful attention to the indexing of all new material, became an increasingly significant source for Manx historical studies.

In 1957, Mrs. Quilliam was succeeded by Miss I. M. Killip as permanent part-time Folk-Life Survey collector and administrator. Miss Killip made a major contribution to this field of study through the publication in 1965 of her re-examination of the *Folklore of the Isle of Man* and she continued to advance the work of the Survey in all areas until her retirement in 1984.

The work of the Manx Museum's Folk-Life Survey continues to record that part of the Manx people's story that might not otherwise be preserved in the annals of "official" history. This rich source material for historical study is provided for today's students through the generosity of individuals from earlier generations who recognised the importance of passing on an understanding of the old way of life; a way of life which has had such an influence on the development of the nation's personality.

However, the work of the Folk-Life Survey continues, for the collection of the "unwritten history" of today's society will be just as important for tomorrow's students and scholars. Memories, tales, dialect, photographs, films, plans and drawings are all still being collected in an effort to document our own times and experiences. Through this work, the Museum is helping to assure that the true voice of the Manx people will be heard in history to fill out the picture left to us by documentary and object sources. That voice may often be shaky with age, but posterity will find it provides an eloquent and vital link into the very hearths and hearts of the Manx people.

Behind the scenes: Walter Clarke, a member of the Museum staff and a collector of the Manx language from the older speakers, transcribes a tape-recorded interview from the Folk-Life Survey's sound archive.

OUR FRIENDS

The work of the Manx Museum and National Trust, although primarily funded by the Manx Government, is provided with most valuable support both financial and practical, by two "Friends" organisations: the Friends of the Manx Museum and the Friends of the Manx National Trust.

In 1938 a Society under the title THE FRIENDS OF THE MANX MUSEUM was established "to acquire exhibits of importance for presentation to the Museum and generally to give such aid to the Trustees as may lie within their power".

Since then the Friends of the Manx Museum have been able to purchase and present to the Island's National Museum many items of great importance. Much of the Museum's collection of Archibald Knox's Art Nouveau silverware pewterware and jewellery originally designed for Liberty, together with rare medals and ancient coinage were gifts from the Friends. Many paintings have been purchased outright as well as help given to acquire such important items as the four Romney portraits of the Taubman Family. The Costume Gallery at The Grove Museum and the audio-visual presentation at Cregneash were assisted by the Friends, who have marked Centenary Year by making a major financial contribution towards the phased programme of new gallery designs at the Manx Museum.

Today's membership of over 500 indicates a healthy spread of support, and the visiting public have in turn responded generously by their gifts in the Friends' collection boxes at the Manx Museum.

Once a year the Friends meet in Douglas for a specially sponsored Lecture followed by dinner. Nine such lectures have enabled them to present the Museum with a substantial number of slides. Not only is their collection thereby augmented but also there now exists a growing reserve of material suitable for regular use.

Thus this "Society of persons interested in furthering the objects of the Museum" is not only privileged to play a valuable role, but also its members are brought into contact with history, visual and written, that makes life in the Isle of Man doubly rewarding for residents and visitors alike.

THE FRIENDS OF THE MANX NATIONAL TRUST were formed shortly after the 1951 Act of Tynwald which nominated the Museum and Ancient Monuments Trustees as being also responsible for the preservation and promotion of areas of scenic beauty and historic interest within the Island. Indeed, much land had been secured for preservation prior to 1951 by a group of enthusiastic individuals and it was the donation of this land which formed the initial basis of the new Trust's responsibilities.

This level of enthusiasm and dedication has been continued by the Friends, which is now a registered charity comprising a body of subscribers to a fund which is administered by a committee elected from its members and which is used either in the acquisition of property or in the improvement of amenities. By joining the Friends, members provide the National Trust with practical assistance in its important work of preserving for posterity the Island's natural beauty and unspoilt countryside and coastline.

Over the years, the work of these two groups of supporters has provided a significant and lasting contribution to the quality and scope of the Manx Museum and National Trust and the public will be able to enjoy many of the fruits of this friendship during the Trust's second century of activity.

Application forms for membership of both Friends organisations are available from the Manx Museum, Douglas.